EGGERTON.

THE FROG BOOK

*North American Toads and Frogs, with a
Study of the Habits and Life Histories of
those of the Northeastern States*

by

MARY C. DICKERSON

*with a new preface
and appendix of nomenclatural changes by
JAMES D. ANDERSON, Professor of Zoology,
Rutgers University, The State University
of New Jersey*

DOVER PUBLICATIONS, INC.

NEW YORK

Published in Canada by General Publishing Company, Ltd.,
30 Lesmill Road, Don Mills, Toronto, Ontario.
Published in the United Kingdom by Constable and Company,
Ltd., 10 Orange Street, London WC 2.

This Dover edition, first published in 1969, is an unabridged
republication of the work originally published by Doubleday,
Page & Company in 1906.
This edition contains a new Preface with table of changes
in nomenclature prepared especially for this reprint by Professor James D. Anderson, Rutgers University, The State
University of New Jersey.

Standard Book Number: 486-21973-9
Library of Congress Catalog Card Number: 69-15901

Manufactured in the United States of America

DOVER PUBLICATIONS, INC.
180 Varick Street
New York, N. Y. 10014

PREFACE

THE FROG BOOK has long been considered a classic work of enduring interest to amateur and professional biologists. One can never find a simple, single reason for a work's continuing importance even though the field of study subsequently expands and matures. This book is often praised for the excellence of its illustrations, especially the color plates that retain their value in spite of many recent publications of high quality. It is also noted for the accuracy and excellence of the descriptions of the life histories and habits of frogs and toads. Less frequently mentioned by scientists, but of equal importance, is the sense of beauty in living things that Miss Dickerson brought to the work. This feeling for beauty, for life itself, pervades all aspects of the book. It is not merely the description of accepted beauty, for even Miss Dickerson considered some of her subjects odd or even ugly, but rather the total beauty of living organisms and natural living systems that has been implanted in the work and conveyed to the reader.

The author, Mary Cynthia Dickerson, was born in Hastings, Michigan, on March 7, 1866. From the beginning she must have seen the world with different eyes from those around her, for she devoted her life to learning, to seeking beauty, and to bringing the knowledge and beauty of nature to others. For Miss Dickerson this was not an easy task. She came from a family that did not place high value on learning and she had to work for all aspects of her own education in a day when that was difficult, especially for a woman. During her early years she devoted great amounts of time to the care of three younger brothers and later took her formal education piecemeal while supporting herself. Between 1891 and 1895 she taught high school in Michigan and Illinois, saving money for courses at the University of Michigan and later at the University of Chicago where she completed her undergraduate studies in 1897. The following eight years were spent as Head of Zoology and Botany at Rhode Island Normal School in Providence. During those years she excelled as a teacher and also developed her skills as a naturalist. The careful observations, notes and photographs done at that time led to the publication of *The Frog Book* in 1906 and the equally beautiful *Moths and Butterflies* published in 1901. Ever anxious to improve herself, to see and learn more, Miss Dickerson then spent two years at Stanford University where she worked with the renowned fish taxonomist, David Starr Jordan. This intensive taxonomic training added another dimension to her background and resulted in several papers with Jordan on the fishes of Fiji and the Gulf of Mexico. When she came to the American Museum of Natural History in New York in 1908, Miss Dickerson assumed even more diverse activities that included being Curator of Woods and Forestry, Curator of Herpetology and editor of the *Journal of Natural History* (now called *Natural History*). Her appreciation of beauty led to the development of excellent exhibits in both Forestry and Herpetology and her love of learning led to the organization and development of an outstanding department of Herpetology. Her early associates in that department, G. K. Noble, K. P. Schmidt and C. L. Camp became leaders in the field, and the department and collections became world famous. Her gifted and devoted editorial work alone could stand as a major accomplishment since *Natural History* has continued to bring to a diverse audience the beauty of nature that she saw so clearly.

Miss Dickerson died in 1923, two years after sustained illness forced her to leave the museum.

The Frog Book is essentially an introduction to the natural history of frogs and toads. A similar book written today would cover the same areas but would place greater emphasis on the voice and on the tadpoles. Unfortunately very little is known about the ecology and behavior of tadpoles although a great deal more is known about the growth and structure of these larval stages. Much of the technical literature on frogs today concerns the functions of the voice. Many studies have shown that frog calls are important mechanisms that prevent interbreeding between species and recent studies indicate that the voice also serves to space individuals of a species in breeding aggregations. Such aspects of the voice were not understood or appreciated at the turn of the century. The calls of many species have been subjected to rather sophisticated analysis and the components of many calls have been presented in audiospectrograms so that the voices of different species can be compared visually. Although these aspects of the voice are extremely important in understanding the biology of frogs and toads and should be mentioned in modern works, they are of little use to the reader who wishes to recognize the frogs calling in a local pond. Perhaps the attempts by Miss Dickerson to describe the calls in terms of familiar sounds or the musical scale are best for introducing people to the variety of frog voices.

Nomenclatural Changes

The following list indicates changes in nomenclature that have occurred since this book was published in 1906. In the main text Miss Dickerson used 7 family names, 63 generic and specific names. Of these 70 names 30 have been changed: 3 family, 4 generic and 23 specific. Such taxonomic changes over more than sixty years do not indicate inaccuracy on the part of the author but rather reflect changes in the philosophy of classification and nomenclature. The changes in the family names, for example, represent a better understanding of the major groups of frogs. The greatest changes in the science of systematics during this century have been in our understanding of the species, and most of the nomenclatural changes at the species level reflect the different species concept employed by systematists today. The modern systematist recognizes that species are composed of populations, the individuals of which vary one from the other, and that the populations of the species vary geographically. The characteristics in which they vary depend on the species. Thus in some groups the voice may differ from place to place, in others the color pattern, in others the body proportions, etc. At the turn of the century many of these variants would have been named as species, but today they are recognized as parts of single polytypic species. Geographic variants are frequently given subspecific names as can be seen in the taxonomic list. Fourteen of the 23 changes at the species level result from the placement of two or more species under one specific name. These changes were necessary in the light of studies indicating that they were not different species but variations of one genetically continuous form. That species are composed of variable populations genetically linked is only one aspect of the modern species concept. An equally important aspect is that species are reproductively (and therefore genetically) isolated from other species. Therefore some structurally similar frogs living in the same area but not interbreeding are considered full species today but might have been placed under one species name in 1906. Five of the changes recorded herein come under this category. The remaining four changes are purely technical and dictated by an international code of zoological nomenclature. One of the most important rules of this code states that the oldest valid name for an animal, in all but a few special cases, takes priority over all subsequent names. The technical name of the Spring Peeper, a species splendidly described in this book, is a good example. The name employed by Miss Dickerson was *Hyla pickeringii*, described in 1839 by Storer. Subsequent studies have shown that the same species was described in 1838 as *Hyla crucifer* by Wied. Thus *Hyla crucifer* is today the officially recognized name for the species. Users of this reprint edition will find the currently accepted technical names in a list appended to this Introduction. In almost all cases, however, the populations so accurately described and depicted by Miss Dickerson are still considered real biological entities, either species or geographic variants of species. For example the Red-legged frog was discussed under both *Rana aurora* and *Rana draytonii*. Although they are now considered as only subspecifically distinct, the descriptions given are totally valid for these geographic variants. In order to correct any impression that all taxonomic problems in frogs have been solved, attention should be drawn to such groups as that called the genus *Chorophilus* by Dickerson but placed in the genus *Pseudacris* today. These Chorus frogs are complex and their relationships poorly understood. The accounts in *The Frog Book* are accurate as long as applied to the exact geographic areas discussed. However, since geographic and individual variation as well as the extent of reproductive isolation are known imperfectly, the questions of species and species borders are not settled. We may expect name changes to continue to occur in this group for some time.

The names used by Miss Dickerson are listed alphabetically in the column on the left. The names on the right are those used today for the same animals. If no name appears on the right, then the name used by Dickerson applies essentially as she used it. Two species names on the right indicates that the name used by Dickerson included two species by modern standards. Subspecific names are used only when it is clear that the name used by Dickerson applied exactly to that population of the species, as in the example for *Rana aurora* above. The list has been kept as simple as possible and unsettled taxonomic questions have been avoided. Frogs referred to as *Hyla versicolor*, for example, are actually two species that can be distinguished only by analysis of the voice. Since so little is known of this, and since recent field guides do not distinguish the species, it seems pointless to include such changes in this list.

Table of Changes

Chorophilus ocularis (p. 162)	*Hyla ocularis*
Chorophilus ornatus (p. 161)	*Pseudacris ornata* and
	P. streckeri
Cystignathidae (pp. 163-65)	*Leptodactylidae*
Discoglossidae (pp. 51-2)	*Ascaphidae*
Engystoma carolinense	
(pp. 166-68)	*Gastrophryne carolinensis*
Engystoma texense (pp. 168-69)	*Gastrophyryne olivacea*
Engystomatidae (pp. 166-70)	*Microhylidae*
Hyla andersoni (pp. 131-33)	
Hyla arenicolor (pp. 122-23)	
Hyla cinerea (pp. 126-28)	
Hyla evittata (pp. 128-30)	*H. cinerea evittata*
Hyla femoralis (pp. 150-51)	
Hyla gratiosa (pp. 124-26)	
Hyla pickeringi (pp. 138-48)	*H. crucifer*
Hyla regilla (pp. 134-38)	
Hyla squirella (pp. 148-50)	
Hyla versicolor (pp. 117-22)	
Hyla versicolor phaeocrypta	
(p. 120)	*H. versicolor*
Hylidae (pp. 117-62)	
Hypopachus cuneus (pp. 169-70)	
Lithodytes latrans (pp. 163-64)	*Eleutherodactylus augusti latrans*
Lithodytes ricordii (pp. 164-65)	*Eleutherodactylus ricordi*
Pelobatidae (pp. 53-62)	
Rana aesopus (pp. 193-96)	*R. aeroleta aesopus*
Rana areoleta (pp. 192-3)	
Rana aurora (pp. 216-17)	
Rana boylii (pp. 221-22)	
Rana cantabrigiensis (pp. 211-13)	*R. sylvatica cantabrigiensis*
Rana cantabrigiensis latiremis	
(p. 212)	*R. sylvatica cantabrigiensis*
Rana catesbiana (pp. 227-40)	*R. catesbieana*
Rana clamitans (pp. 198-205)	
Rana draytoni (pp. 213-16)	*R. aurora draytoni*
Rana draytoni onca (pp. 196-98)	*R. pipiens fisheri*
Rana grylio (pp. 226-27)	
Rana onca (pp. 196-98)	*R. pipiens*
Rana palustris (pp. 188-92)	
Rana pipiens (pp. 171-85)	
Rana pretiosa (pp. 218-21)	
Rana septentrionalis (pp. 224-25)	

Newark, New Jersey   JAMES D. ANDERSON
September, 1968

PREFACE

THE original manuscript for this book concerned Toads and Frogs of Northeastern North America only. It was compiled largely from notes made during a period of some ten years in Minnesota, Michigan, Tennessee, New Hamshire, Massachusetts and Rhode Island. It was written with the direct aim of making these forms known and appreciated by people interested in nature.

Brief accounts of the species of other parts of North America were added later. These descriptions and the photographs accompanying them were made from living material shipped from various parts of the continent. This collection of material is in the American Museum of Natural History, New York, with the exception of specimens of Colour Plates XI and XVI which are in the National Museum at Washington.

The Colour Plates were made from photographs from life, some of the plates representing eight or ten negatives. They were coloured from living material by Mr. Herbert L. Guild of Providence, working under the supervision of the author. Owing to the careful work of Mr. Guild on the originals and to the efforts of the Publishers to obtain accurate reproductions, these plates are unusually true to life. Of course, in many cases, the colour represented may be only one phase in a complex and changing colouration.

Twelve black and white plates showing typical haunts of common toads and frogs are from photographs by Mr. W. A. Dean, Artist Photographer of Providence. Various line drawings introduced to indicate food or enemies or to act as a calendar, were made by Miss Alma Field of Providence. With few exceptions the subjects for these line drawings were taken from photographs from life by the author.

Sincere gratitude is especially due to three people: Dr. J. Percy Moore of the University of Pennsylvania, Philadelphia, who read the manuscript and gave many valuable suggestions; Dr. Leonhard Steineger of the National Museum at Washington who not only allowed study of the National Museum Collection of Salientia but also gave assistance in the identification of specimens; and Miss Maud Slye, Instructor in the Rhode Island Normal School, Providence, who read the manuscript from the standpoint of its English.

Thanks are due to many others also, for help in getting living material, for opportunities for study and so on. Among these are Dr. Frank R. Lillie, University of Chicago; Dr Wm. M. Wheeler, American Museum of Natural History, New York; Dr. Hans Gadow, University of Cambridge, England; Director, C. H. Townsend, New York Aquarium; Dr. A. D. Mead, Brown University, Providence; Dr. J. Van Denburgh, California Academy of Science, San Francisco; and Dr. J. F. Illingworth, Seattle, Washington.

It is hoped that the book not only will introduce the elementary nature student to the fascinations of pond life but that it will suggest to the more advanced student serious work on the classification, life histories and habits of the North American Salientia—for there remains a field of work of such breadth that what has been done seems only a beginning.

MARY C. DICKERSON

Providence, R. I.
June 10, 1906.

CONTENTS

xvii

LIST OF COLOUR PLATES

LIST OF HALF-TONES

xxvii

LIST OF TEXT ILLUSTRATIONS

as in the case of Snakes and Lizards; like the Turtles, possess a bony box-like shell; or like the Crocodiles and many extinct forms, have bony plates in the skin. Unlike the Batrachians, the Reptiles breathe throughout their lives by means of lungs — in certain cases helped by the walls of the pharynx — and when adapted in other ways for water life, remain divers merely.

Batrachian eggs are laid in the water and hatch into so-called tadpoles, different from the adults in appearance and thoroughly adapted for water life. The eggs of Reptiles are laid on land, and they hatch into perfected diminutive Reptiles fully adapted for land life.[1]

II. *Two Orders of Living North American Batrachians — Urodela and Salientia*

The living North American Batrachians differ enough to allow classification into two distinct Orders, the Urodela and the Salientia. The Urodela are the Tailed Batrachians, or Salamanders, with various popular names, such as Mud Puppies or Water Dogs, Tritons, Newts, and Efts. The Salientia are the Tailless Batrachians, i. e. the Toads, Tree Frogs, Frogs, and all Batrachians that have the frog-like form.

There can never be any confusion in identifying a Batrachian as a member of one or the other of these two Orders. The Urodele is always tailed, has an elongated body and legs of nearly equal size; while any member of the Salientia has a relatively short stout body without a tail and with the long hind legs developed for jumping and swimming.[2]

The members of the Order Urodela vary considerably in their habits and life histories. Like all the Batrachians, they usually pass through a larval aquatic existence, after which they

---

[1] The technical differences in the skeletons are as follows:

The vertebræ of Reptilia are gastrocentrous, those of Batrachia never so; Batrachian skeleton never has sternal ribs and a true sternum; Batrachia have two occipital condyles for the articulation of the skull with the vertebral column, Reptilia have only one.

[2] Technical differences of the skeletons are as follows:

The acentrous and opisthocœlous,or amphicœlous vertebræ of the Urodela are many in number. The trunk vertebræ carry ribs or vestiges of them. The shoulder-girdle is simple, mainly cartilaginous, and not a complete circle — the precoracoids not meeting in the midventral line. The pelvic girdle is weak, with the ilia placed at right angles to the axis.

The Salientia have few vertebræ, which are usually notocentrous and procœlous; the last bone of the vertebral column (Fig. 6) is a long solid coccyx to give support to muscles for leaping. This coccyx consists of several vertebral segments coalesced. The pelvic girdle is large and strong; ribs are absent except in Discoglossidæ. The shoulder-girdle is a complete circle overlapping or fusing in front. (See Fig. 5.)

2

INTRODUCTION

I. *Distinction of Batrachians from Fishes and Reptile*

The Batrachians represent a Class of Vertebrat
occupying a position between Fishes and Reptiles. Th
siderable variation in general appearance among th
living members of the Class, so that a Batrachian is no
defined and identified as is a fish, a bird, or a mamm
is no one characteristic by which it may be known, a
in each of these other Classes.

Batrachians, however, are distinguished from Fish
eral easily recognizable characteristics. They usually h
limbs furnished with fingers and toes (pentadactyle li
never have fins stiffened by bony rays (although they
fins soft and filmy in character in the young stages).
exception of one order (Apoda), they do not have scale
sess a skin either smooth and slimy or rough with
nearly dry. Fishes breathe throughout their lives by
gills, but the Batrachians, while usually living in the
breathing by gills in the early stages of life, as a ru
during adult life by means of lungs, and are more c
developed for land life.[1]

A popular distinction from the Reptiles is not ea
since Batrachians and Reptiles sometimes correspond
actly in form. That is, they both have limbs of the pe
type and in the case of Salamanders (Batrachians) an
(Reptiles) both possess tails and elongated bodies. In
of the common Salamanders are popularly called Liza
ing the great superficial resemblance of certain memb
two Classes.

However, Batrachians and Reptiles are very differ
in all fundamental points. Instead of a more or less s
slimy skin, Reptiles have a skin protected by overlapp

---

[1] There are certain technical points of difference in characteristics of the ske
vertebræ of Fishes are never pseudocentrous or notocentrous. The Batrachian has tv
dyles, except in the case of some Stegocephali. The Batrachian is characterized by
fenestra ovalis and stapes and by internal nares.

may remain aquatic or may become terrestrial in habit. (Figs. 1, 2, and 3.) The aquatic forms usually have the tail flattened vertically to aid in swimming; while the terrestrial forms have a rounded tail. A few, like Necturus, keep the gills throughout their lives.

The Urodela represent in numbers about one-tenth of the Batrachian group as known in the world at present, that is, about one hundred species. Of this number between sixty and seventy are American species.

III. *Development and Metamorphosis*

The North American representatives of the Salientia deposit the eggs in water, usually in shallow, stagnant water. The eggs may be laid singly or in small clusters, as in the case of some of the tree frogs (Fig. 167); in large masses, as is the habit among the frogs (Fig. 246); or in long unbroken strings, as in the case of toads (Fig. 34). The eggs are sometimes free in the water, but more often are attached to water-weeds or other objects. If free, the egg mass has such buoyancy that it floats at the surface of the water (*Rana sylvatica*).

The number of eggs in a laying depends on the species and often on the age and size of the individual of the species. The number may be as high as 12,000 in the American Toad. The size of the egg will sometimes help in the identification of a species, but there is great variation in this respect. In the first place, the size of the egg does not correspond with the size of the Batrachian, the largest frog of North America (*Rana catesbiana*) having an egg of less size than that of some of its smaller relatives. Besides, the size varies considerably with the individual. In a large collection of egg masses of *Rana sylvatica* or *Rana palustris*, the difference in size will be so conspicuous that unless one knew the opposite to be true, he would judge the egg masses to have been laid by frogs of different species.

The egg is spherical, and is provided with a large amount of light-coloured yolk. When the eggs are first laid, part of this yolk can be seen occupying the lower portion of the egg under the more or less pigmented upper portion. (Fig. 202.) The dark pigmented portion of the egg at the top (later the whole surface becomes black or brown in colour) allows a greater absorption of the sun's heat than would a lighter colour. So the development which is wholly dependent on temperature is materially aided. Each egg is surrounded by a thin elastic membrane that fits it closely (except in Pelobatidæ) and one or two gelatinous membranes outside of this. These membranes are not visible when the eggs are first laid, but swell after they come into contact with water, becoming very conspicuous, though transparent. These envelopes aid the development; they absorb and hold the warmth from the sun's rays, producing a somewhat higher and more equable temperature than is that of the surrounding water. They also serve to protect the egg or egg mass by converting it into a slippery unmanageable object not easily grasped and eaten by birds, turtles, and others of the Batrachian's enemies about the pond. It is reported that ducks sometimes feed upon frog egg masses. The membranes of the eggs are easily penetrated by leeches,[1] which suck out the contents, and so prove themselves perhaps the most destructive enemy of frog spawn.

The breeding season is likely to occur in early spring, but varies with the species, some of the Salientia being able to endure more cold than others. As a rule, toads are later in their appearance at the pond than are frogs or tree frogs. In eastern North America, *Rana sylvatica* and *Rana pipiens* appear earliest among the frogs, *Hyla pickeringii* and *Chorophilus n. feriarum* among the tree frogs. The latter may be heard as early as February and the two species of frogs appear very soon after. On the Western coast, *Rana draytonii;* and *Hyla regilla* are breeding in January and February in California, and following them closely *Rana pretiosa* and *Hyla regilla* are breeding in Washington. Members of the genus Scaphiopus have been known to breed at various times from March to August, always during a warm rain.

The length of the breeding season varies greatly. All of a given species may resort to the water at about the same time and remain there for a short period only, as in the case of the Spadefoot Toad (*Scaphiopus holbrookii*) or less conspicuously of the Wood Frog (*Rana sylvatica*). On the other hand, they may go to the ponds scatteringly and each individual linger there. In the latter case the breeding season may extend over a period of two or three months, as in the case of *Bufo lentiginosus,* of *Bufo americanus,* and even more remarkably of *Bufo fowleri.*

---

[1] *Macrobdella decora.*

4

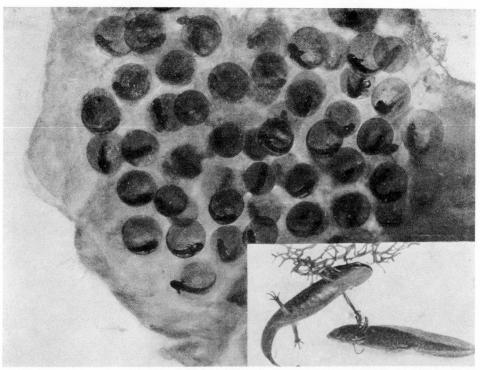

FIGS. 1 and 2.—The SPOTTED SALAMANDER (*Amblystoma punctatum* Linn). Providence, R. I. [Enlarged.] The spherical eggs enclosing the embryos are within an external mass of jelly. The full-grown larva has a tail fin and external gills adapting it to water life.

FIG. 3.—SPOTTED SALAMANDERS 1 year old. Black and yellow. These are typical representatives of the *Urodela* which together with the *Salientia*, or frog-like forms, constitute the two classes of the North American Batrachia.

In May, when birch trees are in their splendour of young leaves, frogs and toads announce spring from all the waterways.

Investigation has yet to prove that any given North American species has more than one true brood each year. The fertilization of the egg is external and the grasp of the male is back of the arms, except in the Discoglossidæ and the Pelobatidæ, where it is inguinal, as among the Salamanders. When several species are breeding in a given pond, they may divide the space and form themselves into colonies. The same exclusiveness is true later of the tadpoles also.

For details of the development of the frog's egg, see pp. 176 to 181, and for those of the toad's egg, see pp. 67 to 71. The Salientia show their close relationship by the similarity in the development of the eggs. The time element varies with the species and with the temperature in the case of a given species. Some embryos hatch in less time than others — in two or three days even (*Bufo americanus*) instead of in as many weeks (*Rana pipiens*) — and thus may be at an earlier stage of development at the time of hatching. They may therefore either pass through a quiescent, clinging stage after hatching (Figs. 35 and 248), or omit this and become active at once. There may be differences in colour, in the extent of the development of the external gills, and in other details, but, on the whole, if we know the story of development in one species, we know what to look for in other species also.

This applies equally to the metamorphosis of the tadpole. (See American Toad, pp. 69 and 70, and Bullfrog, pp. 235 to 238.) The length of life of the tadpole before its change into the frog may vary from two or three weeks to as many years. Some of the interesting points possible to observe during the metamorphosis are the following: The arms and legs develop simultaneously, but the arms are concealed under the opercular membrane. (Fig. 280.) The left arm appears first, because of the presence of the breathing-pore or spiraculum on the left side. (Figs. 284 and 285.) The eyes are elevated, become free, and have movable lids perfected. The lachrymal canal shifts upward and backward toward the eye and enters the lower eyelid. (Fig. 287.) The horny parts of the mouth are dropped and the mouth cavity increases in size. The tail becomes smaller by absorption from within. The tadpole takes on habits of rushing to the surface or of resting wholly out of the water (Figs. 287 and 288), showing that the lungs, which for some time before had been functional in company with the gills, now take on all of the respiratory work (except

5

that performed by the skin). Within a short time after the appearance of the arms, the skin of the opercular membrane has grown to that of the arm and a distinct seam is visible at the line of union. (Figs. 289 and 229.) This seam is sometimes visible in the second year after the metamorphosis.

The metamorphosis may take place in a relatively short space of time, often being hastened by lack of food. Hunger causes earlier degeneration and resorption of the edible portions of the tail and opercular membrane, and hence hastens the metamorphosis. On the other hand, the change may be delayed by good feeding and low temperature, and by any disturbance which results in requiring the expenditure of energy on the part of the tadpole. As the tail becomes smaller and no longer functional, its colour darkens until it is nearly black. This is due to the concentration of the pigment that was previously spread out, giving colour to the tail and its fin.

One of the most interesting structures of the tadpole is the system of the lateral line organs. These are sense organs of the skin that appear to the naked eye as dots of lighter or darker colour, but are really tiny papillæ at the ends of tubules of the skin. They are arranged in curving rows on the top of the head and around the eyes. They also extend backward to the tail or beyond, usually in three irregular rows on each side. (Fig. 4) Their arrangement differs somewhat in the different genera and species and they are more prominent in some than in others. In a given individual they may be more conspicuous at some times than at others, depending on the colour of the tadpole at the time the observation is made. Each papilla is in direct connection with a fibre from the lateral branch of the vagus nerve, and the system of organs is supposed to provide a special sense necessary in some way to aquatic life. Organs of the lateral line are uniformly possessed by Fishes; the organs of the lateral line possessed by the Salientia are known in the tadpole stage only, and disappear at the time of the metamorphosis. (See p. 14.) There has been much difference of opinion as to the exact function of these organs, but they are now regarded as refined organs of touch, making the creature sensitive to vibrations of the mass of water. They have developed from the skin, which is sensitive to waves and currents of water. It is thought that the internal ears have developed from organs of the lateral line, and the ears

PLATE III

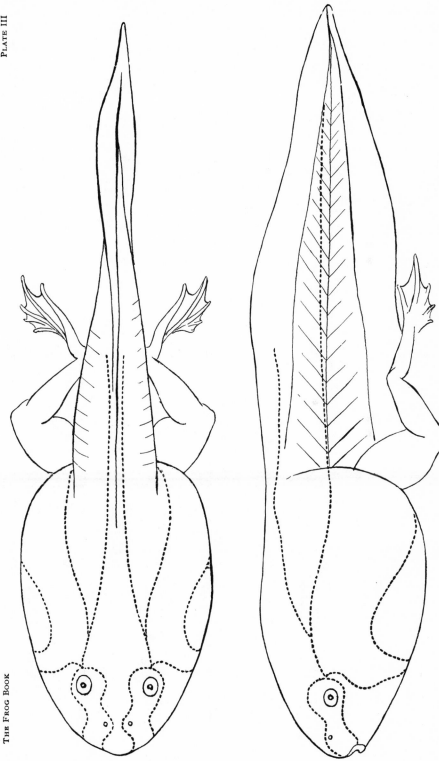

FIG. 4.—Dorsal and side views of Bullfrog tadpole. The dotted lines indicate the location of the lateral line sense organs.

PLATE IV

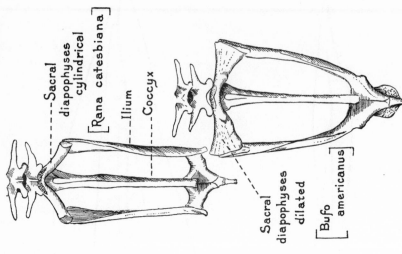

--Sacral
diapophyses
cylindrical
[Rana catesbiana]

--Ilium

--Coccyx

Sacral
diapophyses
dilated
[Bufo
americanus]

FIG. 6.—Dorsal views of pelvic girdles to illustrate the cylindrical and dilated conditions of the wings (diapophyses) of the sacral or 9th vertebra. After Cope.

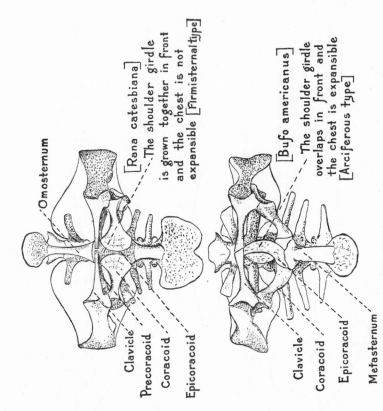

--Omosternum

[Rana catesbiana]
The shoulder girdle
is grown together in front
and the chest is not
expansible [Firmisternal type]

Clavicle
Precoracoid
Coracoid
Epicoracoid

[Bufo americanus]
The shoulder girdle
overlaps in front and
the chest is expansible
[Arciferous type]

Clavicle
Coracoid
Epicoracoid

Metasternum

FIG. 5.—Ventral views of shoulder girdles (seen in front of vertebral columns) to illustrate the firmisternal and arciferous types. After Cope.

are sensitive to the most delicate vibrations of the water producing sound. The sense organs of the skin, the lateral line and the ears, then, are closely related in origin and in function.

IV. *The Families of the Salientia or Tailless Batrachia*

The Tailless Batrachia of North America, as far as known, are represented by seven families, containing together twelve genera and fifty-six species. In addition, there are a few forms that rank as subspecies. All show slight modifications of one narrow plan of structure, and are sometimes distinguished from one another by close discrimination only. Their natural classification rests on minute details of internal structure. It is based, for the most part, first, on the ventral structure of the shoulder-girdle (Fig. 5); and second, on the shapes of the sacral diapophyses, those bones that form wing-like extensions of the sacral or ninth vertebra and connect directly with the ilia or hip-bones. (Fig. 6.)

Order SALIENTIA.

   I. Superfamily Arcifera.

      The two halves of the shoulder-girdle (coracoids and precoracoids) overlap in front so that the chest is capable of expansion. (Fig. 5.)

      A. Sacral diapophyses dilated. (Fig. 6.)

        1. Terminal phalanges of skeleton not claw-shaped.

          a. Vertebra opisthocœlous, ribs present, teeth on upper jaw.

            Family 1. *Discoglossidæ* (Ascaphus, p. 51).

          b. Vertebræ opisthocœlous, or procœlous, ribs absent, teeth on upper jaw.

      Family 2. *Pelobatidæ* (Scaphiopus, etc., pp. 43 *and* 53).

          c. Vertebræ procœlous, ribs absent, teeth absent.

            Family 3 *Bufonidæ* (Toads), pp. 44 and 63.

        2. Terminal phalanges of skeleton claw-shaped and supporting adhesive disks.

          a. Vertebræ procœlous, ribs absent, teeth on upper jaw. *Family* 4. *Hylidæ* (Tree Frogs), pp. 46 and 117.

      B. Sacral diapophyses cylindrical. (Fig. 6.)

      Vertebræ procœlous, ribs absent teeth on upper jaw. (Very like the frogs, except for the arciferous shoulder-girdle.)

Family 5. *Cystignathidæ* (Lithodytes, etc., pp. 45 and 163).

II. Superfamily Firmisternia.

The two halves of the shoulder-girdle meet in front and unite (coracoids and epicoracoid cartilage), so that the chest is not capable of expansion. (Fig. 5.)

A. Sacral diapophyses dilated.

Vertebræ procœlous, ribs absent, teeth absent or present. *Family 6. Engystomatidæ* (Engystoma pp. 48 and 166). B. Sacral diapophyses cylindrical.

Vertebræ procœlous, ribs absent, teeth on upper jaw.

Family 7. Ranidæ (Frogs), pp. 48 and 171.

Family I. Discoglossidæ

This is the most primitive family of the Salientia, resembling the Salamanders in the possession of ribs and in other detailed characteristics of the skeleton. The tongue is round and only slightly free behind, so that it cannot be extended for the capture of food. At the breeding season the clasp of the male is lumbar or inguinal, as among the Salamanders and the Pelobatidæ. The tadpoles have the breathing-pore situated on the midline below, instead of on the left side as in all other families of the Salientia.

Until 1897, when a new genus of the Family was found at Humptulips, Washington, the Discoglossidæ contained only four genera, and were supposed to be unusually limited in distribution. They were reported from Europe, southwestern Asia, northern Africa, and the island of New Zealand only, never having been found in the Western Hemisphere, or in tropical Africa, Asia, or Australia. (Refer to p. 51.)

Family II. Pelobatidæ

This family, related to the Discoglossidæ below and the Bufonidæ above, also shows some primitive characteristics of structure, and the clasp at the breeding season is inguinal. The members of the Family are strictly nocturnal, as is evidenced by the vertical pupil of the eye. They are burrowing in habit. The foot is unusually thick and leathery and is provided with a large sharp-edged digging spur (inner sole tubercle).

The Family is well represented in North America and Mexico and in the Eastern Hemisphere, with the exception of tropical regions. Seven genera are known and about twenty species. North America has four representatives of the one genus Scaphiopus. (Refer to p. 53.)

8

Family III. Bufonidæ

The Bufonidæ includes batrachians differing greatly from one another in appearance. They always have parotoids, and the ear is fully developed. But they may be short and stout or quite the opposite, rough and dry-skinned or smooth and slimy. In habit of life they may be terrestrial, burrowing, aquatic, or even arboreal.

The family includes eight genera, with many more than a hundred species, but, curiously enough, one of the genera, Bufo, includes all but fifteen of these species. The Bufonidæ is the most nearly cosmopolitan of all the families in its distribution; Madagascar, Papuasia, and the small islands of the Pacific, are the only regions not possessing representatives. The greatest number of genera is found in Central America; the greatest number of species, mainly Bufo, of course, occur in Central and South America. The genus Bufo is lacking in the Australian region.

Bufo is the only genus of the family found in North America, but this genus has thirteen species and a few allied subspecies. Texas has the greatest number of these species. (See p. 63.)

Family IV. Hylidæ

This family embraces the arboreal Salientia, or Tree Frogs. It is most nearly related to the Bufonidæ, and is, next to the Ranidæ, the largest family of the Salientia.

The tree frogs are relatively small in size and are often green in colour. The ends of the fingers and toes are provided with adhesive disks, by means of which the creatures climb with great skill. They have large resonating pouches, and voices that are surprisingly loud when compared with the small size of the singers.

Their distribution is cosmopolitan, with the exception of the African region. The rich forests of Central and South America have the largest number of representatives of the family — some one hundred thirty species; Australia has about thirty species and North America fifteen. In the rest of the world, six species only are represented. Of the North American species, ten are members of the genus Hyla; the others belong to Acris, Chorophilus, and Smilisca. (Refer to p. 117.)

Family V. Cystignathidæ

The old family of the Cystignathidæ is nearly as large as the Hylidæ. It is not well defined, but overlaps in its characteristics

9

the Hylidæ, the Pelobatidæ, and the Ranidæ. It resembles the first in sometimes possessing adhesive disks on fingers and toes; the second, in that the sacral diapophyses are in some species dilated instead of cylindrical; the third, in nearly all ways, except the fundamental one that it has a shoulder-girdle of the arciferous instead of the firmisternal type.

The various members of the family show habits aquatic or terrestrial, burrowing or arboreal, and have proportions and structures adapting them to these various existences. The largest number of species occurs in Mexico and Central and South America, but Australia is also well provided with them (twenty species). Outside of these regions, the Family is not known, except for the few forms found in North America, due to the overlapping of the northern and southern zoölogical realms. North American genera are Lithodytes of Florida and Texas and Syrrophus of Texas. (Refer to p. 163.)

Family VI. Engystomatidæ

With some exceptions, these "Narrow-mouthed Toads" have, as the name implies, a narrow pointed head and a small mouth in sharp contradistinction from the type among the Salientia. These structural characteristics of the family are related to the habit of feeding upon ants and minute insects only. The body is usually very stout, making the small size of the head all the more striking. The ear is usually invisible. Most members of the family possess no teeth on the jaw. There are never palatine teeth, but often there is a serrated ridge across the roof of the mouth in front and a second one farther back. These ridges may be a modification in structure due to ant-eating habits.

The shoulder-girdle is always of the firmisternal type, but it differs greatly among the various members of the family in its details of structure. The pupil of the eye may be vertical, circular, or horizontal. The legs may be short or long; the toes provided with disks or not. In fact, outside of the fundamental distinguishing features (shoulder-girdle firmisternal, sacral diapophyses dilated), there are few points of likeness among the members of the family. Boulenger has divided it into three subfamilies, and the unlikenesses are evident also from the fact that there are only about twice as many species as genera.

The Engystomatidæ are tropical in their distribution. The only North American species found outside of southern Texas is *Engystoma carolinense*. This is found in a belt across the continent from Florida to Texas, inclusive, and as far to the north as Virginia (Cape Charles), southern Illinois, and Missouri. (Refer to p. 166.)

Family VII. Ranidæ

The Family of the Ranidæ is the most specialized of the Salientia; it is also one of the most unified families in its structural characteristics. The shoulder-girdle is not only always firmisternal in type, but also usually agrees with the type for the family in its details (such as the presence of the precoracoids and a well-developed omosternum and sternum furnished with a bony style). The cranium also constantly shows the same characteristics (such as the absence of a frontoparietal fontanelle).

The family contains a large number of genera, and it is very widely distributed. Australia, New Zealand, and southern South America are the only parts of the world not possessing representatives of the true frogs. Some two hundred species (by far the largest number) are found in the tropical portion of the Eastern Hemisphere. North America has only one genus, Rana; there are seventeen known species, and one form of the rank of a subspecies (*Rana c. latiremis*). They are most numerous in the eastern part of the continent, though several species are found west of the Sierra Nevada Mountains. See p. 171.

V. *Phylogeny*

It is not until recent years that the Batrachians have been recognized as a distinct Class, intermediate in position between the Fishes and the Reptiles. This is partly because of the relatively high specialization of some of the living batrachian species, a specialization that removes them from the direct line of evolution and makes necessary a large amount of comparative morphological and embryological investigation before their true relationship can be discovered. In France and Germany, in England and lastly in America, this work has been going on since the time of Linnæus in the eighteenth century. Linnæus classified Batrachians, some of the Fishes, and Reptiles together, calling them Amphibia. Since then Batrachians have been classified with the Fishes and again and again in various combinations with the Reptiles. They were first recognized as a group distinct from both Fishes and Reptiles in 1804,[1] and were then called Batrachia.

There is now no question but that the Batrachians, no matter how they differ in form, are closely related to one another and are descendants of the Fishes. Neither is there any question that in the past ages some primitive forms of Batrachians, now extinct, formed the direct ancestors of the Reptiles. An understanding of their relation to other animal races has been facilitated by the discovery of fossil remains of Batrachians and Reptiles. Fossil Batrachia — the Stegocephali[2] — have been found which by the structure of the skeleton show evidences of descent from either the Dipnoi or Crossoptergii (extinct Fishes). Fossil Reptiles — Proreptilia and Theromorpha[3] — have been discovered which in their turn seem to produce a gradually traced line of evolution from these extinct Stegocephali to higher Reptiles.

The Stegocephali are found in largest numbers in the Carboniferous strata of North America and Europe. They thus must have flourished during the Coal Period in North America, that early epoch in the history of the earth following the Age of Fishes and preceding the Reptilian Age. At this time, the continent, which extended from what is now the Appalachian Mountain region west to Kansas and Nebraska only, was in a semi-emerged condition. The great areas of marsh were filled with jungles and rank growths of fern and conifer, with an animal life represented by many of the lower invertebrate forms (among them some of the lower insects), and by the vertebrate classes of the fishes, these early batrachians (the Stegocephali) and a few of the early reptiles. But there were no flowering plants, no moths, or butterflies, bees, or wasps; and the great silence was unbroken by bird or mammal. That the Stegocephali did not flourish much beyond this Coal Period is proved by the fact that their remains are found in ever smaller numbers from the lower Permian (at the close of the Carboniferous era) through the Trias (of the Reptilian era), and that above this, their representatives are almost wholly lacking.

---

1 Brongniart, " Essai d'une Classification Naturelle des Reptiles."

2 Stegocephali (Cope); Labyrinthodontia (Huxley). The latter represents the former in part only.

3 The fossils which have been assigned here may prove to be Stegocephalian instead of Reptilian.

In North America to-day, the Carboniferous strata made in the Coal Period are best represented in the region of the Alleghenies. It is in this region, in the upper Coal Measures of Pennsylvania, Ohio, and adjoining states that the fossils of the Stegocephali are found. They have also come to light in the Coal Measures of Nova Scotia.

These earliest four-footed, air-breathing vertebrates were often of considerable size (several feet in length). This is proved not only by their skeletons, but also by footprints left by them on slabs of sandstone both in Europe and in America. Usually they resembled the Salamanders in shape, sometimes possessing very long tails. The body carried a partial armour of bony plates or scales and the head was heavily armoured. The skeleton is in a relatively generalized condition such as might have developed into the relatively more specialized types found in the lower Batrachians (Apoda and Urodela) and in some extinct Reptiles. The presence of pentadactyle limbs of course proves the Stegocephali higher than all Fishes, but the shoulder-girdle is primitive, resembling that in the Dipnoian Fishes, and the pelvis and cranium present features very different from those of the typical Fishes, but in some respects like those in the Dipnoi and Crossoptergii and some extinct Reptiles. That the Stegocephali are not Reptiles is proved perhaps by the presence of two occipital condyles, whereas Reptiles have but one; it is proved to a certainty by the structure of the vertebræ. (They are never gastrocentrous, as in Reptiles.)

The path of evolution from these extinct Stegocephali to the Urodela and the specialized Salientia is obscure. It is not known whether the intermediate ancestors were forms breathing by mean of gills throughout their lives (Perennibranchiata) or were already air-breathers. In fact, it is not even known whether the Urodela and Salientia arose separately from the Stegocephali or whether they had intermediate common ancestors. The oldest form of the Salientia known is represented by fossils from the Jurassic beds of the Rocky Mountains (representing the middle period of the Age of Reptiles). So little is known of this form, however, that it has little weight. The earliest reliable evidence of anything approaching modern types is given by a small skeleton found in the Cretaceous of Belgium (the latest period of the Reptilian Age, just previous to the Tertiary); this is thought to be a perennibranchiate Urodele (Hylæobatrachus). Probably Batrachia were abundant throughout the Reptilian Age (Mesozoic), but were represented by delicate, marsh-living animals not suited to fossilization. The modern types of the Salientia appear in the Tertiary with about as many genera and species as now.

Not only do the Salientia show their development from the Fishes through fossils, but their structure still tells the story of their descent. In addition to this, some points of the proof are shown in their development through a larval form adapted to water life.

The adult structure which constitutes the main likeness is the three-chambered heart with its valved conus arteriosus and the symmetrical arrangement of arterial arches. Two of the telling points in the development are the presence of lateral line sense organs previous to the metamorphosis (p. 6), and the existence of four or five gill arches in the larva. It is thought that the gills of the tadpole are not phylogenetically related to the gills of true Fishes, but that they are so related to the external gills possessed by some of the Dipnoi and Crossoptergii, or that they have developed in response to the needs of the tadpole in its adaptation to a water environment. This is true even of the so-called internal gills, which replace the first external gills and are covered by the opercular membrane. They have been called internal because they were under this opercular membrane, not because they were homologous with the internal gills of Fishes.

The lowest of the Salientia and the most nearly related to the primitive Batrachians are the Discoglossidæ (outside of the Aglossa, which are not represented in North America). These have not only the primitive characteristics of the skeleton (vertebræ opisthocœlous, distinct short ribs, etc.), but they have other structures also in primitive condition. Such is a tongue adherent to the floor of the mouth, so that they must capture food with the jaws, as do the Urodela. The Pelobatidæ are perhaps intermediate in position between the Discoglossidæ and the Bufonidæ and lead also to the Cystignathidæ. These last, in their turn, point towards the Hylidæ. The Ranidæ are thought to be the highest among the Salientia.

Thus, historically, Batrachians are more interesting than any other vertebrate Class. They bridge the greatest gap in verte-

14

brate evolution: they made the change from water life to land life at the time when the earth reached the condition in which land existence was possible.

Their small numbers now — only one-eighth that of the Fishes, one-fourth that of the Reptiles, and one-tenth that of the Birds — and the few fossils found would seem to prove that they never became a dominant group. Not remaining perfectly adapted for water life, as are the Fishes, never becoming independent of water and fully adapted to land life, as are the Reptiles, they have been at a disadvantage as a race. They have been limited in their distribution to moist situations near water, and have been wiped out of existence in large numbers when conditions changed, because they were not able to migrate over dry regions until they again found a proper habitat. Also, during those ages when the earth was occupied by Fishes, Batrachians, and Reptiles only, the Batrachians could not but be unequal to the situation, pitted against two devouring races, the Fishes in the water and the Reptiles on land.

VI. *Temperature and Hibernation*

All Batrachians, like Fishes and Reptiles, are cold-blooded, i.e. they have a variable body heat, depending on the temperature of the environment. In this they are distinguished from Birds and Mammals, which have an unvarying body temperature.

Because of this variation of the body temperature with that of the surroundings, Batrachians can endure extremes of heat and cold, but are greatly influenced by them. With decreasing temperature the processes of respiration and circulation gradually slacken speed, and the animals become more and more lethargic until they sleep. With rise of temperature to a limit varying from 20° to 30° Centigrade in the different species, they gain increased activity.

Members of the Salientia can endure an astonishing amount of cold; even freezing in the water of a pond or in the mud at its bottom will not of necessity cause death. The circulation and all life processses may stop, but if the blood and protoplasm of the heart do not fall much below freezing-point, the frozen parts will recover. Since sleep is induced in specimens at varying temperatures below 10° C., it is easy to understand why Batrachians are not found in the extreme north.

In the autumn, when the frog or toad feels this slowness and inactivity of the body functions, it creeps away into some protected place or burrows into the soil. (Refer to p. 33.) The burrow is pushed to a greater or less depth, depending on whether the place chosen is at the bottom of a pond, under logs or stones, or in the open earth of gardens or fields—depending also on the species and on the age and consequent size and strength of the individual.

This hibernation or sleep induced by cold continues until a return of high temperature. If by any cause climatic conditions of the spot chosen should change, or if chance led the batrachian into a deep well, cave, or other cold situation so that a sufficiently high temperature never returned, hibernation would continue for years perhaps, until, still sleeping, the creatures died from exhaustion of vital forces. Frogs that have been frozen are always found in the hibernating position.

The Salientia can endure a greater degree of cold than of heat. It is thought that in water death occurs at 40° C. Thus tadpoles and water frogs are often killed in large numbers in the shallow pools of Texas. Land frogs and toads hide away in cooler situations under moss and stones in shaded regions and pass through a period of æstivation till lower temperature returns. The tree frogs can endure much higher temperature than can dry-skinned toads or water frogs. It is said that they can sit in the sun at a temperature of 60° C. (120° F.). This is possible because of the moisture secreted by their skins. The fact is that they do not actually experience this high temperature because evaporation keeps the surface cooled to a much lower point.

VII. *The Poisonous Character of Frogs and Toads*

When annoyed or when taken roughly in the hand, members of the Salientia squirt out from the urinary bladder a transparent fluid wholly harmless in character and usually odorless. When handled very roughly by an enemy, a secretion is given out in minute quantities from glands in the skin. This is not harmless if taken into the system of an animal; it is a poison varying in amount and intensity with the species.

The skin of the Salientia is thickly set with glands. These may be so small that they are invisible to the naked eye, the skin appearing perfectly smooth. On the other hand, they may be larger, and if large, are either few and scattered or many and aggregated — the latter condition being illustrated by the warts and parotoids of the toads and by the lateral folds of some of the frogs.

It is thought that these glands are of two kinds, slime-glands and poison-secreting glands. The slime-glands have for their chief function assistance in the process of respiration by the skin. But it is thought by some that their secretion serves a secondary purpose of protection; that it is an alkaloid and acts as a narcotic. The larger poison-secreting glands are sometimes so few and scattered as to be invisible to the naked eye, but often are gathered together in conspicuous elevations. In these aggregations of glands the openings are sometimes plainly visible to the naked eye. (Parotoid glands, Figs. 48 and 89.) The secretion is milky in appearance and acid in character and is thought to act as a convulsive.[1]

The value of the secretion lies in its protection of the Batrachian from enemies who would otherwise devour it. This poison is not aseptic, as is the case in poisonous snakes, but acts upon the heart and central nervous system. That of the European toad *Bufo vulgaris* has been compared to Digitalis and Erythrophlæum.[2] Numerous experiments have proved that toad poison injected into the system will kill any vertebrate, the dose being proportionate to the size of the animal.

If a young dog takes a toad into its mouth, it will never repeat the act, and perhaps suffers much discomfort for twenty-four hours or more because of this first offence. Snakes eat toads without any apparent discomfort. Skunks are fond of toads as an article of food, but before they eat them they roll them roughly under their paws on grass or other low vegetation until the poison has been sent out from the glands and rubbed off on the grass. *Rana œsopus*, the gopher frog of Florida, eats toads, but ejects the poison from the mouth almost immediately after swallowing the toad. If the frog is in water, this poison floats at the surface in conspicuous white foamy masses.

Frogs have less poison in the skin than toads have, and serve as food for all sorts of animals, especially for birds. Herons feed

---

[1] Physalix, 1890.

[2] Boulenger, 1897.

largely on bullfrogs; leopard frogs have been found in the stomach of a loon;[1] bronzed grackles have been observed eating wood frogs,[2] and so on.

The poison secreted in the skin of the Salientia concerns only the enemies who feed upon them; it does not affect man. The secretion, even if rubbed on the hands, cannot cause the formation of warts; however, it will produce an irritation and smarting if transferred from the hands into the mouth or eyes. It is said that German violinists purposely handle toads before playing, and that the secretion prevents the hands from perspiring greatly.[3]

VIII. *Regeneration of Lost Parts in the Salientia*

In the Urodela the power to regenerate lost parts is very great. Not only the gills and the tail of a salamander, but the limbs also, will be reproduced perfectly if bitten off by some hungry beetle or fish, or torn off by one of its own kin.

This power of regeneration extends also to the more specialized group, the Salientia, but the reproduction of the lost part is the more perfect, the younger the specimen. The tadpole's tail may be bitten off or injured again and again, and each time it will grow to its previous size.[4] This is true even at the time when the period for the resorption of the tail has almost been reached.

If the hind limb of a metamorphosing tadpole be injured, even amputated, above the knee, before the completion of the metamorphosis, it will be regenerated completely. After the frog form is attained, the power of regeneration is largely lost, although the injured limb will always show some tendency toward replacing the lost portion.

IX. *Voice among the North American Salientia*

All members of the North American Salientia can produce sound. This sound is caused by air passing over vocal cords in the larynx of the throat, and so it constitutes a true voice. The loud croaking given during the breeding season is produced

---

[1] Hills (T. M.), Zoölogical Society Bulletin, N. Y. Zoöl. Soc., April, 1904.

[2] Miller (W. De W.), Plainfield, N. J., Bird Lore.

[3] Boulenger.

[4] For the relation of this regeneration to the notochord, see Bryn Mawr College Monographs, 1902. Morgan (T. H.) and Davis (S. E.).

usually by the males only of a given species. The air enters at the nostrils (the mouth is kept closed) and passes back and forth from mouth to lungs over the vocal cords. The sounds can be produced under water, and often are in the case of our common bullfrogs.

The Salientia possess internal vocal sacs in the region of the throat or on each side at the shoulder. These, when inflated, may push out and stretch the loose outer skin of the body, and thus show as external vocal pouches. The vocal sacs are filled with air, through openings from the mouth, and act as resonators, increasing the volume of sound. Single external vocal pouches at the throat are possessed by Engystoma and Hypopachus, by *Bufo fowleri, Bufo punctatus, Bufo lentiginosus, Bufo americanus, Bufo l. woodhousei,* and by all members of the Hylidæ. (Fig. 7.)

Fig. 7. The Common Tree Frog—(1) in resting position with lungs inflated and body large, and (2) singing, the air from the lungs forced into the throat vocal pouch.

Vocal bladders inflated from the middle of the base of the throat are to be found in *Bufo cognatus, Bufo compactilis,* and *Bufo quercicus.*[1] (Fig. 8.) Vocal pouches visible at the shoulder are

[1] Living male specimens of *Bufo hemiophrys* and *Bufo debilis* have not been examined.

19

Fig. 8. Bufo compactilis with vocal bladder extended from base of throat.

conspicuous in *Rana pipiens* and *Rana sphenocephala*, *Rana areolata* and *Rana æsopus* and in *Rana virgatipes* and *Rana grylio.* (Fig. 9.) Other North American members of the Salientia, as far as examined, have internal vocal sacs which show their positions during the croaking but do not inflate so greatly as to have the skin over them become thinned.

Each species has its typical call, or " song," with definite pitch and quality of tone. The calls are exceedingly simple, seldom involving anything like rhythm or melody. However, several of the calls contain notes of different pitch usually sliding into one another (*Bufo fowleri, Rana catesbiana*), and all are given with an emphasis and expression peculiar to the given species, so that we cannot say that the calls lack character. In a few cases they are decidedly musical and pleasing to the ear.

The typical call of the Salientia consists of a single note. The note

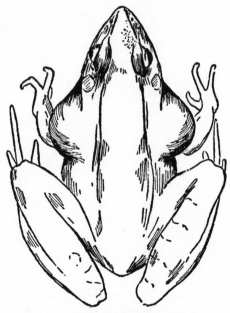

Fig. 9. Leopard frog, drawn to show vocal pouches extended at the shoulders.

may be short and repeated in very rapid succession, as that of *Acris gryllus*; or longer and given in less rapid succession, as is that of *Hyla pickeringii*; or decidedly prolonged and given at

20

still greater intervals, as in the case of *Bufo americanus*. This single note may be of any pitch whatever, high or low; and frogs of the same species may give calls of different pitch; in fact, there seem to be two or three prevailing tones in the case of some species. This is decidedly true of *Bufo fowleri* and *Hyla pickeringii*. Again, the note may be smooth and unbroken (*Hyla pickeringii*), vibrated so rapidly that it reminds one of the buzzing calls of some Orthopterous insects (*Engystoma carolinense*), or trilled in a pronounced fashion (*Hyla versicolor*). The quality may vary as greatly as the pitch, being sweet and musical(*Bufo americanus*), sonorous and musical (*Rana catesbiana*), harsh and squawking (*Bufo compactilis*), like the rattling of pebbles (*Acris gryllus*), and so on. The character and expression in many cases is easily recognizable: for instance, the song of *Bufo americanus* is reposeful, almost serene; that of *Hyla versicolor* suggests comfort, just as the purring of a cat does; *Bufo Fowleri* voices woe and desolation with every note; and *Bufo quercicus* would seem to be expressing most active distress in its tones like those of a lost chicken.

Enough to say that these calls of the Salientia are easily recognized after being once heard and identified, and although they are less complex and musical than those of the birds, nevertheless we get much pleasure from the recognition of these primitive songs of a primitive race. They not only act as tolerably accurate barometers, thermometers, and calendars, but in our travels through new parts of the country announce to us something concerning the fauna of the place without investigation on our part.

During spring and early summer we are likely to hear not the voice of a single performer of a given species, but the complex sounds produced by a chorus of performers. The result of the many voices may be a harsh and discordant medley or an effect of harmony, depending on the species, the number singing and the vigor and rapidity with which they are producing the sounds. *Rana catesbiana* and a few others do not sing in chorus.

The females, as a rule, produce less loud and emphatic calls than those given by the males. They never show external vocal pouches. In some cases they seem to be voiceless. However, many that were thought voiceless have, during later investigation, been heard to produce sounds. Further investigation will probably prove all to have the power of producing weak sounds of some sort. Many frogs and toads, both male and female, give a high-pitched cry when greatly annoyed, and some of the frogs open the mouth and produce a scream so loud and so much like the human voice that it is startling in effect. The female bullfrogs (*Rana catesbiana*) of Wisconsin can give the low-pitched "jug-o-rum" call with a vigor almost equal to that of the male, also swelling the internal vocal sacs to a size almost equal to those of the male.

X. *Colour and Colour Change*

Colour in the Salientia is largely due to pigment in the skin. This pigment may be black, red, yellow, or metallic. The black pigment is granular and is enclosed within cells (chromatophores) which have the power of changing shape. With a low power of the microscope, these dark, branched cells can easily be seen in the thin web of a frog's foot or in the fin of a tadpole's tail. There

is usually a layer of black pigment cells just below the epidermis, which, itself, is white and transparent. These pigment cells may contract or expand, radiating many branches. If they contract and retreat, the surface of the frog is left light in colour (Fig. 10); if they expand, stretching out black anastomosing branches toward the transparent epidermis, the skin appears dark (Fig. 11). Each cell is connected by means of a slender nerve fibre with the sympathetic nervous system, which

Fig. 10. When the pigment cells retreat and contract, the resulting color of the skin is light.

in turn is connected with the central nervous system of the animal. Therefore the cells can act in harmony and as the result of a common stimulus. This stimulus may be brought to the cells by reflex action from outside influences (such as light and heat) acting directly on the skin, or by outside influences (such as the colour of the surroundings) acting through the eye.[1] Or, on the other hand, the stimulus may be sent from within the animal by reflex action, and may have its origin in the character of the food or some item of the physiological condition of the creature.

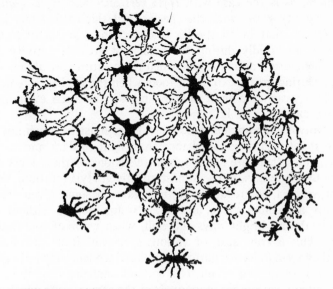

Fig. 11. When the pigment cells send out interlacing branches the resulting color is dark. After Lister.

It is easily proved that certain definite stimuli bring about definite results. Bright light or heat causes the cells to contract and the skin to become lighter in colour. Darkness or cold causes expansion of the cells and resulting dark colour of the skin. Thus hibernating frogs are dark-coloured; the same frogs sitting in bright light are so light-coloured that they would seem a different species to the casual observer. Absence or presence of moisture, other conditions being equal, seems also to play a part in causing the pigment cells to contract or expand. Toads kept in a dry

---

[1] Blind specimens change colour much less rapidly than do those that are normal.

place or found along a dusty road are light in colour, while those kept or found in moist surroundings will prove to have the pigment cells spread so that the skin is dark-coloured. Activity on the part of the toad or frog has a marked tendency to produce a change to lighter colours; this is true even when there are counteracting influences, such as darkness.

The change from light to dark and *vice versa* may take place in as short a period of time as ten minutes (*Hyla regilla, Hyla squirella*, etc). Again, the time necessary is habitually a half-hour or more, as is the case with *Hyla versicolor* and *Hyla gratiosa*. The rapidity varies with the species; but this further fact is always true, that in all species colour changes are likely to take place more rapidly during the season of greatest activity (the breeding season) and at a time when the creatures are abundantly fed. During great scarcity of food, when the vitality is reduced, the frog assumes a light colour, and retains such even under strong counteracting influences.

Notwithstanding all these facts, there must be much not yet understood regarding the change from light to dark and the reverse, since there are so many contradictions of these facts that come under observation. Almost any given Hyla (gratiosa, versicolor, cinerea, squirella, regilla) may take on some given colour, usually a medium shade, and retain it for months without any change during bright days and dull, when warm or cold, wet or dry. This is true, also, of various species of Rana, perhaps of all; they seem to have a natural individual tendency toward a given colour or shade and retain it in spite of changing conditions and in company with other individuals of the same species which constantly respond to these changes.

Again, frogs and tree frogs sometimes surprise one by becoming their lightest when kept in complete darkness and when all conditions would seem to point towards their taking on their dark dress. This is noticeably true of *Hyla pickeringii* and *Hyla cinerea*. Again, some species of tree frogs, *Hyla squirella* in particular, will change back and forth again and again very rapidly for hours at a time when the conditions remain the same. Thus the process of change would seem not to be a wholly automatic one nor the result entirely of reflex action. There are probably internal factors to be taken into account, factors that have to do not only with the physiological condition, but also concern the primitive sensations and emotions of the frog. Some scientists go as far as to say that changes of colour in Batrachia "can be inhibited by the will and can be produced at will."

A frog that possesses a layer of black pigment cells under the epidermis will, as indicated, change from light to dark, but if there are no other pigments or other structures, the shades passed through will be dull browns and greys. If yellow pigment is possessed also, the changes will be from black through bright browns to light yellowish shades. Green colour is not produced directly by a pigment, but as the result of black and yellow pigments and a structure, namely, the so-called interference layer. This is a single layer of polygonal cells between the epidermis and the black pigment layer. These cells contain minute yellow particles, which crowd to the sides of the cells next the epidermis. If these cells were empty, the result would be simply that the black pigment layer would be farther from the surface and would be seen through the interference layer. This would make the colour appear blue instead of black, giving the ordinary colour phenomenon of dense media, as seen in the colour of the sky (i. e. all the light waves of great wave lengths are absorbed and only those of short lengths are reflected). When the interference cells contain yellow, the blue is seen through the yellow and the resultant colour is green.

The green colour thus produced may be more blue or more yellow, and may change to brown when the black pigment cells expand greatly and press close about the cells of the interference layer, thus diminishing the density. A fragment of the outer skin of a green tree frog examined from underneath, of course appears black, because we are looking directly at the black pigment layer. The same piece looked at from above and against the light appears brown, but examined from above with light from above, it appears green and shows the polygonal cells of the interference layer.

Therefore frogs that have the interference layer and black and yellow pigments appear green or brown and can change from one to the other with great rapidity. Sometimes to these pigments and the interference layer are added pigments of other colours, red, white, and metallic, or iridescent. Consideration

25

of all these facts gives us some understanding of the astonishing changes and combinations of colours seen in some of the North American tree frogs, such as *Hyla regilla*.

As a rule, the colouration of the Tailless Batrachia is seldom plain green or brown but is more or less spotted, mottled, or striped, so that the animal blends with the detail of its background and is more or less invisible. There are no Salientia in North America that, like some of the black and yellow salamanders, present sharp contrast of striking colours, and so warn their neighbours of their poisonous character.

Broadly speaking, the lower Families have less complex pigmentation and skin structure than the higher forms, so that their colours are likely to be greys, browns, and olives, with some admixture of red and yellow. This is true of the Discoglossidæ, Pelobatidæ, and Bufonidæ. The most complex colouration is possessed by the Hylidæ and Ranidæ. With exceptions, they have the interference layer well developed, and so are brown or green, changing from one to the other and through many shades of each, besides having additional effects produced by red, white, and metallic pigments. Of the Ranidæ, *Rana palustris, sylvatica,* and *virgatipes* represent some of the species that, as far as observed, are never green; *catesbiana, grylio, clamitans,* and *pipiens* are among those that change rapidly from green to brown.

The colours of the upper parts of the frog or toad make it harmonize with its surroundings. Many Hylidæ and Ranidæ have bright colours on portions of the body concealed during rest, but displayed in leaping and swimming: witness the orange yellow of *Hyla versicolor, Hyla andersonii,* and *Rana palustris,* and the bright red of *Rana draytonii,* as well as of *Rana pretiosa* and *Rana aurora* of the Pacific Slope. These brilliant colours are called flash colours.[1] They may act as recognition marks for others of the same species, or may serve to startle the enemy and warn of the more or less poisonous character of the possessor.

The colour patterns of the Salientia are interesting when we consider their origin in past ages. They have come into existence slowly, through the influence of light, and probably as a direct result of the alternating spots and bars of sunshine and shadow cast on the creatures by the sun shining through the foliage of their environment. The pigment was gradually mar-

---

[1] Hans Gadow, Cambridge, England.

shalled into definite arrangement, and those frogs in which the arrangement was such as to be helpful in hiding them in their environment were missed by enemies, while others were destroyed. The protective arrangements were inherited and again emphasized through generation after generation until we have in the Salientia of to-day animals wellnigh invisible in their haunts. When we do see them against their background of water and foliage, it is wonderful how greatly the elongated spots and horizontal bands of light and dark that make up the pattern on the back and that cross the folded legs resemble the alternating sunshine and shadow made by the sun shining between plant stems and grass blades. The light-edged rounded spots of *Hyla gratiosa* and *Rana pipiens* are marvellously like the shining sun-spots that dance on the ground when sunlight is streaming through dense foliage.

One of the most complicated conditions exists in the cases where a given pattern is vividly displayed when the frog wears a dress of some medium shade and is wholly obscured in the light and dark phases of colouration. This is true of the colour pattern of *Acris gryllus, Smilisca baudinii, Hyla gratiosa, Hyla versicolor*, and others among the Hylidæ, and of *Rana catesbiana, Rana grylio, Rana onca*, and perhaps others among the Ranidæ.

The origin of the colour of Salientia is still a problem. It is largely a chemical problem, closely connected with the food of the species and with the conditions of the chosen environment. The pigments are thought to be mainly excretory in origin, waste products deposited in the skin — perhaps through the influence of light and heat—instead of disposed of in the ordinary fashion. The white pigment is thought to be guanin, related to uric acid, and the metallic pigments are named from their composition "guanin cells" or " iridocytes."

XI. *Animal Behaviour*

" How intelligent is the creature?" is a question of interest in the study of any animal. How many of its actions are the result of automatic response to the various stimuli of the environment? How many can be explained wholly as instincts, that is, racial habits inherited through a long line of ancestry and performed alike by each and every member of the race? How many actions denote intelligence higher than this?

Watch a tree frog leap, catch a swaying branch with precision of aim, and balance itself perfectly on the frail support. See the toad that has jumped to the top of the aquarium balance itself for a few minutes on the edge of the thin glass while it makes an examination of the surroundings before proceeding. Watch a frog that is sitting on some support adjust itself as you tip the support now in one direction and now in another. These actions look as wonderful as the feats of a rope-walker. They are, however, automatic actions, and could be done by a frog whose brain had been removed. The frog has a nervous system that makes most delicately co-ordinated muscular response through an elaborate system of reflex actions.

Frogs and toads are sensitive to various forces in their environment and give response according as they are acted upon by these forces. For instance, the earth's gravity affects the tree frog so that it is not at ease unless its head is uppermost. Watch the frog turn again and again in desperate effort to keep its head uppermost when its support is alternately held upright and reversed in position.

On a warm day the frogs are in full view among the late vegetation of the pond. The next day, after a drop in temperature, not a frog can be found. Frogs in captivity remain out of the water or sit with head and shoulders protruding until the air becomes colder than the water. At this time they disappear and lie with flattened bodies and lowered heads at the bottom of the aquarium until a return of higher temperature. Thus frogs give automatic response to temperature stimuli.

The frog's method of eating is attended with much nervous alertness, and sometimes with unsatisfactory results to the frog. The food consists, in general, of living worms and insects, which are seized and swallowed alive. The frog uses his hands to help put the food into his mouth. The mouth has the sense of touch highly developed, but the sense of taste is present in only small degree. In all cases, movement of a small living object gives the visual stimulus, and, psychologically speaking, brings to the frog the suggestion of something to eat. Long experience of the race has taught that only immediate and swift motor response will result in capture of the food — the miller or grasshopper may take wing, the slug disappear under a board, or the caterpillar roll into a ball and "play dead." Usually, the result of the immediate seizure of the moving object is satisfactory, since almost all small insects and worms are part of a toad's or frog's menu. But sometimes lack of examination of the object brings dire results. Such is the case when a large stag beetle is swallowed. Its huge pinching mandibles produce terrible effect at once in the frog's stomach. Fortunately, the frog has a wide, short œsophagus, so that any disagreeable object can be disgorged immediately.

This lack of examination of food has made possible various stories about the toad: that is, that the American toad will seize and swallow shot rolled toward him until he is heavy with it, and that the Southern toad will again and again swallow the burning ends of matches, mistaking them for fireflies. It also explains an incident related in an old " American Naturalist." A toad was seen to pick up an elm twig that had just fallen from the tree above him, and the observer amusingly interprets that the toad used the hands to play with the twig as though playing upon a flute before finally dropping it.

However, although frogs and toads do, as a rule, seize moving objects without examination and will try to eat even one's finger or pencil, nevertheless there are many exceptions. Especially in the case of the toads is a more intelligent method often pursued. The moving object, if it is at all large or formidable, may be stalked some distance and examined closely. In fact, the toad may discriminate the forward-moving end and make special effort to take the creature head first. If grass or earth are taken with the food, the mouth distinguishes these through the sense of touch, and the toad removes them, or tries to, using the hands awkwardly for the purpose.

Also after swallowing a stag beetle or a very large unmanageable earthworm, the toad learns by his experience and cannot be tempted again by the same or similar objects. The permanency of the lesson has not been tested. Experiments with labyrinth tests have proved that the green frog can profit by experience.[1] The learning is very slow indeed, but after fifty to one hundred experiences, a habit is perfected, and when tested after the lapse of a month, still persists.

The frog's sense of sight is fundamental not only in the cap-

---

[1] The Instincts, Habits, and Reactions of the Frog. Robert M. Yerkes. Harvard Psychological Studies, Vol. I.

ture of food. It is the sense on which almost total dependence is placed for protection.

We are walking along the grassy margin of a lake. In a small cove ahead, screened by shrubbery, a green frog gives a vigorous croak. A second frog, a third, then many others, join till there is a harsh medley of sounds. This continues for some time; suddenly one loud voice stops, and instantaneously all are hushed. Why? We were trying to see through the shrubbery, and although perfectly silent, set a long flexible branch swaying, which the frog evidently saw. Shall we say, as do myth and story, that frog orchestras have leaders who intentionally signal the others when to begin, are on the watch, and again give an intentional signal on the approach of danger? Not at all. Human interpretations will not serve for the frog world. The following is the explanation.

Frogs are extremely alert in sight and hearing, especially in sight. There was no movement anywhere in the horizon of the pond, and one frog gave expression to the physical joy of existence. This croaking was evidence to all the other frogs that there was no danger present; their eyes gave the same proof of safety that the first frog had gained, and one by one they joined in the chorus. The bushes moved. One frog saw the motion (not necessarily the frog that croaked first), was frightened, and responded with instant silence. Perhaps others saw also; if not, the sudden hushing of the one voice implied danger, and every frog obeyed an impulse of fear and became silent. That is all. Except that we have reasoned it out, while the frogs felt and acted only.

Frogs see small objects best at a distance of three or four feet. They will very often let a fly or worm crawl immediately under their " noses " while they are staring with eager eyes far ahead. Toads are less far-sighted than frogs. However, frogs may see an approaching enemy — a person, a bear, or a large bird — ten or more feet away, that is they may give a motor response when the enemy is at that distance.

There is the familiar " splash " ahead. One frog has seen us. A second "splash," and a third, long before we can approach near enough to see the frog blending as it does with the colours of the bank. These second frogs and others ahead have the advantage in escape over the first, for they were put on the alert by the ominous meaning of the splash of the first. The sudden splash made by a frog leaping into water is associated with danger, since a frog is not likely to leap into the water unless it is startled — it walks or jumps short distances to the edge of the water, slips lightly into it, and swims. This splash, then, puts a frog into a waiting state of unusual keenness of sight and alertness of muscle. The frog may lift the head or take on a more attentive pose, but usually the only external evidence of this alert state is a changed rate of breathing. The throat movements are more rapid, except in cases where the attention demanded, or the fear induced, is relatively intense; in such a case, the breathing movements may cease altogether for several seconds at a time.

It is not only the result of out-of-door observation, but it has been proved by experiment that a frog does not give a motor response to sound alone (an illustration of a true inhibition phenomenon), but that a sound stimulus intensifies the effect of an accompanying visual or other stimulus. This explains not only the instances given, but many others. It means, for instance, that if the frog hears an insect before seeing it, he is put on the alert, so that when he sees it his dash for it is more vigorous and effective than it would have been with the visual stimulus alone. The gopher frog of Florida, sitting at the mouth of its burrow, hears a crunching on the sand or a crackling of twigs, and because of the warning of his ears is ready to beat a more vigorous retreat when the enemy appears than he otherwise could. It is unfortunate for the frog that the approach of the snake is so soundless, and that the heron hunting at the pond is so often statuesque and silent.

Frogs can hear sounds made in air, whether the frog's ear is in air or under water. It is thought that the hearing is keenest when the ear-drum is half in air and half in water. Frogs can hear sounds of both high and low pitch. The green frog is said to hear sounds varying in pitch from 50 to 10,000 vibrations per second. In captivity, frogs prove constantly that they hear sounds of all sorts. They often respond with croaking when the sound stimulus is non-startling in character, whether that stimulus be the croaking of another frog, the sound of running water, or of human voices. It is probable that one of the most ominous sounds in the ears of a frog is the pain-scream of one of its own species. This is a high-pitched sound produced with

31

the mouth widely opened. It is given only when the frog is injured by an enemy or is in a state of great fear. The cry expresses distress in large measure, and must imply to the listening frogs the presence of great danger.

The frog's ear has the functions of balance and orientation as well as the sense of hearing.[1] Sometimes in spring, after the breeding season, a frog is found that has the ear badly injured. Such a frog keeps the head lowered on the wounded side. It cannot progress directly, but moves in a circle instead. The automatic action of the frog's ear in the work of orientation is interestingly seen when we move a frog in its aquarium or moss garden from one part of the room to another; or when we walk from one place in the house to another with a toad or frog sitting on some support which is carried in the hand. At each corner, even at the slightest change in course, the frog turns its head to adjust itself to the new direction.

Sight and hearing are correlated senses, serving in the capture of food and the escape of enemies. The sense of sight and the temperature sense are correlated in receiving stimuli which result in various protective actions. In normal temperature, frogs are attracted by light and move towards it (positively phototactic). That a frog jumps into the water when frightened, instead of landwards, probably illustrates the fact that a frog moves toward the stronger light or more brightly illuminated surface.

Frogs in captivity constantly illustrate this relation to light. In trying to escape from an opaque pail, they leap upwards; in a glass aquarium they struggle to get directly through the glass (even when the glass is covered with white paper so that they cannot see through it). A tree frog will try for hours to get out at the upper end of a glass beaker turned upside down; darken the upper part and the frog will go to the source of light below and find the opening. A frog moves not only towards diffused light but towards direct sunlight as well. However, it does not remain in the sunlight, but takes a station near it, in diffused light or shadow.

Frogs do not distinguish between a lighted space and a white solid. They will turn towards a white card or paper and try

---

[1] The static and acoustic functions lie in the labyrinth organs (connected with the tympanum by means of the columella), since there is no organ of Corti, as in mammals. It is thought that the papilla basilaris (the nerve end organ from which originates the organ of Corti in mammals) is the most concerned in the acoustic function.

to jump through it, and they may struggle at the impossible task of working their way into the solid white surface made by the leaf edges of a closed book.

That frogs are attracted by light and have definite orientation in regard to it sometimes produces interesting results when frogs are in captivity, where the light comes strongly from one or two directions only. The same response to the same stimulus may place six or eight pickerel frogs in a row, each in resting position with toes tucked under and head resting meekly on the body of the frog in front of him; or a half-dozen green frogs may make burrows in the moss side by side in a row and sit in the burrows all facing the same way — six pairs of bright eyes alert and contented.

In increased temperatures the positive response to light is still greater up to a temperature of 30° C. Above this, the frogs move away from the light instead of toward it. In decreased temperatures, the response is less until at 10° C. frogs move away from the light (negatively phototactic). This is true whether the frogs are in air or water. Experiments [1] which have proved this are interesting because of the explanation they give of the æstivation habits of the Salientia in the high summer temperatures of Texas and Mexico and the hibernation habits during the winters at the north. Green frogs kept in a moss vivarium in winter remain out on the moss in normal temperatures, but disappear under the moss at once if the temperature of the room drops much below normal, or if a window is opened and the cold wind is allowed to blow over them.

Many North American frogs and toads show protective instincts or racial habits, the immediate cause of which seems to be unusually strong stimuli acting on the nervous system. When a toad, frog, or tree frog is disturbed suddenly, it may fill the lungs with air until they puff out at the sides, making the creature as broad as long. At the same time, the head is lowered to the ground and the frog certainly looks on the defensive. It seems reasonable that it would prove well-nigh invulnerable to the attacks of an enemy like the snake that expected to swallow it whole and head first.

A toad very often flattens and spreads the body and remains motionless on the ground when startled by the approach of an

---

[1] The Response of the Frog to Light. E Torelle. American Journal of Physiology, vol. 9.

enemy. This makes it almost invisible, because of the likeness of its skin in colour and texture to the soil. Many of the Salientia play dead in response to an unexpected tactual stimulus. The common toad will often hold the legs tight against the body and inhibit all movement — even the breathing vibrations of the throat — when seized by a dog or other enemy. The leopard frog may stretch the legs backwards stiff and straight, fold the arms on the breast, and inhibit the breathing movements. It certainly looks like a dead frog as it lies motionless in one's hand for fully a minute; suddenly with a lightning movement it is gone before the hand can be closed over it. The cricket frog plays dead in water. Taking a position with arms and legs rigid and throat collapsed, it floats about helplessly like any stick or leaf.

A very different protective instinct is possessed by some members of the group. For instance, the gopher frog of Florida has a ludicrous method of spasmodic instead of continuous activity. When trying to escape an enemy, it remains motionless for some seconds, after which it moves a short distance with indescribable swiftness and stealth, and then appears statuesque again in a new spot. This is repeated several times till the frog is two or more feet from the enemy, when a few successive prodigious leaps take him far out of reach. The tree frog *Hyla evittata*, when startled, may leap to a twig and take a position behind it. Here, hugging the twig closely, it will keep out of the range of vision of the enemy by moving alternately back and forth, to the right when the enemy moves to the left, and *vice versa.* This instinct is probably possessed by many of the tree frogs, though observed in this one only.

On the whole, it would seem that frogs and toads possess but a low order of intelligence. There are but few glimmerings of anything above automatic response to stimuli, behaviour resulting from reflex actions and hereditary instincts. They certainly form crude ideas of food and enemies. They evidently associate certain stimuli with crude ideas, such as the coming of an enemy or something to eat. It has been proved by experiment that they may associate two kinds of stimuli: after having received an electric shock on touching given wires, they afterwards leap as soon as they touch the wires and before the electric current is turned on.

They feel discomfort from hunger, cold, and lack of water; physical comfort from food, warmth, and moisture. They feel physical joy and express it in song. They certainly possess the one emotion, fear. Frogs are more excited by fear than are toads. A frog when frightened will dash into anything or from any height. A toad will proceed to the edge of a table or window, and stop to examine the surroundings before jumping.

Frogs and toads can be tamed somewhat. They will come out of their burrows for food at a given time and will take it from the fingers. They will get used to the movements of people and to all kinds of sounds. On the other hand, they walk over one another, and in fact pay no attention to one another outside of the time of the breeding season. Occasionally there is an exception to this. The sexual instincts of the green frogs are excited even in winter when the frogs are fed. Also, on occasions, *Rana pipiens* and *Rana onca* will snap at the head of a companion frog who has taken a worm that he was trying to capture. Whether this is an exhibition of anger, or the frog is still trying to get the moving worm which is gradually disappearing and finally disappears in the other frog's mouth, is a question not easily settled. Judging from the general meekness of toads and frogs, it would seem more probable that the latter explanation is the correct one.

XII. *Geographical Distribution.*

The Tailless Batrachians are widely distributed. Toads, or representatives of the genus *Bufo* (about 100 species), are found all over the world except in Australia and Madagascar. The genus *Hyla*, the largest among the Salientia (150 species), is almost cosmopolitan in its distribution, being found everywhere except in Africa. The genus *Rana* (140 species) has a range extending all over the northern world, though it is practically lacking from Australia, Africa, and South America.

Most of the North American Salientia belong to these three genera, *Bufo*, *Hyla*, and *Rana*. There are only four genera (*Ascaphus, Scaphiopus, Acris*, and *Chorophilus* [1]) peculiar to the continent, and of these, two (*Ascaphus* and *Acris*) possess a single species each, and one of these (*Ascaphus*) has, as far as known, an unusually limited range.

[1] Chorophilus has one representative in the Neotropical realm (Peru).

35

The more specialized a race of animals and the more perfectly it is adapted to life in a given haunt, the more dependent is its distribution on the physical features of a continent. The Salientia, though members of a relatively generalized Class, are in several respects most highly specialized; and they are illustrations of such perfect adaptation that they are helpless in the face of any condition radically different from those of the chosen environment.

For instance, they are cold-blooded, and so cannot live in extreme northern latitudes or in the highest altitudes, because of the attendant decrease in metabolism with lowered temperature. (See p. 15.) To a large extent, they breathe through the skin and absorb water through the skin, hence they must live in moist situations. They have not endurance enough to migrate even short distances over dry regions. Again, no Batrachian can live in salt water,[1] and not only is salt poisonous to them, but lime is, also. Therefore they can neither live in limestone regions or in those impregnated with salt, nor can they cross such regions.

Thus the North American Salientia must be dependent on the physical features of the North American continent. We shall not expect to find them north of a line of 0° C., annual mean temperature, because just north of this the ground remains frozen the year through, except at the surface. We shall not, moreover, expect to find as many species for some distance south of this limit as there are in the southern part of the continent. We shall not look for them in the bordering salt marshes, gulfs, and bays, nor in Salt Lake nor on the salt plains of the West. There must be relatively few of them on the dry Western plains, in the Rocky Mountains, and in the desert and plateau regions of California, Nevada, Utah, Arizona, Mexico, New Mexico, and Texas. Also, the species living in these latter places must be the species least dependent on moisture, namely the Toads; or those that live in deep burrows, never leaving these burrows except during rain (the Spadefoot Toads). We shall not expect to find tree frogs (Hylidæ) in treeless though fertile regions, such as the prairies of the Middle West. However, this point is less certain, since the condition is less vital. Moisture and other conditions being right, tree frogs can adapt themselves to life on the ground, and may

---

[1] Certain species can endure water with 1% salt; sea water has about 3.2%.

suffer retrogression in the structures which facilitated arboreal habits.

The distribution that we should expect from the physical features of North America is exactly the one we find on a study of its Salientia. The thermal barrier to their spreading gives only a few species to southern Canada. Very few species are reported from the Western plains and Rocky Mountain region; among them are the burrowing Spadefoot Toads, which are almost peculiar to the region. The dry plateaus of the Southwest yield mainly toads, some six species. The tree frogs are almost wholly limited to southern and southeastern regions, with eminent exceptions, such as *Acris gryllus*, the Cricket Frog, which has the disks of the toes reduced, and may be found on the ground either in forest regions or prairie districts. The riches of the continent in genera and species of Salientia are found in the moist forest-covered southeastern United States, in Florida, the Gulf States, and eastern Texas. The northern part of the Pacific Slope west of the Sierras also has some abundance of species.

A comparative study of the distribution of living and extinct animals, together with a study of the geological history of the world, has resulted in a division of the globe into faunal regions, each of which has its subregions. The western hemisphere has a tropical region (Neotropical) at the south, made up of South America, Central America, the West Indies, and Mexico. A boreal region at the extreme north consists of Canada from Newfoundland to Alaska, with a southern boundary corresponding in general to the northern outline of the United States (the main exceptions to this correspondence are due to southerly extensions along the mountain chains). The stretch of temperate America between these two is the austral [1] region, which is very nearly confined within the limits of the United States.

The Austral region has been divided into life zones that stretch across the continent south of the boreal zone from coast to coast. Their boundaries are very irregular. Along the east and west coasts the southern Austral zones penetrate far northward, and in the high altitudes of the eastern and western mountain districts the more northerly austral zones, and the Boreal also, reach long arms southward. The eastern wooded

---

[1] The Austral and Boreal of Merriam (1892) correspond to the following: Nearctic of Slater (1858); Medio-columbian and Aqulonian of Blanford (1890); Sonoran and Holarctic of Lydekker (1896); Medio-columbian and Holarctic of Cope (1896).

portions of the austral zones, counting from north to south, are known as the Alleghenian, Carolinian, and Austroriparian faunas, respectively. In a consideration of the distribution of the Salientia the first two may be taken together for the sake of convenience and called the Eastern subregion. The dry portions of the austral zones from the elevated plains to the west coast are known as the Transition, Upper Sonoran, and Lower Sonoran faunas. [1]

The Eastern subregion presents throughout similar conditions of environment for the Salientia. Everywhere are fertile fields or prairies, extensive wooded tracts, and a multitude of lakes and ponds, rivers and brooks, all affording suitable haunts and an abundance of insect food. Because of the thermal conditions, there are more species near the southern limits, and they diminish in number toward the north. This part of the continent is the home of the genus *Rana*, possessing eight species.

The species distributed throughout the extent of this subregion are as follows: *Rana clamitans, Rana palustris, Rana pipiens, Rana sylvatica, Bufo americanus, Hyla versicolor,* and *Hyla pickeringii.* Species not found outside its boundaries are *Rana palustris, Rana sylvatica, Rana virgatipes, Bufo fowleri,* and *Hyla evittata. Bufo fowleri* is reported only from Massachusetts, Rhode Island, and New York near the coast; *Hyla evittata, Hyla andersonii,* and *Rana virgatipes* are found only in the country east of the Alleghenies, New Jersey to Virginia. [2] A few species found in a more or less limited section of this subregion are reported from other subregions also; such are, *Chorophilus nigritus triseriatus, Hyla andersonii, Acris gryllus,* and *Scaphiopus holbrookii.*

The boreal region has but few representatives of the Tailless Batrachians. At the east it has *Rana septentrionalis* peculiar to itself and gains *Rana clamitans, Hyla pickeringii, Bufo americanus,* and a few others from the austral zones just south. At the west it has *Rana cantabrigensis* and its subspecies *latiremis, Bufo boreas, Bufo hemiophrys,* and *Chorophilus n. septentrionalis.*

The *Austroriparian* subregion consists of the southeastern United States, i. e. the coast region south from isothermal 77°

---

[1] For boundaries of Merriam's Life Zones, see chart in Bulletin No. 10, U. S. Department of Agriculture.

[2] The eastern part of the Carolinian division of Verrill or the Cisalleghenian division of Cope.

(Norfolk, Virginia), and those states bordering the Gulf of Mexico, Georgia, Florida, Alabama, Mississippi, Louisiana, and the eastern one-third of Texas. It also contains the country along the Mississippi to southern Illinois. West of the Mississippi, its boundary line extends southward from Missouri to the mouth of the Rio Grande in Texas.

This subregion has a large number of toads and frogs. It is the richest of all the subregions in members of the Hylidæ. Its forest areas and many streams, its relatively high temperature and humid air, make it peculiarly well adapted to the needs of this group. The subregion has many species peculiar to it; namely, *Hyla cinerea, Hyla squirella, Hyla gratiosa, Hyla femoralis, Chorophilus ornatus, Chorophilus ocularis, Chorophilus occidentalis, Engystoma carolinense, Bufo quercicus, Bufo lentiginosus, Rana grylio, Rana æsopus,* and *Rana sphenocephala.* Of these species peculiar to the subregion, many are found in the eastern sections and Texas as well, but *Bufo quercicus* and *Rana grylio* are not found west of the Mississippi and *Hyla gratiosa* and *Rana æsopus* are not found outside of Florida. Peninsular Florida is a faunal region distinct from the Austroriparian, but the evidence of this does not rest largely in the distribution of the Salientia. Florida has a member of the Cystignathidæ (*Lithodytes ricordii*), a wanderer from the West Indies.

The Austroriparian overlaps the Sonoran subregion in Texas. The species that it gains from the Sonoran in this overlapping are either toads or members of the Cystignathidæ adapted to live in rocky ravines or among limestone cliffs. They are the following: *Bufo compactilis, Bufo debilis, Bufo valliceps, Bufo punctatus, Bufo l. woodhousei, Lithodytes latrans,* and *Syrrophus marnockii.* This subregion, though itself poor in toads, gets so many additions from the two adjacent subregions that it makes a showing of seven species, possessed mainly by Texas, of course.

The Sonoran subregion is made up of the Upper and Lower Austral zones from the Western plains inclusive to the Pacific Coast. At the south it includes Lower California, Arizona, New Mexico, and western Texas, as well as the northwestern part of Mexico. At the north it extends into Montana east of the Rocky Mountains, to British Columbia between the Rocky Mountains and the Sierra Nevadas, and not quite as far north as Oregon west

39

of the Sierras. It is greatly broken into by the colder and less dry Boreal and Transition zones that extend southward in the high altitudes and moister valley regions of the mountains.

The whole subregion is made up of arid elevated plains and plateaus, of desert regions and mountain ranges. It is notable for its lack of Batrachia, the only genera of the Salientia at all well represented being Bufo and Scaphiopus. There is no species common to the whole Sonoran subregion. Unlike the Eastern Austral zones, it presents great natural barriers to the spreading of animal races, and so is cut into divisions, each having its more or less peculiar fauna.

That part of the subregion east of the Rocky Mountains is grass-covered, but relatively dry and treeless. It not only has an arid atmosphere, but it is so elevated that the temperatures are low. It has but few species of Salientia; two almost peculiar to it are *Bufo cognatus* and *Scaphiopus hammondii bombifrons.*

In Texas this dry region is separated from the moist Austro-riparian subregion of the eastern one-third of the state by the boundary of the first plateau (one of the series of three steppes which present a terraced rise westward from near sea-level to 4,000 feet above). This line passes near Fort Worth, Austin, and San Antonio, Texas, to the valley of the Rio Grande. In topographical, climatic, and faunal conditions, western Texas is as different from eastern Texas as Colorado is from Missouri. Austroriparian Texas is a plain with low hills of red sand and with shallow valleys and ravines. It is largely forest-covered, has a great fertile prairie in the central region, and many swamps in its southern portion. It is well watered also by the moist winds from the Gulf. In sharp contrast with this, the Sonoran portion — especially the region of the first plateau — is of peculiar interest. It is dry because of its elevation and because all prevailing winds are depleted of their moisture in crossing eastern Mexico or eastern Texas. It is picturesque with deep forest cañyons. The lower levels are covered with buffalo grass and with various species of cacti and yuccas. Species peculiar to this district are *Lithodytes latrans* and *Syrrophus*[1] *marnockii.* But from the surrounding sections of country the following long list of species is gained: *Hyla cinerea, Smilisca baudinii, Chorophilus n. triseriatus, Rana areolata, Rana pipiens, Engystoma*

---

[1] Lithodytes and Syrrophus are both Mexican genera.

carolinense, Scaphiopus couchii, Bufo debilis, Bufo punctatus, Bufo compactilis, and Bufo valliceps.

The country between this western section of Texas and the Western plains north of it, on the one hand, and the Sierras on the other, presents little besides barren mountains, desert valleys, and areas of sagebrush. It possesses two species of toads and one spadefoot; namely, Bufo l. woodhousei, Bufo cognatus, and Scaphiopus hammondii. However, this part of the Sonoran subregion is penetrated even as far as Arizona and New Mexico by the less dry Transition zones, and so this part of North America has a few other species of toads and frogs; these are Rana onca, Rana pipiens, and Bufo boreas nelsoni. The last is the southern mountain subspecies of Bufo boreas which is found at the north — both east and west of the Sierras. Rana pipiens, abundant in eastern North America, in Texas, and on the Western plains, reaches its western limit just east of the Sierras.

At the south, in Arizona and New Mexico, in addition to Bufo cognatus, Bufo l. woodhousei, and Rana pipiens, are found Bufo halophilus, Bufo alvarius, Bufo punctatus, and Hyla arenicolor, the latter two entering from Mexico.

The peninsula of Lower California has no species of Salientia peculiar to it. It reports Rana draytonii, Hyla regilla, Bufo punctatus, Bufo halophilus, and Scaphiopus couchii.

The narrow stretch of country between the Pacific and the Sierra Nevada, made up of California, Oregon, and Washington is arid in its southern portion (Sonoran)[1], humid and forested at the north (Transition). At the south are found Bufo halophilus, Hyla regilla, Rana draytonii, and, rarely, Rana boylii. The north has a longer list; namely, Bufo boreas, Bufo halophilus columbiensis, Hyla regilla, Scaphiopus hammondii, Rana draytonii, Rana boylii, Rana pretiosa, and Rana aurora. These are, for the most part, species not found elsewhere in North America. Some of them follow the temporary streams of the rainy season into the desert regions of California and Nevada on the eastern slope of the Sierras. Hyla regilla, for instance, is often found in springs from fifteen to forty miles distant from other water, having been stranded there during flood times of previous years, when the springs were temporarily in connection with streams.

[1] Named Diegan division by Dr. John Van Denbergh, San Francisco.

41

FIG. 12.—To explain fundamental structural characteristics mentioned in the keys.

FIGS. 13 and 14 (1 and 2).—*Scaphiopus holbrookii* Harlan. Raleigh, N. C. Very scared looking when first awakened. The skin of the side and upper arm is free from the muscles underneath and drops down in a fold over the lower arm when the creature is resting. The black pupil is vertical.

FIGS. 15 and 16 (3 and 4)—An uncanny-looking fellow Photographed to show wide front and the unbroken curve of the jaws, also the black horny thickening of the first and second fingers. The parotoid gland is round. The ear is distinct (in front of and below gland).

KEYS FOR THE IDENTIFICATION OF NORTH AMERICAN SALIENTIA[1]

(For terms used in Keys, refer to Fig. 12. For method of using Keys, see footnote 2.)

PRELIMINARY KEY TO FAMILIES

(See page 7 for internal characters determining classification into Families.)
I. Pupil of eye vertical.
    A. Inner sole tubercle small; ear not visible; parotoid glands present; size small. Northwestern United States (Washington).

        Ascaphus, of the Family *Discoglossidæ*. (See p. 51.)

    B. Inner sole tubercle large, with extensive cutting edge.

        Pelobatidæ. (See First Key, p. 43.)
II. Pupil not vertical; either horizontal or round.
    A. Parotoid glands always present.

        Bufonidæ. (See Second Key, p. 44.)
    B. Parotoid glands lacking.
        1. Fingers and toes more or less enlarged at tips, to form adhesive disks.
            a. Disks T-shaped, small; undersurface of frog smooth.

            Cystignathidæ. (See Third Key, p. 45.)

            b. Disks round, large or small; undersurface more or less granulated.
            Hylidæ. (See Fourth Key, p. 46.)
        2. Fingers and toes without disks.
            a. Head narrow and mouth small; a fold of skin on top of head behind eyes; ear not visible; size small (1½ inches, or less).

            Engystomatidæ. See Fifth Key, p. 48.)

            b. Head not unusually narrow; mouth large; ear distinct; size 2 inches or more (except in immature).

            Rqnidæ. (See Sixth Key, p. 48.)

FIRST KEY. SPECIES OF PELOBATIDÆ (*Spadefoot Toads*)

I. Ear distinct; parotoids round, flat; black granulations on top of head; two curved yellowish lines on back. Eastern North America.

        Scaphiopus holbrookii. (See Colour Plate II, also p. 53.)

---

[1] These keys are more or less artificial. Unfortunately, they cannot be based on colour, because of the great variation and the lack of stability in both colour and colour pattern in the members of this order. Also, it has been impossible to avoid detail and combine brevity with definiteness, because of the similarity of the various species.

[2] *Method of using Keys.* As long as the specimen agrees with the characteristics named in the Key, read continuously until a technical name is designated at the extreme right. As soon as the specimen disagrees with the Key characteristics, skip from the point of disagreement to the number or letter next in order.

In all instances where size is not mentioned, medium size (about 3 inches) is understood.

II. Ear indistinct; parotoids lacking.
    A. Skin smooth; head arched between the eyes in front, sometimes black and horny here, and on the end of the muzzle; size small (2 to 2½ inches). Western Plains.

           Scaphiopus h. bombifrons. (See Fig. 26, also p. 61.)

    B. Skin rough, with closely set tubercles; head not arched between the eyes in front.
        1. Muzzle truncate in profile; short, thick through at end; two or four light bands on back present or not. North America, west and south of Rocky Mountains.

           Scaphiopus hammondii. (See p. 59.)

        2. Muzzle rounded in profile; with or without intricate arrangement of light bands on back and sides. Southwestern North America.
           Scaphiopus couchii. (See Colour Plate II, also p. 57.)

SECOND KEY. SPECIES OF BUFONIDÆ (*Toads*)

I. Parotoid glands short, either roundish or triangular.
    A. Head rounded above, thick through; cranial crests not present; glands on tibiæ; size large.
        1. Muzzle relatively long, sloping in profile; skin very rough, with warts of many sizes; tendency to arrangement of warts in dorsal rows. Northern Pacific region.
           Bufo boreas. (See Fig. 133, also p. 115.)

        2. Muzzle short, steep in profile; skin warty, but relatively smooth on and between the warts; femur extremely short. Southern Pacific region.
           Bufo halophilus. (See Fig. 121, also p. 113.)

    B. Head flat, thin through; skin evenly and closely tubercular.
        1. Cranial crests high, sharp-edged, conspicuous. Mexico and Texas.
           Bufo valliceps. (See Colour Plate V, also p. 108.)

        2. Cranial crests not present; granulations on various parts of head; size small (two inches). Southwestern North America.
           Bufo punctatus. (See Colour Plate V, also p. 110.)

II. Parotoids longer, oblique, descending on shoulders.
    A. Cranial crests not present; skin evenly tubercular.
        1. Head flat and thin through; granulation on muzzle; parotoids unusually large; toad very small (1¾ inches). Southwestern North America.
           Bufo debilis. (See p. 112.)

        2. Head thick through, short; femur very short; sole tubercles unusually large; size medium. Mexico and Texas.
           Bufo compactilis. (See Fig. 93, also p. 102.)

B. Cranial crests straight; head short; leg short; underparts unspotted.

    1. Crests thick, divergent backward from a bony elevation above and between nostrils; two large sole tubercles, each with cutting edge. Western Plains and Rocky Mountains.

Bufo cognatus. (See Colour Plate V, also p. 99.)

    2. Crests narrow, inconspicuous; skin very tubercular, spinous on legs and arms; size small (1¼ inches). Southeastern United States.

Bufo quercicus. (See p. 104.)

C. Cranial crests curved around eyes; glands on tibiæ; size large. Arizona.

Bufo alvarius. (See Colour Plate V, also p. 106.)

III. Parotoids oval (sometimes kidney-shaped in C), extending straight backwards from the posterior angle of the eye.

A. Head long (three and a half times in total length); cranial crests greatly elevated, and swollen into knobs behind; underparts unspotted. Southern United States.

Bufo lentiginosus. (See Colour Plate IV, also p. 89.)

B. Head very short (five times in total length); cranial crests variable, usually parallel on a raised occiput; underparts unspotted, except on breast; sole tubercles large; size large. Rocky Mountain region and southwards.

Bufo l. woodhousei. (See Colour Plate IV, also p. 91.)

C. Head medium in length (four times in total length); cranial crests divergent behind; warts often large, and arranged singly in dorsal spots; underparts spotted. North America, east of the Rocky Mountains.

Bufo americanus. (See Colour Plate III, also p. 63.)

D. Head short (four and a half times in total length); cranial crests variable, usually parallel; warts never very large, usually arranged several in each dorsal spot; underparts unspotted. Eastern United States, near coast.

Bufo fowleri. (See Colour Plate IV, also p. 93.)

E. Head short (four and a half times in total length); muzzle vertical in profile; cranial crests parallel; no crests behind eyes; tendency to arrangement of warts in dorsal rows; underparts spotted. North Dakota and Manitoba.

Bufo hemiophrys. (See p. 98.)

THIRD KEY. SPECIES OF CYSTIGNATHIDÆ

I. Leg short (length to heel equals length of body forward to ear); muzzle rounded in profile.

A. Posterior femur spotted; head long (one-third total length); muzzle pointed, as seen from above; ear round; size small (1½ inches). Texas.

Syrrophus marnockii. (See p. 165.)

45

B. Posterior femur unspotted; head shorter (one-fourth total length); muzzle rounded; ear a vertical oval; size 3 inches. Texas.

Lithodytes latrans. (See Colour Plate II, also p. 163.)

II. Leg longer (length to heel equals length of body forward to eye, or some point anterior); muzzle truncate in profile.

A. Head longer than wide; sides somewhat tubercular; size small (1 inch). Florida.

Lithodytes ricordii. (See p. 164.)

FOURTH KEY. SPECIES OF HYLIDÆ (*Tree Frogs*)

I. Disks on fingers and toes of medium or large size (never so small that they are difficult to discern).
A. Skin coarsely granulated above, like undersurface; fingers webbed; head broad, short; size 2 to 2½ inches. Florida.

Hyla gratiosa. (See Colour Plate X, also p. 124.)

B. Skin rough, with small warts.
1. Posterior surface of femur reticulated with yellow and black; size 2 inches. Eastern North America.

Hyla versicolor. (See Colour Plate VI, also p. 117.)

2. Posterior surface of femur not reticulated or spotted; size 1¾ inches Southwestern North America.

Hyla arenicolor. (See Colour Plate X, also p. 122.)

C. Skin smooth, or nearly so.
1. Posterior surface of femur spotted or blotched.
a. Head short, relatively narrow; body long; white spot under eye and one at arm insertion; a black spot on shoulder; size 2 to 2½ inches. Mexico and Texas.

Smilisca baudinii. (See Fig. 178, also p. 151.)

b. Head broad, flat; form stout; upper surfaces green, bounded with line of white (even across wrists and heels); green extends in scallop on throat; size 1¾ inches. New Jersey and South Carolina.

Hyla Andersonii. (See Colour Plate VII, also p. 131.)

c. Muzzle pointed, projecting much beyond the line of the jaw; fingers not webbed; an oblique cross on the back; size 1 inch. Eastern North America.

Hyla pickeringii. (See Colour Plate X, also p. 138.)

d. Muzzle rounded, projecting but slightly beyond the jaw; no light spot under eye, nor distinct line along jaw; fingers slightly webbed; there may be a pattern of spots and bars similar to that of *Hyla versicolor* (Fig. 134); size 1½ inches. Southeastern United States.

Hyla femoralis. (See p. 150.)

2. Posterior surface of femur not spotted.
   a. Frog long and slender; colour plain, i.e. no evanescent pattern of spots and bars on head, back, and legs; size 1¾ to 2¼ inches.
   (1) Light bands from the muzzle along the sides, also on the tibiæ. Southern North America.

Hyla cinerea. (See Colour Plate X, also p. 126.)

   (2) No light bands; colour plain green above, white below. Virginia, Maryland.

Hyla evittata. (See Fig. 161, also p. 128.)

   b. Frog not unusually long and slender; light line along jaw (immediate edge of jaw dark).
   (1) Form robust; head thick through; canthus rostralis very prominent; back marked with evanescent pattern of bands and elongated spots; size 1½ inches. Pacific Slope.

Hyla regilla. (See Colour Plate VIII, also p. 134.)

   (2) Form more delicate; head not so thick through; canthus rostralis well marked, but not sharply angled; back marked with evanescent pattern of rounded spots; size 1¼ inches. Southern United States.

Hyla squirella. (See Colour Plate X, also p. 148.)

II. Disks on fingers and toes so small that they are scarcely discernible.
   A. Skin rough; webs very large; muzzle long and pointed; legs long; size 1 inch or less. North America, east of Rocky Mountains.

Acris gryllus. (See Fig. 184, also p. 153.)

   B. Skin smooth; webs minute, or lacking.
      1. Muzzle truncate in profile, long, slender; upper jaw edged with white; legs very long; size under 1 inch. Southeastern United States.

Chorophilus ocularis. (See p. 162.)

      2. Muzzle rounded in profile, slightly projecting beyond line of jaw.
      a. Posterior surface of femur unspotted.
         (1) A light line along jaw; usually longitudinal bands on back, the middle one forking posteriorly; size 1 inch, or slightly more.
            (*a*) Leg to heel equals total length.
            Head long.

Chorophilus nigritus. (See p. 157.)

47

Head short.

Chorophilus n. feriarum. (See Fig. 185, also pp. 157 and 160.)

(*b*) Leg shorter (length to heel equals length of frog forward to eye); head long. Middle and Western United States, east of the Rocky Mountains.

Chorophilus n. triseriatus. (See pp. 157 and 160.)

(*c*) Leg short (length to heel equals length forward to shoulder or ear); head long. Northern North America.

Chorophilus n. septentrionalis. (See pp. 157 and 160.)

b. Posterior surface of femur spotted; a light blotch above the dark edge of the jaw; leg short (length to heel equals length forward to ear or eye); size 1½ inches. Southern United States.

Chorophilus ornatus. (See p. 161.)

FIFTH KEY. SPECIES OF ENGYSTOMATIDÆ (*Narrow-mouthed Toads*)

I. Two large sole tubercles; toes with short webs; muzzle short in front of eyes (less than twice the longitudinal diameter of the eye); size 1½ inches. Texas.

Hypopachus cuneus. (See Colour Plate II, also p. 169.)

II. One small sole tubercle; no webs; muzzle in front of eyes longer (more than twice the longitudinal diameter of the eye).
A. Skin very smooth; form slender; head to shoulder one-third total length size 1 inch. Texas.

Engystoma texense. (See Fig. 193, also p. 168.)

B. Skin finely tubercular; form stout; head to shoulder one-fourth total length; size 1¼ inches. Southern United States.

Engystoma carolinense. (See Colour Plate II, also p. 166.)

SIXTH KEY. SPECIES OF RANIDÆ (*Frogs*)

I. Lateral folds present.
A. Skin with longitudinal folds between the lateral folds; definitely outlined spots on the back and sides; leg to heel equals or exceeds total length.
1. Spots squarish; undersurfaces of legs bright orange-yellow. Eastern North America.

Rana palustris. (See Colour Plate XIII, also p. 188.)

2. Spots rounded.
a. Head long (two and a half times in total length); circular white spot at centre of ear; spots on back not outlined with light. Southern States.

Rana sphenocephala. (See Colour Plate XII, also p. 186.)

48

b. Head shorter (three to three and a half times in total length); spots outlined with light. North America, east of the Rocky Mountains.

Rana pipiens. (See Colour Plate XI, also p. 171.)

B. Skin corrugated with elongated warts between the lateral folds and on the sides; definitely outlined rounded spots on back and sides; length of leg to heel not as great as total length.

  1. Head long (two and a half times in total length). Florida.

Rana æsopus. (See Colour Plate XIV, also p. 193.)

  2. Head shorter (one-third total length). Southern United States.

Rana areolata. (See Fig. 223, also p. 192.)

C. Skin relatively smooth between the lateral folds.

  1. Ear of male larger than eye; legs short; no black cheek-patch.

    a. With definitely outlined spots on back and sides; size small (2½ inches); web large. Nevada, Utah.

Rana onca. (See Colour Plate II, also p. 196.)

    b. Without pattern of spots; size 3½ or 4 inches. Throat of male yellow. Eastern North America.

Rana clamitans. (See Colour Plate XIII, also p. 198.)

  2. Ear of male not larger than eye; legs long; black cheek-patch usually present.

    a. With red in the colouration.

      (1) Leg to heel equal to total length; skin unusually smooth. Northern Pacific region.

Rana aurora. (See Colour Plate XIV, also p. 216.)

      (2) Leg to heel not equal to total length; skin may be tubercular in old specimens; size large. Pacific region.

Rana draytonii. (See Colour Plate XV, also p. 213.)

    b. No red in the colouration; brown or grey.

      (1) Length of leg to heel exceeds total length. Eastern North America.

Rana sylvatica. (See Colour Plate XIV, also p. 205.)

      (2) Length of leg to heel just equals total length, or is less than total length. Northern United States and Canada.

Rana cantabrigensis. (See p. 211.)

D. Skin very tubercular over the whole upper parts; webs conspicuously large and broad.

  1. Leg short (length to heel equal to length of body forward to ear); sole of foot rough with tubercles; eye set obliquely. Northern Pacific region.

Rana pretiosa. (See Colour Plate XVI, also p. 218.)

49

    2. Leg long (length to heel equal to total length); ear obscure, covered with tubercles; size small (2½ inches). Pacific region.

Rana boylii. (See Colour Plate II, also p. 221.)

II. Lateral folds not present; ear of male larger than eye; legs relatively short; webs large.
  A. Webs quite to the tips of the toes; head long (two and a half times in total length); size large (4 to 5 inches). Southeastern United States.

Rana grylio. (See Fig. 269, also p. 226.)

  B. Webs leave one joint of fourth toe free; body stout.
    1. Head narrow; size medium. New York to Minnesota and Canada.

Rana septentrionalis. (See p. 224.)

    2. Head broad; size very large (7 to 8 inches). Eastern North America.

Rana catesbiana. (See Fig. 276, also p. 227.)

  C. Webs shorter (two joints fourth toe free); head narrow, long; size small (2½ inches). New Jersey.

Rana virgatipes. (See Colour Plate XIII, also p. 222.)

FAMILY I. DISCOGLOSSIDÆ: THE DISCO-GLOSSOID TOADS[1]

THE AMERICAN DISCOGLOSSOID TOAD

Ascaphus truei Stejneger

IDENTIFICATION CHARACTERISTICS

Colour: Dull reddish brown, with a few indistinct blackish markings on the back. A dusky band between the eyes. The top of the head in front of this band pale reddish grey narrowing in the midline in front and bordered on each side below the line of the canthus rostralis by a band of black. This black band extends backward through the eye to the shoulder along the lower border of the parotoid gland. A black spot below the arm insertion. Posterior surface of arm irregularly spotted. Femur, tibia, and under side of foot edged by an irregular dark band which is sometimes edged with white. Underparts light, clouded with dark, especially across the breast. Fingers and toes tipped with light.

Measurements: Size small; i.e. length $1\frac{1}{2}$ inches. Head slightly broader than long. Nostril nearer to the eye than to the tip of the muzzle. Space between eyes equal to width of eyelid. Arms and legs relatively long; arm, 1 inch; leg (total length), $2\frac{1}{4}$ inches. Length of leg to heel equals length of body forward to eye. Tibia longer than femur.

Structure: Skin granular, slimy, wrinkled, and irregularly warty above. Smooth and wrinkled below. Parotoid gland elongated, extending from the eye backward toward the shoulder. A narrow elongated gland on the side, corresponding in position to the lateral fold of frogs. Head flat; muzzle elongated, abruptly descending on the sides, obtusely pointed in front. Canthus rostralis prominent. Ear hidden. Fingers long and slender; three palm tubercles, no tubercles under the joints. Foot but slightly webbed; no tarsal fold; inner sole tubercle medium in size; no tubercles under the joints.

Range: One specimen only of *Ascaphus truei* has been found. Humptulips, Washington, 1897.

---

[1] Refer to pp. 7, 8, and 43.

This curious little batrachian (a member of the Discoglossidæ, (see p. 8) is the lowest known form of the Salientia in North America. In fact, no other Discoglossoid toad has been found in the Western Hemisphere, and the discovery of this one in 1897 marks one of the most important steps in the history of the Batrachology of North America.

Although having the form of the Tailless Batrachian, and many of its structural characteristics, such as parotoid glands and a tongue free behind, it has a skeleton showing the fundamental features in a primitive condition, as in the Tailed Batrachians or Salamanders. It thus supplies an important item in the story of the evolution of the Salientia. (See p. 14.)

The geographical distribution of the Discoglossoid toads has been most interestingly worked out by Dr. Leonhard Stejneger, of the National Museum.[1] He makes the region southeast of the Himalayas, in Asia, the original home of the family. From here they radiated to New Zealand, in early Cretaceous times, to western America (over the land bridge that existed between Asia and North America) in upper Cretaceous times, and to western Europe in early Tertiary times. Curiously enough, although at the moment of publication of his theory no Discoglossoid toad had ever been found in the region indicated as the centre of radiation, a new species[2] was announced from there one month later by Boulenger.

---

[1] 1905. A Résumé of the Geographical Distribution of the Discoglossoid Toads, in the Light of Ancient Land Connections. Leonhard Stejneger. American Geographical Society, vol. xxxvii, No. 2, pp. 91-94.
Oct. 20, 1905. Science, p. 502. The Geographical Distribution of the Bell-Toads. Leonhard Stejneger.

[2] *Bombina maxima* Boulenger. Tong Chuan Fu, province of Yunnan.

FAMILY II. PELOBATIDÆ: THE SPADEFOOT TOADS [1]

THE HERMIT SPADEFOOT

Scaphiopus holbrookii Harlan

IDENTIFICATION CHARACTERISTICS

Colour: Greenish, yellowish, or ashy brown above, with or without a curved line of yellow extending backward from each eye. (See Fig. 17.) Iris golden. Light yellow colour about upper jaw, on sides, and on outer margins of the legs and arms. In the case of the female, the yellow is replaced by yellowish white. The under parts are dingy white, becoming purplish posteriorly. (For colouration, see Colour Plate II.)

Measurements: Size somewhat below medium, i. e. length 2½ inches. Female not much larger than male. Body stout and toad-like. Head large and with very wide front. (See Fig. 15.) Lower leg shorter than upper leg. Legs short; i. e. length of leg to heel about equal to length of body (to posterior margin of ear). (See Fig. 17.)

Structure: Skin relatively smooth, though close inspection shows small tubercles plainly visible on back and sides. No bony crests on the head. The thin skin is completely adherent to the cranial bones and is penetrated by small black bony granules. The eyes are exceedingly prominent; pupil vertical. Ear distinct, smaller than the eye. The upper jaw lacks the indentation common among toads. (See Fig. 15 and compare with Fig. 110.) The parotoid glands are small and round. (See Fig. 16.) The inner tubercle of the sole is a large black spade-like process; there is no outer sole tubercle. (See Fig. 19.)

Range: *Scaphiopus holbrookii* is found in every part of eastern North America, including Texas and Florida. It is reported from Martha's Vineyard, which fact, as Cope says, may indicate the late separation of that island from the mainland.

A strange weird-looking creature is the Hermit Spadefoot when he is turned out of his ground burrow. At first sight he

[1] Refer to pp. 7, 8 and 43.

looks like a small brown ball of earth, but almost immediately air is expelled from the lungs, so that the inflated sides collapse, and two elevations rise at the smaller end and become two round staring eyes (Fig. 13) of so brilliant a gold that they seem wholly out of place in such a dusky surrounding. In the centre of each golden circle is a very narrow black vertical slit, which gradually broadens into an oval black pupil. Awkward hands are lifted one at a time and rubbed over the eyes. The Spadefoot, now quite awake and alert (Fig. 15) begins trying to escape. He does not stealthily creep away as do many of the toads; he does not startle one with a prodigious leap, as do the frogs and tree frogs. He begins sinking out of sight into the soft earth, and in less time than it takes to tell it, has wholly disappeared from view.

If we wait a moment and then remove the earth carefully from over him, we find him cosily settled in his usual hibernating position. His head is bent downward so that his chin rests on his front feet. These feet and the back ones are tucked closely under him, his eyes are shut, and his sides are puffed out because of the expansion of the lungs within.

If we take him out and put him on a piece of paper or some other solid substance, instead of directly on the ground, we can observe the backward digging movement of the feet and can hear the scratching and scraping as the horny parts of the feet (Fig. 19) are vigorously rubbed against the hard surface. By this time, however, the creature is thoroughly awake and greatly frightened. (Fig. 18.) Finding its digging efforts unavailing, it creeps stealthily forward or hops in regular toad fashion for a short distance, and then tries again to dig a burrow in which to hide.

The Hermit Spadefoot is not well known. It burrows into the ground and sleeps days or weeks, perhaps years, at a time. A gravedigger once found one 3 feet 2 inches from the surface of the ground, with no evidence of entrance or exit to the burrow.[1] The Spadefoot is seldom discovered in garden or orchard; but it is certainly true that if a Spadefoot toad were turned out of its burrrow by the plough, the casual observer would not give it a second glance, because it looks so much like an ordinary dingy brown toad, unless one sees its eyes.

The mystery surrounding the life of the Spadefoot is increased by the fact that when he does leave his burrow it is always under

[1] Vol. I, No. 7, Bulletin of Amer. Museum of Nat. Hist., Col. Nicholas Pike.

cover of the darkness of night. Toads are lovers of the dusk; the Spadefoot is wholly nocturnal in habit, a fact which might be inferred from the cat-like vertical pupil of the eyes.

There is one time when the Spadefoot Toads make themselves conspicuous. This is when they come out of their burrows, hundreds strong, and go to the ponds or temporary pools for the purpose of depositing the eggs. This time is usually in the spring,[1] and is always coincident with a very heavy rainstorm or with a long-continued, warm drizzling rain. They are likely to remain in the pond only one night, or two at most, but during this time keep up a continual chorus of loud calls that can be heard at a great distance. The Spadefoot Toads swim and float awkwardly, sit on projecting stones and tufts of grass, and in fact turn the dead and shallow temporary pool of the meadow into a scene of great activity. The females make a low, grunting sound; the loud calls are given by the males only. Each call is relatively short, and is somewhat louder than that of the common toad. Its carrying power is greatly enhanced by a throat-sac which acts as a resonator. This sac swells to three times the size of the creature's head. The call is often started while the Spadefoot is floating with his body horizontal and his legs outstretched. Increase of air in the throat region changes the centre of gravity so that the body is thrown forcibly and instantaneously into a vertical position in the water.

The chorus is somewhat unusual in quality, and when it is heard at night it takes on an extra note of weirdness from the surroundings. An idea of its effectiveness can be gained by reading the accounts of it given by various observers. Now it is described as "a loud bellowing," again it is said to consist of "weird plaintive cries," or of "shrill ear-piercing groans." One writer calls it "a deafening, agonizing roar, hoarse and woeful."

After the eggs are laid, the Spadefoot Toads disappear entirely, leaving no trace of their hiding-places. In fact, it is not known whether they burrow in the neighbourhood of low land where temporary pools are likely to form, or whether they go a considerable distance into higher land before they burrow. At any

---

[1] F. S. Smith, April 29, 1879. New Haven, Conn.
C. C. Abbot, May, 1874. April 10, 1884. June 26, 1884. Trenton, N. J.
C. W. Hargitt, August 10, 1887. Martha's Vineyard.
C. S. Brimley, May, 1895. Raleigh, N. C.

rate, these facts are well authenticated: They disappear with never a stray one left behind, and they may not appear again in the same locality for many years.

They leave the pond filled with eggs — strings of eggs fastened to grass blades or stretched from weed to weed. In most of the cases observed, the ponds dried up before there was time for the development of the eggs, and in all cases the development seemed to be hastened because of the drying of the pond. The eggs hatch in from seven to fifteen days, according to the temperature.

The tadpoles appear velvety black in water, but when examined closely are rich brown in colour. They are short and stout-bodied, with narrow, spotted tails. In about two weeks after hatching, the delicate thread-like arms appear and the absorption of the tail begins. They leave the water while the tails are still quite long. Like toads, they will drown if they have no opportunity to get out on land. The tadpoles may show the yellow dorsal lines characteristic of the adults even before the front legs appear.

The first instinct of the little Spadefoots is to burrow. The feet are supplied with the apparatus for digging, although it is not as hard and horny as it becomes later, and so necessitates making the burrow in soft earth. The diminutive creatures have been observed to feed greedily on flies and young spiders.

One observer records an exodus of thousands of young Spadefoot toads from their native pond. For hours they "trudged" in leisurely fashion up a steep hill, apparently not stopping for food on their way.[1] When picked up in the hand, they made a faint squeaking noise.

The adult Spadefoot is an unintelligent and somewhat uncanny-looking creature—its appearance quite matching its mysterious habits and underground life. (Fig. 15.) The wide, rounded head bears two extremely prominent eyes set far apart. The vertical pupil has a narrow downward-projecting slit at the lower end. The iris has a black triangular indentation at its anterior margin. One-fourth inch behind the eye and about equalling it in size, is a round parotoid gland.

The skin is smooth, compared with that of the common toad,

---

[1] The life history of the Hermit Spadefoot is taken from the accounts of various observers cited in Bibliography, pp. 241 to 250.

PLATE VII

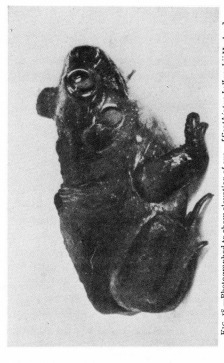

FIG. 18.—Photographed to show elevation of eye. [*Scaphiopus holbrookii* Harlan.]

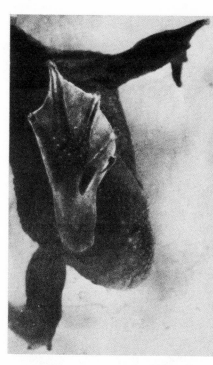

FIG. 19.—The webbed foot of the Spadefoot Toad. The inner tubercle is a black digging spur.

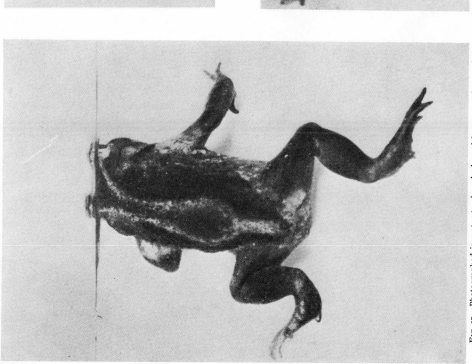

FIG. 17.—Photographed in water to show body and leg proportions and the **curved** yellow lines extending from the eyes backward. [Male *Scaphiopus holbrookii* **Harlan.** Raleigh, N. C.] For coloration see Colour Plate II.]

PLATE VIII

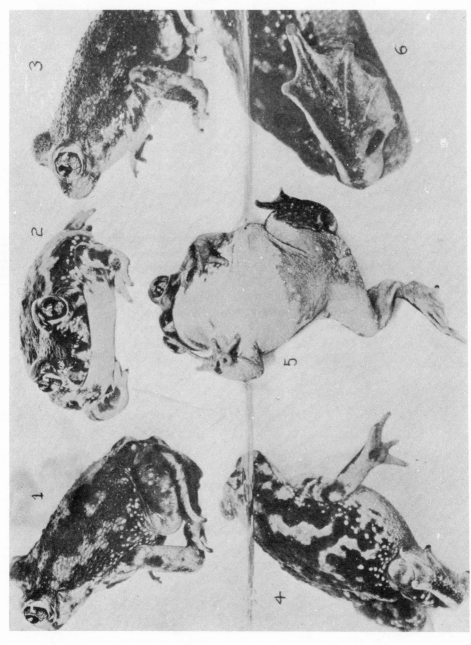

FIGS. 20 to 25 (1 to 6).—*Scaphiopus couchii* Baird. Brownsville, Texas. Length 2¼ in. Photographs (4, 5 and 6 in water) to show natural positions and structural characteristics. (See pages 57 to 59. For one possible coloration see Plate II.)

but on close examination is seen to be finely warty. While attached firmly in the region of the head, it is loosely attached on much of the body, and wrinkles at every turn. (See Figs. 16 and 18.) When the Spadefoot is in resting position, the loose skin of the upper arm extends in a fold down over the lower arm and hand. (See Fig. 13.)

The fingers are thickened at their tips; there is a black, horny thickening of the upper surfaces of the two inner fingers. (See Fig. 15.) The foot is depressed, and the skin covering it is thick and somewhat horny in character, converting the foot into a living spade. At the base of the shortest toe is a long, black, horny spur to aid in digging. The same black horny substance is seen at the tip of this inner toe. (See Fig. 19.)

Except during the breeding season, the Spadefoot is found only by accident. It sits in its burrow, showing only its peculiar golden eyes at the doorway. The turnip-shaped burrow is about six inches long and somewhat oblique in position. The earth on the interior is hard and smooth, packed into this condition by a continued energetic turning-about on the part of the owner of the burrow. The Spadefoot is solitary in habit, and will not tolerate the presence of a neighbour in the burrow.

SCAPHIOPUS COUCHII, BAIRD

IDENTIFICATION CHARACTERISTICS

Colour: Variable; green, olive, or brown — bright or dull — of light or dark shade. Streaked or banded more or less irregularly with light (bright yellow or dull yellowish). These bands may be continuous and symmetrically placed, producing a regular pattern, or may be so irregular and broken as to give the appearance of spots only. Small tubercles of the anterior back and head are black; those of the sides, posterior back, and tibia may be yellow. Buttocks with white tubercles. Iris metallic yellow, sometimes reddish. Underparts light, skin transparent and purplish posteriorly. Hands and feet light-coloured. (See Colour Plate II, also Figs. 20 to 25.)

Measurements: Size below medium; i. e. length 2 to 2½ inches, Head ¾ inch long (specimen of 2¼ inch length). Space between eyes equals or slightly exceeds width of eyelid. Leg short; length

57

to heel equals length of body forward to ear or eye. Tibia shorter than femur. (Fig. 24.)

Structure: Skin rough, with small tubercles on head, back, sides, and tibias. Skin of underparts slightly rough, smooth anteriorly. Parotoids small, flat, covered with tubercles; indistinct. Head rounded in front; slight indentation in upper jaw. Muzzle slightly projecting, with gradual slope to the jaw. Ear round, indistinct. Pupil vertical, with narrow slit in iris below. Iris has triangular indentation at front. Nostrils nearer to the end of the muzzle than to the eye; they are directed upwards. Hand with one large and two small palm tubercles; third finger longest; first and second black and horny (male). Foot large, fully webbed, and supplied with a large black inner sole tubercle. (Fig. 25.)

Range: Scaphiopus couchii (Baird) is reported from Mexico, Lower California, and Texas. In Texas, it has been found at Brownsville, Waco, and Helotes.

This Southern Spadefoot is an attractive and alert-looking creature, very different from the uncanny, smooth-skinned Eastern Spadefoot (*Scaphiopus holbrookii*) and the Northwestern form *Scaphiopus h. bombifrons.* It is often very bright in its colouration and shows habits of jumping and walking instead of constantly burrowing; it would thus seem more adapted to terrestrial existence than are its near relatives. The adaptations for subterranean and nocturnal life are well marked, however, in the development of the inner sole tubercles and in the vertical pupil of the eye.

There is great variation in the arrangement of the colour. The bands of light may be so reduced as to give an irregularly spotted appearance merely. On the other hand, they may be so broad as to make the creature appear light-coloured banded with dark. The typical arrangement of the light is as follows: A curved or V-shaped band between the eyes anteriorly, with the bend pointing backwards; second and third larger, more elongated V-shaped bands more or less parallel to this, starting backward from the eyelids on the top of the head posteriorly and from the posterior angles of the eyes respectively. The third meets, in the midline of the back, oblique converging bands from the lower posterior sides. In addition, there are lateral bands from above the ear backward, and conspicuous short ones (usually seven in number) on the muzzle and side of the head and neck, extending from above downward to the line of the jaw.

When several of these Spadefoot Toads are kept in captivity, they protest noisily until they get accustomed to the new environment. The voice is low-pitched and harsh; the sounds are made both by the male and female. A vocal pouch, in the case of the male, expands not only at the throat region, but also at the sides — over the arm insertion and on the sides of the breast — giving the creature a broad ludicrous front.

Scaphiopus couchii was found breeding in the pools at Brownsville in July, 1905.

THE WESTERN SPADEFOOT
Scaphiopus hammondii Baird[1]

IDENTIFICATION CHARACTERISTICS

Colour: Brown or grey, with or without two (or four) curved dorsal stripes of lighter colour. Tubercles tipped with red or orange. Muzzle not barred vertically with light (as in *Scaphiopus couchii*). Underparts light, unspotted. Throat of male black.

Measurements: Size medium or below, i. e. length 2 to 3 inches. The total length of leg and foot exceeds very slightly the total length of head and body

Structure: Upper surface closely set with relatively coarse tubercles. Skin of underparts smooth. Parotoids lacking or obscure. Ear obscure. A fold of skin back of the angle of the jaw. Outline of jaw from below, acuminate oval (more acute than in *Scaphiopus couchii*). Muzzle short, thick, perpendicular when seen in profile. (Muzzle more truncate and protruding, but less thick than in *Scaphiopus couchii*). No canthus rostralis.

Range: Scaphiopus hammondii Baird is widely distributed. It is found both east and west of the Sierras and also has an extensive range north and south. It is reported from Mexico, south-

[1]*Spea hammondii* Baird, and judging from the type specimens in the National Museum, *Spea hammondii intermontana* Cope, also. (Cope's Batrachia of North America.)

ern California, New Mexico, Texas, Utah, Nevada, northern California, and Washington.[1]

This Western Spadefoot resembles *Scaphiopus couchii* in having a tubercular skin and the parotoids either obscure or lacking. It differs in having a more pug-dog expression produced by the shorter, more truncate, and projecting muzzle; also, the ear is more obscure. There can never rise confusion in distinguishing it from *Scaphiopus holbrookii* or *Scaphiopus hammondii bombifrons*, both of which are comparatively smooth-skinned. The lack of parotoid glands and black granulations of the head will also distinguish it from *Scaphiopus holbrookii*, and it differs from *bombifrons* in having the cranium between the eyes flat instead of arched.

There is considerable variation in colouration and in size in the species. The pattern of dorsal lines may be present in whole or in part only, or may be obscured. The northern specimens attain a larger size than those in southern California and Texas.

This species, like the other Spadefoot Toads, is interesting because of its adaptation to existence in dry regions. It remains in subterranean burrows throughout the year except during continued or heavy warm rains. It is said to be very noisy during the breeding season. Young specimens were obtained from San Diego, California, in early April. They measure three-fourths inches long, having a blackish skin already covered with reddish warts, and feet that show the black horny spade well developed. They have the characteristic thick projecting muzzle and obscure tympanum.

Scaphiopus hammondii has been known to deposit its eggs in pools formed by heavy rains, in July and August. It is likely to appear in gardens and vacant lots in cities as well as in more isolated country places.

---

[1] San Diego, Olancha, Redding, California; Painted Desert, Arizona; Helotes, Texas; Pyramid Lake, Nevada; Salt Lake City and Provo, Utah; Fort Walla Walla, Wash.

THE SPADEFOOT OF THE WESTERN PLAINS

Scaphiopus hammondii bombifrons Cope

IDENTIFICATION CHARACTERISTICS

Colour: Yellowish olive. Muzzle darker through midline. Indistinct curved dark band on the head between the eyes. Two curving (more or less parallel) dark bands, extending backward from the eyes. These bands are made up of closely placed spots, each spot containing a smooth orange-coloured tubercle at its centre. Similar spots with orange-red tubercles are scattered irregularly over the sides and posterior portion of the back. There may be four distinct light yellow bands running lengthwise along the back. There may be a dark spot on the canthus rostralis. Iris golden. Tibia spotted irregularly or vermiculated with dark. Underparts dingy white, purplish posteriorly; throat blackish.

Measurements: Size small, i. e. length 2 inches. Space between eyes equal to or greater than width of eyelid. Leg short; length of leg to heel equal to length of body forward to shoulder or ear. Tibia not longer than femur.

Structure: Skin smooth and fine in texture, with a few tubercles on the sides, posterior portion of the back, and on the tibias. Muzzle short in front of eyes (no longer than horizontal diameter of eye). Outline of jaw as seen from below, acuminate oval. Truncated muzzle elevated. Eyes face forward and outward; pupil vertical. Nostrils slightly farther apart than distance between eyes. No canthus rostralis. Ear indistinct. Top of head between the eyes anteriorly is horny-looking, also in front of this beween the nostrils and on the end of the muzzle. It is not only horny-looking, but it is elevated in two arches from the front backward. (See Figs. 26 to 30.) Parotoids obscure or lacking. Hands unusually small and fingers short. Whole palm horny, so that the palm tubercles are not easily made out. Foot extensively webbed, but the webs are deeply indented. Inner sole tubercle not only large, but greatly extended, so that it is most effective in digging.

Range: *Scaphiopus hammondii bombifrons* is typical of the northern part of the Western plains. It ranges from northern Texas to Montana. It is reported from Montana, Dakota, Idaho, and Colorado.

This Spadefoot is especially characteristic of the elevated plains of the Western part of the continent. It has the habits of the Eastern Spadefoot (*Scaphiopus holbrookii*), in that it burrows during the greater part of the year, only coming out during heavy and continued rains. In its range it is very abundant, and so when it does appear, every ditch and pool of water may show representatives. Being dependent on rain, its breeding season varies greatly from year to year. Cope observed specimens in Montana in which the metamorphosis was completed August 20th. He observed in Idaho the full-grown, fat larvæ with the tails unabsorbed trying to feed upon animal food. They were in small burrows that they had made in the wet sand some distance from the lake margin. Some of them, in which the metamorphosis of the mouth had proceeded so far that there was a wide gape, had whole grasshoppers[1] in their mouths or partially projecting from them. This observation also was in August.

This Spadefoot croaks vigorously when taken in the hand. The throat swells into a resonating pouch wider than long, and widest just back of the jaws, in a line with the front of the arm insertions. The creature is very active and alert in habit. It burrows into sandy soil dexterously and rapidly, using the feet and legs to good effect. The curved horny elevations on the head combined with the shortness and thickness of the muzzle, produce a most curious pug-dog expression. The horny arches are probably closely connected with the burrowing habit, the head being used to keep the burrow open in front. The amount and hardness of this horny growth of the epidermis of the head varies in different specimens: there may be a thin dark-coloured layer only, or the horn may be thick and as black and hard as is the inner sole tubercle. In some specimens this black horny substance is found not only on the head but also in a broad dorsal band.

---

[1] *Caloptenus spretus.*

PLATE IX

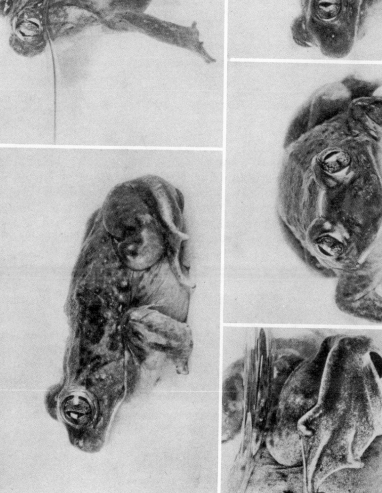

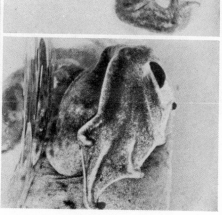

FIGS. 26 to 30.—The SPADEFOOT of the Western plains. *Scaphiopus bombifrons* Cope. Denver, Colo. Length 2 in. Photographed to show the vertical pupil, the curious shape of the head, the smooth skin and the great development of the inner sole tubercle.

FIG. 31.—Toads go to the ponds in early May. The male sits more erect in the water. His throat is dark-colored when not distended in singing.

May 1st.—" The spreading leaves of the skunk cabbage and the unrolling fronds of the cinnamon fern."

FAMILY III. BUFONIDÆ: THE TOADS[1]

THE AMERICAN TOAD

Bufo americanus Le Conte

IDENTIFICATION CHARACTERISTICS

1. *Colour*: Extremely variable; usually yellow-brown, light or dark in shade, with or without patches and bands of lighter colour. A light vertebral stripe may be present. There may be much bright red and yellow on the warts. There are likely to be four irregular spots of dark rich colouring along each side of the vertebral line. Under parts light, with few or many spots. (See Fig. 52.) Throat of male, black. Female much brighter and more variegated in colour than male. (Fig. 47.) (For colouration, see Colour Plate III.)

2. *Measurements*: Male 2½ to 3 inches in length; female much larger. Head large; its length contained 4 to 4½ times in total length. Legs medium in length — length of leg to heel equal to length of body forward to eye.

3. *Structure*: Skin conspicuously warty. Parotoid glands medium in size, more or less reniform in shape; situated just back of eye. Straight, narrow, diverging bony ridges extend backward between the eyes; each meets at right angles a second bony ridge extending back of eyes to a point above ears. The first ridge extends a little beyond the point of meeting with the second. There is little or no evidence of a ridge extending between the end of the second ridge and the parotoid gland. (See Fig. 48.) Inner sole tubercle of foot conspicuous because of size and black colour. Outer tubercle smaller. (See Fig. 44.)

Range: Bufo americanus is the common toad east of the Rocky Mountains from Mexico to the Great Bear Lake. It shares the Southern States with *Bufo lentiginosus,* and southern New England and New York with *Bufo fowleri.* The species varies considerably in different parts of its range, the variation showing itself in intensity of markings, prominence and arrangement of the cranial crests, and in size.[2]

---

[1] Refer to pp. 7, 9 and 44.

[2] *Bufo copei* Henshaw and Yarrow (James Bay, type locality) seems to be a small, prominently spotted *Bufo americanus,* judging from the type specimens in the National Museum. *Bufo aduncus* Cope may possibly be *Bufo americanus.* The type specimen is lost, and the species has not been rediscovered.

The unrolling fronds of the Cinnamon Fern.

It is the first of May, late in the afternoon. We stand at the edge of a pond, under a maple brilliant with its fringes of red keys. A marshy place at our left is yellow with "cowslips." Farther back from the water are the broad spreading leaves of the skunk cabbage and the unrolling fronds of the cinnamon fern. Everywhere about the margin of the pond the green arrowhead leaves are just thrusting their pointed ends above the water; the new red leaves of the yellow pond-lilies are resting on the surface or struggling up to it.

Suddenly out in the centre of the pond hundreds of small fish leap from the water to escape some enemy below, and drop back, making overlapping circles of motion that widen and spread until all is placid again. There is no silence; all is life. The red wings are indulging in a lively conversation in the marsh near at hand. The ever-present green frogs are croaking from the ooze and immersed brown leaves just in front of us. They are so near that we can see their yellow throats and green sides expand again and again as the explosive calls are repeated.

What is the new sound? Very near at hand, there is a sweet tremulous call that continues for several seconds, then stops abruptly. There it is again, but from another direction, and slightly different in pitch. Now it comes from all quarters — many voices answering and blending into harmony.

It is not difficult to locate the singers. They are toads, with throats distended into conspicuous light-coloured sacs astonishingly larger than their heads. They are quite unconscious of our presence as they sit erect in shallow water, showing their bright eyes and their enlarged throats. (Figs. 31 and 83.)

The sounds are of such quality that they influence us to loiter. We sit down on the dry exposed roots of the maple to watch, and to listen to these creatures expressing the glad life within them. The simplicity and quiet joyousness of it all take hold upon us.

Suddenly there is a slight commotion in the shallow water

The shining leaves and flowers of the Cowslips.— May 1st.

at our left, and out comes a snake, making its way along the bank towards the mass of golden "cowslips." But such a queer snake one never saw. It has two long legs extending straight out from the neck. It is the work of but a moment to stop its course and hold it firmly to see what strange monster is here. Do you see? The snake has partially swallowed a large toad, headfirst, and the toad's long hind legs are extending on each side from the angle of the snake's jaws. It is one of our singers, too intent on his singing to see the stealthy approach of his enemy. Pity wins the day; we must save the toad, although the snake will lose a good dinner, and probably a well-earned one. So we increase our pressure on the snake slightly, and the toad is released. With eager hops he proceeds back to the water. The snake goes on until hidden under the shining leaves and yellow flowers of the "cowslips." Humbly and thoughtfully we continue our walk. The crooning tones of the singers in the pond become more and more indistinct until they are lost altogether, and we come again into the busy world of men.

In late May, go to the woods, when the new wintergreen leaves are coming up red. Proceed to the pond at the edge of the woods, especially if it be late afternoon. Stand and look out over the water with its opening yellow pond-lilies, some of their leaves still wearing their baby red. See the brilliancy and delicacy of the columbines that cluster with the ferns at your right. Look for the broad leaves and flower-like fruits of the "cowslips" along the pond margin at the left. Hear the emphatic call of the oven-bird at your back, the love notes of the

The broad leaves and flower-like fruits of the Cowslips.—May 20th.

chickadee far away among the trees, and the merry tinkle of the bobolink in the meadow beyond the blue flags. By this time, however, you have probably heard sounds from the pond itself. The explosive note of the Green Frog proceeds from the shallow water; the purring trill of " the Tree Toad " comes from some spot impossible to locate. But listen! The toad's lullaby note [1] comes from the far margin, sweeter than all others if we except the two notes in the chickadee's spring call. We could never have believed it to be the voice of a toad if we had not seen and heard on that first May day. The sustained note is not only high-pitched and

 tremulous; it seems to have a dual character, as though a low note were droned at the same time that a high one was whistled. Imitate the call by whistling the upper and at the same time humming the lower of the following two notes. [1] The imitation may be good enough to bring response again and again.

If we go to a pond at night, we shall have every opportunity both to see and to hear toads, especially if we carry a lantern. Instead of being frightened by the light, they are attracted by it and may gather about it. If the lantern is set on the ground, they sometimes try to climb to its top. An especially enthusiastic one may sit on the toe of our boot, swell out his throat and sing. Even taking them into our hands will not quell their ardour at once. They continue to sing even while we take hold of the distended throat, which is hard from the pressure of the air within.

If we row on river or lake, pond or park lagoon, some moonlight night late in May, their voices, which seem somewhat woeful in the silence of the night, make a fit accompaniment to the slow dip of oars and the low gurgle of water at the boat's stern. We are reminded that this song has been compared to the slow opening movement of Beethoven's " Moonlight Sonata."[2] As late in the season as this there will be heard also an occasional deep bass note from a bullfrog, a loud and somewhat startlingly weird sound of the night, not at all in harmony with the gentle, drowsy song of the toads.

---

[1] In late May and June we can hear at the ponds of Rhode Island and Massachusetts the call of the Fowler's toad. This call is far more conspicuous and much less musical. (See p. 95.)

[2] " Familiar Life in Field and Forest." F. S. Mathews.

FIG. 32.—The toads may be removed to an artificial pond and the eggs will be laid as though there had been no disturbance.

FIG. 33.—Toad's eggs laid June 12, 1903. Photographed June 13, 24 hours later. Eggs enclosed in curling, cylindrical jelly-masses.

FIG. 34. Photographed June 15, 1903, three days after time of laying. The coils are straightening; the jellymass is much less solid; the eggs show the head and the tail ends of the tadpoles.

FIG. 35.—Toad tadpoles are hatched June 16, 1903, four days after the eggs are laid. The jelly-mass is almost wholly disintegrated.

The American toads are in the ponds from late April until July. They may appear much earlier if the spring is early. The males — who alone do the singing — are the first arrivals. During a large part of these months they sing both day and night. If the season is unduly cold, they may be silent for days or weeks together, reappearing on the return of a higher temperature.

The eggs which are laid[1] in long curling masses (Figs. 33 and 36), (likely to be tangled among the waterweeds and stretched from object to object in secluded, shallow parts of the pond), are black above and white underneath. They are arranged in a single row, in a transparent jelly-like mass cylindrical in shape, and are fertilised in the water as they are laid. The toads may be removed from the pond to an artificial one, and the eggs will be laid as though there had been no disturbance. (Fig. 32.)

The jelly-like substance about the eggs is scarcely visible when the eggs are first laid, but it swells in contact with the water until it becomes very conspicuous. Perfectly clean and transparent in the beginning, it soon becomes discoloured by the sediment of the water until one may look directly at coils of the eggs and not see them, because of their resemblance to débris at the bottom of the pond.

The eggs are small (less than $1\frac{1}{2}$ mm. in diameter). Their number is incredibly high. Various layings counted have yielded between four and twelve thousand eggs each. If the eggs are laid early, the development is comparatively slow. But if the eggs are laid later, when the temperature is more steadily high, or if they are kept in the warm atmosphere of the house, the development is remarkably rapid.

Those figured here were laid Friday, June 12, 1903, indoors. They were photographed on Saturday, twenty-four hours later, when they were very much increased in size and all the fertilised eggs were entirely black. (Fig. 33.)

Monday they were photographed again. (Fig. 34.) · The jelly-mass is now much less solid; the coils are straightening, but still hold their cylindrical shape. The eggs are no longer eggs, but young tadpoles in which head and tail are easily distinguished. What is our surprise twenty-four hours later — just four days

---

[1] April 14, 1890; April 6, 1891. Baltimore, Md. T. H. Morgan.
Bufo americanus breeds in April and May, sometimes in July. C. F. Hodge, Worcester, Mass.

from the time of laying — to find the tadpoles out of the jelly-mass clinging to its outer surface or to nearby waterweeds. (Fig. 35.) The rounded head is uppermost, the tail with its thin fin hangs downward. At the place where we should expect the mouth to be, there are two small black elevations, called suckers. (Fig. 210.) These secrete a sticky substance by means of which the young tadpoles attach themselves to weeds or grasses. The jelly-mass is now almost wholly disintegrated and the unfertil-ised eggs are very conspicuous swollen gray-and-white objects. These are masses of foul matter, which should be removed if the tadpoles are developing in a small amount of water under arti-ficial conditions.

By Thursday the head, body, and tail are still more clearly differentiated one from another, and finger-like extensions from the neck are conspicuous when the tadpole is viewed from above or below. These are the gills for breathing; they have been present fully forty-eight hours, but were so small and delicate that they were very difficult to see. Ever since the tadpoles emerged from the jelly-mass (which has now totally disappeared), they have moved with a vigorous wiggling of the tail whenever disturbed. Now they are becoming more active and start off on short circuitous voyages when there seems to be no visible disturbance.

On Friday, when they are a week old, their activity is still greater. The head is apparently much larger, but the gills are less conspicuous than before and seem to be farther back on the neck. The fact is, a membrane is growing backward from the anterior part of the head. This membrane will eventually cover the gills and the neck region, making the tadpole look as though it consisted of a large head and a tail, but no body, because head and body become so thoroughly blended.[1]

On Saturday they are still clinging quietly, except for occa-sional sallies to neighbouring weeds by very circling routes. The gills are wholly covered, except for two minute finger-like ends on the left side. (See Fig. 211.)

On Monday, the tenth day, we have veritable " pollywogs," as black as tiny coals, with tails that are in a continual wiggle, and small round mouths that are in constant search for something to eat. For the mouths are now open for the first time. These

---

[1] For details of the development, see Leopard Frog, pp. 176 to 181.

mouths are provided with horny jaws for scraping the tiny plants from their supports and for biting off the delicate ends of larger plants.[1] The baby toad is not different from other babies in being very hungry when it first comes into the world. He finds the minute green plants just to his taste, and perhaps, too, the microscopically-small animals that are in the ooze of the pond bottom or in the slime at its top, or that cling to water weeds between.

At any time between the middle of June and the middle of July, the shallow water of ponds will be found swarming with toad tadpoles in every stage of development from the fully-formed tadpole just described to the perfect little toad. (Figs. 37-40.) They are exceedingly attractive little creatures. The younger ones may change to toads within the twenty-four hours, so rapid is the development.

The whole length of the tadpole when it is from four to six weeks old and is approaching the last stage of its development is about one inch. The tail with its filmy fin constitutes three-fifths of its entire extent. The soft skin is nearly black, but when we look at it closely — especially with a lens — we can plainly see a fine stippling of gold. The two nostrils are very prominent, showing as small white openings. The eyes are small; the pupil is round and black, and is surrounded by an iridescent iris.

The tadpole now breathes by internal gills[2] situated at the sides of the throat. The water enters at the nostrils and at the mouth — which is continually opening and shutting for the purpose — passes through openings in the side walls of the throat, thence over the gills, and out through an opening at the left side.[2] This opening is shaped like a funnel with the small end outermost.

When the tadpole begins to change into the toad, the first sign which we can observe is the appearance of the hind legs. (Figs. 37-38.) These are mere rounded buds in the beginning and project straight backward. Soon the division into toes can be seen, and the joints are perfected. Then the leg is bent and the foot projects outward. Now the tadpole begins using the legs, as well as the tail, in swimming.

In ten days or two weeks after the appearance of the hind legs,

---

[1] The tadpole of *Bufo americanus* has the following mouth structure : The broad upper lip has two rows of teeth; the broader lower lip has three rows of teeth; the border of the lower lip is fringed with papillæ and is doubled in at the corners of the mouth.

[2] See Leopard Frog, pp. 180; also Bullfrog, pp. 236.

69

the front ones suddenly appear, fully formed. The fact is they have been growing for quite as long a time as the back legs have, but were concealed under the membrane that covers the gills. (See Fig. 28o.) When ready for activity, the left one is extended through the breathing-pore, and the right breaks directly through the skin. We now have a strange-looking creature like a little toad with a long tail. For, before the front legs appeared, changes had begun in the region of mouth and eyes. The small mouth has been replaced by a large one,[1] the opening of which extends far back under the eyes. The eyes have increased in size, and have become elevated so that they look like the toad's eyes as we know them in the adult. Now the tail seems mysteriously shorter. It continues to become shorter (absorbed from within), until it is a mere stub (Fig. 39), and finally disappears altogether. These visible changes with the marvellous and radical transformations that have taken place within, convert our black wiggling " pollywog " into a perfect toad. But so smooth and small! There is no sign of a wart on his brown back and he is smaller than the majority of our tiny tree-frogs at a corresponding stage of development.

Late June—The little Toads leave the ponds when the Arrowhead begins to bloom

For some time before the completion of the metamorphosis, the tadpoles prefer to be wholly or partially out of water. This fact shows that lungs have quite taken the place of the internal gills, and that our little water animals have been converted into land animals. If confined in deep water, tadpoles constantly rush frantically to the top to exchange a bubble of foul air for one of fresh (Fig. 39), and they will finally drown if not given opportunity to stay above water.

Just as soon as they lose the tails, toads are likely to

---

[1] See Bullfrog, pp. 236 to 238.

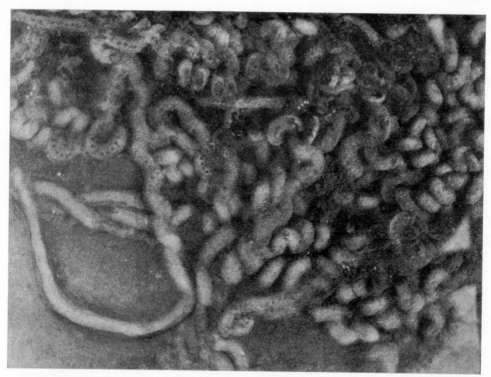

FIG. 36.—A small portion of an extended coiled mass of toad's eggs found at the bottom of an irrigation ditch. [May 2, 1904, Rhode Island.]

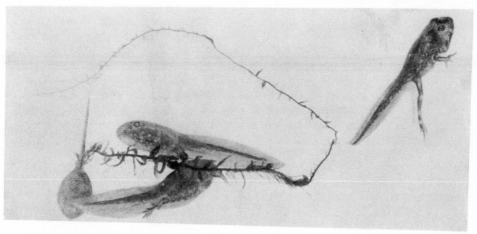

FIG. 37.—By the middle of June, the shallow water of ponds is swarming with black toad tadpoles in every stage of development. [Enlarged.]

FIG. 38.—The hind legs appear. They project straight backward. The joints are perfected and the foot projects outward. The legs and the tail are used in swimming. Visible changes are occurring in the region of the mouth and eyes. The arms appear. [Enlarged.]

FIG. 39.—The tail becomes mysteriously shorter. The little toad constantly rushes to the surface of the water for air. [Enlarged.]

FIG. 40.—Just toads.

FIG. 41.—They stick up their paws in ridiculous fashion as they "come to" after playing dead. [6 weeks old.]

FIG. 42.—One-year-old toads are so tame and confiding that we involuntarily wish them good luck whenever they cross our path.

leave the pond[1] —a whole army of atoms of life, so small and so like the ground that if their numbers were few we should scarcely see one of them, or if we did, might think the little hopping thing merely a cricket. (Fig. 40.)   But sometimes the day of their final transformation coincides with the day of a gentle rain.   A happy coincidence it seems for them, but it is likely to prove rather tragic instead.   They cover the sidewalks and the roadways; and before each individual of the migrating multitude finds a sheltered corner he can call home, many hundreds have lost their lives under the wheels of carriages and the feet of hurrying pedestrians.   The same apparent " deluge " of toads may come if a warm rain occurs shortly after the time of their change to land animals.   They are so delicate at first, so used to life in the water, that they travel only when the air is moist.   This means that they will leave their native pond at night, and that until they are less sensitive must remain secreted during the daytime under stones and chips, in the cracks of board-walks or under the protecting cover of leaves and grasses.   But let a rainfall come before they are too widely scattered or their ranks too greatly thinned, and — truly it seems as if the toads must have rained down!   For the great warm drops splash down on the boards, and see, there are baby toads just where the raindrops struck.

The wet margin of river and pond in early July may be alive with baby toads.   When the toads have been out of water for a few days they are found farther back in the grass.   They congregate in large numbers on sunny brown earth patches.   These they match so well in colour, that, as we approach, their simultaneous hopping into the shelter of the grass gives the illusion that the whole patch of earth is moving.

Those that have been out of the water for two or three weeks differ greatly in general appearance from the tiny black things with fragile legs that we see on the wet mud nearer the water. They are one-half inch long, very fat-bodied and show spots of bright red-brown.   In six weeks they may measure one inch in length and are correspondingly fat.   They may be light orange-brown in general colour with bright orange on the two large warts behind the eyes and on the under sides of hands and feet.   When they are handled they play dead for seconds at a time and finally

[1] This happens generally between the middle of June and the middle of July, according to the advancement of the season.   For the enemies of the toad tadpoles in the pond, see " Leopard Frog," pp. 181, 182.

71

" come to life " sticking up their little orange paws in most ridiculous fashion before they tumble over and hop away (Fig. 41.).

We cannot see the army of toads as it leaves the water without wondering what will be the fate of these defenseless creatures. We try to get ten of them all at once into our closed hand. It is no easy task, although there is plenty of room. As fast as one little fellow goes in, another hops out on the other side. But while they hop out of our hands, they themselves hop, without fail, into our hearts. The midgets have such bright eyes, wise expressions, and alert ways, and their legs seem so inadequately small, even for such tiny bodies. We know that if they proceed along sidewalks and roadways, unavoidable danger comes crashing down upon them, and that if they hunt the mosquitoes and other small insects of the fields and meadows, they must meet enemies unnumbered. Among these are snakes, crows, and several hawks and owls[1], besides ducks and hens. These are enemies not only of young toads, but of the full-grown ones also. The full-grown toads do not eat the young ones. In this they are very different from most of their relatives. For the young toad, the most to be feared among these enemies is perhaps the hungry baby snake, who finds him a most palatable morsel.[2] Probably many of the small toads succumb also to severe cold or rapid changes of temperature during the winter.[3]

However, in the spring, one-year-old toads are numerous. They have grown greatly. There is considerable variation in their size, showing that all have not had equally good conditions or did not start out with equal vigour. They have gained the rough coat and the colour-pattern of dress of the older toads, in fact they lost their smoothness of skin long before they went to sleep for the winter. Toads at this stage are so tame and confiding that we involuntarily wish them good luck whenever they cross our path. (Fig. 42.) Toads do not resort to the ponds for the breeding season until they are three or four years old.

---

[1] A. K. Fisher.—" Hawks and Owls from the Standpoint of the Farmer." Reprint from the Yearbook of the U. S. Department of Agriculture for 1894.

[2] These young snakes seem to be fully aware that they have the advantage of the toads, and the toads are equally aware of the situation. It is no unusual thing to see a baby snake much smaller than one's lead pencil pestering an old toad of considerable size. The great gentle fellow never turns in retaliation—although he might easily swallow the snake if he tried—but proceeds hopping desperately along the roadside, getting nipped on the haunches every few moments.

[3] It is thought that young toads burrow much less deeply into the soil for their winter hibernation than do toads of more years of experience and more physical strength.

During these years they make their home in field and garden and have for their main interest in life the capture of their insect food.

Toads live to be very old. Authentic record gives the story of one that lived to be thirty-six years of age and then was killed by accident. However, there is much fable connected with the stories of their being found imbedded in rocks and trees. It is certain that other conditions being right, the toad can live for some time without food. This time may be stretched into months or possibly into years if the temperature is continually such that the toad is kept in a hibernating state.[1]

The rapidly growing toad sheds its outer horny skin every few weeks to take care of the increase of size within; the older toads moult at least four times a year. The skin is shed in one piece (Fig. 43) and is swallowed. The process is not often seen, except by one who has toads under special observation, for it requires but five minutes or even less time, and is not preceded by any peculiarities of behaviour. When the toad is about to shed his skin, he takes a position with his back greatly humped, his head bent downward, and his feet drawn under him. The outer skin over the whole external surface of the toad becomes naturally free or loose from the skin underneath, and splits of itself along certain definite lines; namely, along the midline of the head and back, across the posterior end of the body, along the midline of the under side of the body, and across the breast from arm to arm. (See Fig. 43.) The splitting is difficult to see, because the skin is thin and dark in colour, like the new skin, which is exposed by the splitting. In fact, the whole process of the moult is difficult to see, not only because the old skin is thin and dark, but also because throughout the operation the old skin adheres closely to the wet surface gradually exposed. To understand the moulting, it is necessary to know that the skin of the head is continuous over the lips with the skin of the mouth, and that the skin that covers the lips is also shed.

After the skin has split along the lines described, the toad begins a process by which the loosened skin is drawn into the corners of the mouth. In fact, throughout the moulting it is the mouth that does the work of getting off the skin. The process

---

[1] Careful experiments have been made by Buckland to test the matter. Toads were confined in boxes of limestone and of sandstone and were buried three feet deep in a garden. At the end of thirteen months when the sandstone boxes were opened, the toads were dead; those in the limestone died before the end of two years.

consists of repeatedly opening the mouth widely and expanding the body so that the loosened skin (which is split at the posterior end and along the back) is forced slightly forward, then shutting the mouth. By this method the skin is gradually sucked and dragged into the mouth at the angles of the jaws. The toad sometimes uses the front feet as hands to help him get the skin down from over the eyes.

This method of sucking the skin in at the angles of the jaws might eventually remove the whole skin if it were not for the obstacles presented by the legs and arms. The hind legs are removed from their coverings by bringing them forward under the toad and pulling them backward, rubbing them forcibly against the body. This is done in just the manner in which we might remove the arm from its sleeve, provided we had no other hand to help. However, the problem is rendered much less difficult by the fact that the skin of the leg and foot splits on the under side almost to the tip of the longest toe. (Fig. 46.) The skin of the foot is sometimes turned wrong side out during the process, but more often it remains in its usual position.

After the toad has removed the back legs from their coats and has dragged into the mouth as much as possible of the freed skin, he has so far completed the moulting that the hind parts are all free and the old skin, much wrinkled and plainly showing the warts on its surface, lies in a dark thick band extending from the angles of the mouth around the upper parts of the arms. In fact, strange as it may seem, that part of the skin which covers the throat and arms and is nearest the mouth is the last part of the skin to be shed. A few more vigorous efforts on the part of the toad, and the skin slips off the hands, the black bands of skin are pulled into the mouth and the process is over. The skin is pulled off the arms with little difficulty, because the splitting extends from the line across the breast out under the arms to the base of the first finger. The skin of the hands is usually turned wrong side out in the process.

Certainly, the easiest way of completing the process seems to be to swallow the skin which has gradually been accumulated under the tongue. Occasionally the skin is swallowed as it is shed, in two long black cords extending down the throat from the corners of the mouth so that the skin that covers the feet is already in the stomach before the skin of the hands is shed. If the skin

PLATE XV

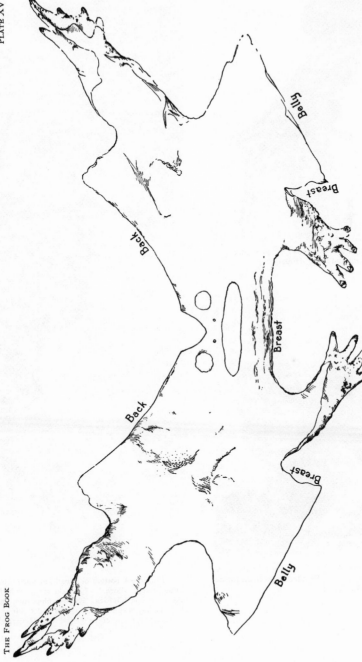

Back

Belly

Breast

Breast

Back

Belly

Breast

Breast

FIG. 43.—The skin of the toad is shed in one piece, making a pattern for a toad. (When the skin is fully stretched out, the edges along the back form a continuous horizontal line more or less parallel to the lines of the ventral surface).

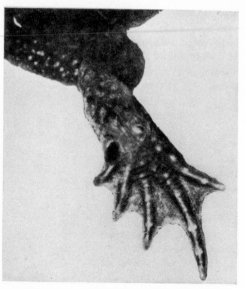

FIG. 44.—The right foot of the toad, photographed from underneath to show webs and spur. [Enlarged.]

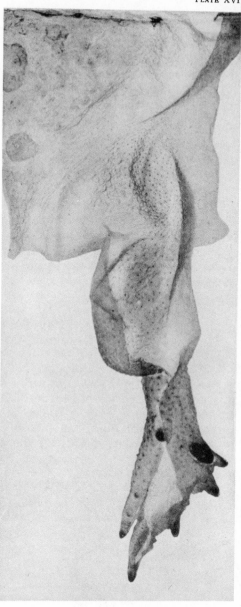

FIG. 45.—In July and August the toad still retains to a certain extent his desire to sing. He often sits with his throat partially distended. [Michigan.]

FIG. 46.—A portion of a toad's moulted skin, rescued as it was being swallowed. The skin of the left half of the back and of the left hind leg. Photographed from underneath to show the line of splitting along the under side of the leg and foot to the horny tip of the longest toe. [Enlarged.]

has been accumulated in the mouth, the toad proceeds to swallow it with much effort. The eyes above and the throat below are compressed convulsively several times, then the cavernous mouth is slowly opened and shut, again and again. Finally, the discomfort seems past. The alert look, which tells that the toad is again awake to his surroundings with all their possibilities, comes back to the bright eyes; the erect position is resumed; the wet skin dries; the colour darkens, and our toad is quite himself again.

The process of moulting may easily be observed in the old toads in July and August after they have left the ponds and taken up their places in the garden or field. On the whole, this is one of the best seasons for getting acquainted with the toad. He is very hungry indeed, for in his arduous life at the pond he has fasted to some extent. He still retains in a measure his desire to sing. He often sits with throat partially distended. (Fig. 45.) Sometimes in the early night he sings.[1] His voice is feebler, but not less sweet than it was a month or more ago.

Hold the toad gently in your hand, so that his hind feet are without support, and hear him " talk." He is annoyed, and demands to be released. His tone is not irritated, however. It is, instead, a gentle chirping sound that reminds one of a newly-hatched chicken, only that the voice is sweeter. See! the throat puffs out and the trilled note is given while the toad is in your very hand. He twists his head about and looks at you brightly. He pushes with his hands, and wiggles his feet in a helpless fashion. All the time he is " talking "—the chirping notes coming thick and fast, while his throat and sides are vibrating rapidly. Again the throat is extended and the musical trill is continued for a few seconds, leaving you elated that you have heard, but with a sense of loss that the sound is so short-lived.

The throat-pouch is a single sac with air entering it from the mouth through two slits. These slits are on the floor of the mouth, at each side of the forward end of the tongue. The air enters the mouth through the nostrils; the mouth is kept closed. The toad can give voice to its call under water with nostrils and mouth both closed. In this case the air passes back and forth from throat-sac to lungs over the vocal cords in the throat. When the call is given

---

[1] I have heard this feeble note of the toad in August only some half-dozen times. When I first heard it (the toads were under observation in " moss gardens " in the house), I accredited it to the snowy tree-cricket, whose voice is so familiar a sound during August evenings.

75

with great vigour, the air from the side slits in the mouth presses on the side walls of the throat-pouch with such force as to make the pouch look as if it were made up of two sacs, i. e. the wall at the midline is not as forcibly distended as are the side walls.

If we hold a toad in our hands, we realize certain details of his appearance which we should not have noticed if we had looked at him at longer range.

The two oval black nostrils are very conspicuous. Each is situated on a line between the inner corner of the eye and the end of the muzzle, and is somewhat nearer the former. There may be rhythmic movements of the membrane bordering the openings which show that air is being taken in.

The throat also moves rhythmically in and out as if in breathing, but more rapidly than the nostril membranes. Timing the movement of the throat, we find that the pulsations occur at the rate of about three per second.[1] The movement is confined to the floor of the mouth and throat, and is, in truth, a swallowing act, necessary to force the air down into the lungs. The necessity arises from the facts that the nasal tubes leading from the external nostrils open into the front part of the mouth (see Fig. 279), instead of far back in the throat, as they do in higher forms, and that the toad has no ribs, and so cannot have chest movements to suck the air into the lungs.

The elevated eyes are very brilliant and very beautiful.[2] The pupil is a black horizontal oval and is surrounded by a broad rim (iris) of gold. While we watch, the eyes are shut, both together or one at a time. The process seems mainly one of making the eye level with the surrounding surface by lowering it into the

---

[1] The rate varies with temperature and other conditions. It is much slower when the toad is sleeping or hibernating. The throat movements may cease altogether for a minute or more at a time. This occurs when the toad is eating or is " playing dead."

[2] The toad's eye is so beautiful that it gave rise in past ages to the fable of the " jewel " of the toad's head. This jewel was supposed to be a precious stone found within the toad's head. It acted when worn as a talisman protecting the wearer from all sorts of evil.

Possibly the supposed venomous qualities of the toad gave the toad-stone special value, for the old theory that " like cures like " was fully believed, and all sorts of poisonous plants and animals were used as charms and talismans.

The jewel in the toad's head is referred to again and again in literature and history.

" The fayrer the stone is in the toad's head, the more pestilent the poyson in his bowelles." —*Lyly.*

" There may be many that ware these stones in Ringes beeing verily perswaded that they keep them from all manner of grypings and pains of the belly."— *Topsell.*

head (into the roof of the mouth, really[1]), but there is also a thin transparent nictitating membrane that rises, and so helps in the process. (See Fig. 274.)

There are two straight narrow ridges or crests passing backward between the eyes from above the nostrils to a point behind the eyes. Here each crest turns a sharp angle (very nearly a right angle) and passes downward back of the eye to a flat, brown spot posterior to and somewhat underneath the eye. (Fig. 48.) These crests are made by the bones of the crown of the head.

The flat vertical oval (Colour Plate III) is the external evidence of the ear. There is no external ear, and this spot is the tympanum or drum of the ear, which is at the surface of the body, protected only by the skin which covers it.

The hand has four fingers. The foot has five toes connected by short thick webs. A short black spur (inner sole tubercle), which is strong and horny, extends downward from the inner margin of the foot just back of the first toe. There is a smaller tubercle opposite this, on the sole of the foot. (See Fig. 44.)

The entire dorsal surface is rough with rounded wart-like elevations of various sizes. Two very large elongated ones (parotoid glands) are situated just behind the eyes. (See Figs. 47 and 48.)

If we examine many toads during the summer, we find that the colour is usually dull brown, with or without lighter markings forming patches and bands. There is usually a line of lighter shade down the middle of the back. Very often the ground colour is yellowish brown, perhaps darker at the head. The smaller, wart-like elevations may be tipped with red. Those above the ear are often of a bright orange hue. Sometimes there are four larger elevations, or spots of colour, arranged along each side of

---

" Sweet are the uses of adversity,
Which like the toad, ugly and venomous,
Wears yet a precious jewel in his head."— *Shakespeare*.

" The ungainly toad
That crawls from his secure abode,
Within the mossy garden wall,
When evening dews begin to fall.
Oh, mark the beauty of his eye,
What wonders in that circle lie!
So clear, so bright, our fathers said—
' He wears a jewel in his head.' "—*Shakespeare*.

[1] See Bullfrog, pp 231, 233.

the white line in the middle of the back. These may be bright red-brown conspicuously bordered with black, the black in its turn being ringed with yellow, and may thus give the effect of yellow-rimmed eyes. The two large swellings (parotoid glands) behind the eyes may have the same colour as the background, or they may differ, being yellow or red-brown when the toad is dull brown, or dull brown when the skin as a whole is yellow or red in tone.

The female is larger than the male, and is usually lighter and more variegated in colour. In both sexes the granular under-surface is light, sometimes tinged with yellow, red, or brown, and having either few or many dark spots. (See Fig. 62.) The adult male has a blackish throat.

At the close of a hot summer's day we sit on the doorstep of a country house, delighting in the coolness and repose, and watching the lengthening shadows of grape-trellis, well-curb, and house. A fat toad comes out from under the doorstep, where he has been quietly sleeping all day; another, clean and bright-eyed, comes from under the sidewalk at our feet. They start off with leisurely hops toward the garden to search for caterpillars and other delicious morsels of a toad's menu. We watch their retreating backs (Fig. 47) until they disappear among rows of beets and lettuce, and we wish them " good hunting." Night after night, summer after summer, toads come out in search of food. They become a part of the place. They help to make the home and contribute their share in its work.

Toads choose cool, moist places in which to live. They are often found in cellars, under porches and sidewalks, and in various dark or damp hiding-places.[1] They seek such locations not only for the shelter, but also for the moisture. A toad never has the pleasure of drinking water in the usual way. All the water that he gets is absorbed through his skin. A toad kept in a dry place grows thinner and more distressed-looking, and is likely to die within a few days; whereas one provided with plenty of moisture remains plump and contented as the weeks go by, even when there is a scarcity of food.

It would, however, be a great mistake to think that a toad does not take pleasure in drinking. He sprawls out in shallow water or on a wet surface and has a contented expression in his

---

[1] From this fact probably originated the epithet " loathsome," in connection with the toad.

FIG. 47.—We watch their retreating backs.   [Male toad at the left ; female at the right.]

FIG. 48.—The AMERICAN TOAD.   Photographed to show the narrow bony crest of the head.

FIG. 51.—The toad swallows the red-legged locusts (*Melanoplus rubrum*) before they have time to pour out their "molasses." [Enlarged.]

FIG. 52.—The toad eats the sowbugs (*Oniscidæ—Crustacea* that live in damp places) that destroy the roots of plants. [Enlarged.]

FIG. 50.—The meadow grasshopper (*Orchelimum vulgare*) may help to furnish the toad a meal. [Enlarged.]

wonderful eyes as he literally " soaks in " the water. In the country in midsummer, when pools and springs are dry, toads very often travel long distances to spend the night on the wet ground about a well of some sort.[1]

In their search for moisture, they sometimes unwittingly fall into wells to lead a most sombre existence, feeding upon the few low forms of life that live there and upon unfortunates who become prisoners in the same way that they themselves did. Release may come if the well has a bucket, but more likely their fate is a tragic one. Their crushed bodies have been taken from pumps into which they have been sucked. They have sometimes been found hibernating in old wells, where they must have been for ten or fifteen years, judging by the amount of débris under which they are buried.[2]

We always have been, and still are, somewhat prejudiced against the coldness of the toad. He is less fortunate than we are, in being wholly, instead of only partially, dependent on the sun for his warmth. On a warm day his temperature may be very high and on a cold day he is very cold indeed,[3] so cold that he may snuggle deeper into his bed and sleep all day. Our epithet " slimy " he does not deserve at all. In fact, he is quite dry and comfortable to the touch, at least he is so when we first take him up. A moment later — if we seized him too quickly and vigorously — he may be somewhat wet; for among his pro- tective habits is the one of pouring out a colourless, odourless fluid upon the enemy. But even with this he is quite harmless.[4]

In addition to this fluid, the toad has another, which is slightly poisonous, and which is secreted by the skin. This secretion is especially abundant in the parotoid glands, the two large swellings behind the eyes. When the toad is in very great agony — as, for example, when he is seized by the teeth of an enemy — he pours out this fluid in sufficient quantity to cause it to appear in milky drops on the gland-like swellings. This fluid has a disagreeable effect on the mucous membrane of the mouth, and so protects the

---

[1] Wild Life near Home. By Dallas Lore Sharp.

[2] J. A. Allen. Amphibia Found in the Vicinity of Springfield, Mass. Proc. Bost. Soc. Nat. Hist., XII, 1865.

[3] Cold-blooded vertebrates have a variable temperature, dependent on the temperature of surroundings.

[4] The toad can in no possible way produce warts.

79

toad from many enemies. Watch the dog's behaviour towards toads that have taken up their residence in the garden or about the house. He either gives them a wide berth or simply teases them, being careful not to take them into his mouth. A young dog may bite a toad, but the experience is likely to prove so disagreeable that he does not repeat it. The irritating secretion is not poured out at all unless the toad is in severe pain. This fluid can do no injury to man, unless it gets into the mouth or eyes.[1]

The toad has been greatly maligned by stories of its poisonous effects on man and man's belongings. Instead of bringing ill luck, the gentle fellow is one of our great blessings. The toad has come to our gardens and to the very doors of our houses because he can get an abundance of food there; also, because as one of man's domestic animals, he escapes some of his natural enemies. As for man, he may well look upon the toad at his door as a good fairy—somewhat in disguise, we must admit. In fact, we might let the toad remain wrapped in the veil of magic that the superstition of past ages put upon him, but change the import of the magic to good instead of evil.

That the toad is the gardener's ally has been proved beyond a doubt.[2] The economic value of the toad has been recognised in this country as well as in others. For many years, gardeners in France have been glad to buy toads in order to have them as insect-destroyers.

The toad remains quietly sleeping through the greater part of the day, thereby keeping himself from being a nuisance and also saving himself from the danger of being stepped upon. But at sunset, or often earlier than that, he comes out from his bed under porch or shrubbery and starts on his regular tour over lawns and through gardens.

The hunt is an exciting one, for the toad eats living, moving

---

[1] I have seen it naturally exuded but once in the several years of my observation of the American toad. This secretion has no power to produce warts. See p. 16.

[2] We are just finding out how many allies man has in his work of tilling the soil. We know now that birds of many sorts are of infinite value. Rose-breasted grosbeaks will keep a field cleaned of " potato-bugs." Kingbirds eat so many grasshoppers that they save a large share of the hay harvest. Bob-whites and even crows are of great value in destroying cutworms.

And humbler even than these, the insects cross-pollinate flowers, making possible fruits of all kinds and seeds for new crops and new varieties of economic plants.

The earthworms actually plough the ground, slowly but certainly converting sterile into fertile land. Even the bacteria of the soil can be used by man to increase his crops greatly. (" Bacteria and the Nitrogen Problem." Geo. T. Moore. Reprint from Yearbook of Department of Agriculture for 1902.) The farmer need not work alone; he has at his command a whole army of helpers.

food only. He must "lie low," approach cautiously but rapidly, move most alertly at the final moment, and perhaps meet with disappointment after all, as the grasshopper takes wing or the caterpillar rolls into a motionless ball. Then there is always the possibility of a lurking enemy. It may be a snake that lives under the wood-pile and is out on his afternoon hunt, or an owl that nests in the hollow oak and in the dusk approaches so silently that the first intimation of her nearness is the clutch of sharp claws. Or a skunk may roll the toad under his paw, preliminary to swallowing it.

The chase must always be an eager one, because the toad is always hungry. His gastronomic ability is so great that he must have four meals per day, or rather his stomach must be filled and emptied four times in each twenty-four hours. He must therefore hunt and eat almost incessantly in order to get as much as he needs.

The tongue of the toad, with which he catches his food, is admirably adapted to its work. It has a sticky surface, from which escape of the prey is impossible, and it is fastened at the front instead of at the back. The latter fact makes it possible for the toad to throw the tongue well out of the mouth. (Fig. 49.)

The toad eats almost all kinds of small living things that are out in the late afternoon and at night. He may sit for an hour or more on the back step and catch the flies and mosquitoes that come to the screen-door in their attempt to get into the house. He sits with head bent forward and eyes looking very bright and intelligent. When he sees a fly alight within two inches of his nose, he makes no perceptible movement of the head or body.

Fig. 49. To show the movement of the toad's tongue in catching an insect. The tongue is fastened in front instead of at the back and can be extended fully two inches, in an exceedingly rapid movement. Its surface is sticky.

The toad eats the black crickets[1] that are said to damage the strawberry crop.

The mouth opens and the fly is gone. When the fly alights farther away, the toad springs forward on his strong hind legs, then easily slips back into a sitting posture again. That is all that we can see, but again the fly is gone.

Look once more. There are many chances to observe, for he is bobbing back and forth as fast as possible, and the flies are constantly disappearing. The free hind end of the tongue is thrown out and pulled back so quickly that we can scarcely see the flash of pink. The tongue touches the fly, however, which adheres to its sticky surface, and so is carried far into the back of the mouth.

The toad walks over the lawn and catches the crickets, the locusts, and the grasshoppers there, not in the least objecting to their hard coats, their long spiny legs, and the " molasses " of the locusts. (Figs. 50 and 51.) He may swallow even a bee or a wasp found on the low clovers or dandelions, and seems to feel much less uncomfortable afterward than one might suppose.

Farther out in the garden, he snaps up the beetles and bugs that are running close to the ground or eating the potato, squash or cucumber leaves.

He rejoices as a blundering May beetle noisily sheathes its wings near him. (Fig. 53.) Before it has time to begin the task of laying its many eggs, it furnishes a mouthful that makes the toad shut his eyes hard several times to get the big thing swallowed. For, strange as it may seem, the large eyes of the toad can

The wingless grasshopper (*Ceuthophilus*) of the ground.

[1] Gryllus abbreviatus.

82

PLATE XIX

FIG. 53.—The toad eats the blundering May beetle (*Lachnosterna*—Herbivorous beetle.)

FIG. 55.—He eats the caterpillar of the mourning cloak butterfly (*Vanessa antiopa*), spines and all. From " Moths and Butterflies," Ginn & Co.

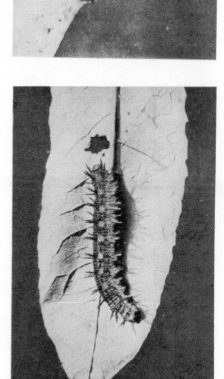

FIG. 54.—He spies out the white-marked tussock caterpillar (*Notolophus leucostigma*) From "Moths and Butterflies," Ginn & Co. [Enlarged.]

FIG. 56.—The toad sees and captures the tent caterpillars (*Clisiocampa Americana*). From " Moths and Butterflies," Ginn & Co.

FIG. 57.—The toad eats the gray slug that leaves a slimy track. The photograph represents the slug and its eggs
—[Enlarged.]

be pressed down into the mouth as far below its roof as they rise above the head, and the movement aids effectually in swallowing. If the farmer could see, he would surely smile with satisfaction, for this May beetle is the mother of the white grubs that feed on roots and underground stems, and so ruin his pasture and spoil his potato crop.

It is not beneath the dignity of the toad to sit and feast on the plant-lice that live on the lettuce. He swallows any spiders he may catch. He may sit in one place for a long time and eat the ants that are about an ant-hill or that gather on a decaying apple or pear. He loiters about the roots of the corn and attacks the cutworms as they come out from their day hiding-places and start to climb to the leaves they devour at night.

The dusk changes to night, but as long as there is any light, the toad can see. His eyes are large and placed on the very top of his head. The golden iris contracts more and more, the pupil becomes correspondingly larger until the eye seems a great black hole in the toad's head. He can see nothing when it is totally dark, but there is usually enough light to see moving objects. He can see the tent caterpillars (Fig. 56) that have left their silken homes on the apple or cherry tree and are hurrying over the ground to find sheltered spots in which to build cocoons. He can see the caterpillar of the mourning-cloak butterfly (Fig. 55) on a similar search, and swallows it, spiny coat and all. He has no difficulty in spying out the white-marked tussock caterpillars that are changing their feeding-grounds from rose bush to snowball or honeysuckle. (Fig. 54.) He does not seem to mind in the least if a caterpillar is thickly set with hairs; in fact, small one-year-old toads will seize and greedily eat the common hairy caterpillars. Click beetles that have been in hiding all day are often captured. This would surely rejoice the heart of the farmer, if only he could see; for the young of these are the much-fought wireworms[1] that damage the growing vegetables and grains.

The following statistics are valuable not only in that they introduce us to the real worth of the toad, but also because they are accurate, being the results of scientific investigation of the matter.[2]

---

[1] Family Elateridæ

[2] A. H. Kirkland. "Habits, Food, and Economic Value of the American Toad." Bulletin, 46, Hatch Experiment Station, Amherst, Mass.

It is found that 88% of a toad's food consists of insects and other small creatures that are considered pests in the garden, grain-field, or pasture. It is estimated that in three months a toad will eat 9,936 injurious insects, and that of this number 1,988 (16% of all its food) are cutworms. Counting the cutworms only, the estimated value of a single toad is $19.88 per year, if the injury done by a single cutworm be put at the low figure of one cent per year.

During the pest of army-worms, one toad examined was found to have eaten fifty-five of the caterpillars. During the siege with gypsy-moths there were found sixty-five larvæ in the stomach of one toad. Another toad which was examined was found to have eaten thirty-seven full-grown tent caterpillars. The farmer and the market gardener, in the light of these statistics, and face to face with their almost endless struggles against insect pests, are beginning to value toads. They have shown their recognition of the value of toads by asking for legislation to protect them, similar to that which protects birds.

The toad does good service, too, in destroying slugs. (Fig. 57.) These are the gray slow-moving creatures that leave shining, slimy tracks wherever they go. They are seldom seen except on dark, rainy days, because, although they are busy all night eating the tender leaves of the lettuce and other low-growing plants, they are sound asleep under boards and stones when the morning light comes. Unless the gardener sees the shining tracks of the slugs, he blames the caterpillars and beetles for all the damage done to his plants.

Celia Thaxter, in "Island Garden" tells of her struggles with slugs. There were so many that every green leaf that appeared was eaten off by them during the night. Some one suggested that the toad was the enemy of the slug, so she sent for toads, as there were none on the island. Two boys caught sixty toads and sent them to her in a wooden box containing earth, with wire netting. on top. When the box reached her there were three dry and dusty toads sitting on the top of the earth. They were so dusty that she showered them with water, but she was not prepared for the result. "The dry baked earth heaved tumultuously; up came dusky heads and shoulders and bright eyes by the dozen." The toads sat there and blinked and "talked" with delight. She turned the box on its side and set the whole sixty free in the garden, and as the summer went on they "grew fatter and fatter till they were round as apples," and her garden became very beautiful.

Toads are especially valuable in greenhouses. In fact, toads and frogs, also, if kept in greenhouses, will free the place not only from slugs and snails, cutworms and injurious beetles, but also from sowbugs, the small crustaceans that eat the roots of all sorts of plants. (Fig. 52.) The fact that a toad will eat earthworms adds to his value to the keeper of a greenhouse; for although worms are of inestimable value in nature, when they are confined in a greenhouse, where their work is not needed, they become an actual nuisance.

It is interesting to watch a toad eat a large earthworm — or rather, try to eat it, for, if the earthworm is an unusually large one, success may not follow the toad's most vigorous efforts. He sees the moving object, walks toward it cautiously (Figs. 58-60), makes a dash, and seizes one end of it in his mouth. But the worm is fully aroused to the situation, and begins vigorous efforts to escape. The toad uses his front feet like hands to push the worm into his mouth, and if he is quick enough and strong enough he may succeed in getting it all in and swallowing it, or at least all but the "tail" of it, which remains for some time hanging out of one corner of his mouth. But more likely the worm gets out of his mouth as fast as he can put it in, because it is slimy and can stretch to be very long, and because the toad has no teeth to hold it. He is likely to give it up in disgust. If he succeeds in swallowing it after persistent effort, he is likely to have a disgusted look, for he does not like the slime that covers the worm. He will sit for a long time opening and shutting his cavernous mouth as if he were not feeling comfortable, and nothing can induce him to take another worm.

When the toad catches an earthworm, he takes it head first, walking past or around the tail, and making his attack at the forward-moving end. This is interesting, since the worm has four rows of backward-projecting spines along its whole length, so that if it were taken tail end first it would be a rather uncomfortable object to swallow. A toad can eat a small earthworm almost as easily as he can a caterpillar. It is likely that on rainy days toads eat many of the worms that come out of the ground to escape drowning.

It is estimated that about one per cent of a toad's entire food consists of earthworms. This one per cent, compared with the sixteen per cent of cutworms, nine per cent of tent caterpillars, and nineteen per cent of weevils and other injurious beetles, gives a very convincing ratio as regards the toad's relation to valuable workers in nature and to destructive ones.

In addition to his practical value in the protection of the garden, the toad is of interest to us from quite another standpoint. The beauty of the flower and the song of the bird make a direct appeal to us. However, there is a beauty other than that of colour, form or sound. There is a deeper beauty that grows out of the relation of one thing to another. This beauty makes an especial appeal to us when it concerns living forms, involving as it does an understanding of the life of a creature in its home and in contest with its enemies. This beauty of relation includes not only harmony, but the discord that by contrast makes the surrounding harmony more beautiful. It involves not only that which is commonly called beautiful and peaceful, but also the fearful and the wonderful, and probably the tragic. It considers not only the individual or even the race, but the universe of individuals and races in the great balance of life.

Considered in this light, the toad, in its perfect adaptation to the needs of life, becomes one of the most interesting of creatures, and the beauty of use behind each element in its appearance and its actions brings a revelation to the thinking mind.

Its very ugliness becomes attractive when we realise that this ugliness has gradually come about through thousands of generations of struggle against enemies and adverse conditions; that every ancestor not fitted by its every point of structure and by every habit of life to escape its foes and to procure food in plenty, was weeded out of the ranks by those very foes or because of that very lack. And now at last the survivor of the long line of life, our common toad, is one of the most protected and the best adapted to its needs of all our animals.

Its dull brown skin, rough with warts of all sizes and shapes, is so like the soil of garden or of field (Fig. 61) that an enemy passes without suspecting that a toad is near. The toad is the more easily passed by because he "lies low," quite motionless with chin touching the ground and body flattened as much as possible.

FIG. 58.—The toad walks cautiously toward the worm.

FIG. 59.—The toad walks around the worm until he can take it head first.

FIG. 60.—He looks very eager as he is about to make the seizure. Eyes shut during swallowing. The end of the worm still hanging out ot the toad's mouth.

FIG. 61.—To show the resemblance of the toad's skin to garden earth, both in colour and texture.

FIG. 62.—Structure study of the undersurface of the American Toad.   (Providence, R. I.)

Among green foliage and in bright light the toad's coat becomes conspicuously spotted and striped, so that he blends perfectly with the details and the alternating light and shadow of the grasses and leaves about him. (Colour Plate III, also Fig. 81.) Even his size and shape tend to make him seem to the passer-by a mere bit of rough wood or stone or a lump of earth.

The colour of the toad's skin can change through a long range, i.e., from light grey or yellowish to almost black. The toad on the sandy road in sunshine is light yellowish with a few darker markings. The sleepy toad just out of his burrow is rich dark brown, probably without markings of any sort. On a bright afternoon the toad in the grass of lawn or meadow becomes light or dark brown, but conspicuously striped with cream colour or light brown, and perhaps has touches of red. (Colour Plate III.)

This change to a colour which corresponds with the colour of his surroundings (often making the toad as invisible as though he carried the magic fern seed in his pocket) may take place within a few minutes, but any decided change usually requires considerable time. Then, too, all the toads that are subject to the same general conditions may not take on the same colouration.

However, his colour and his power of changing it are not the only means by which the toad is adapted to life. By every detail of structure from the tongue with its free hinder part and muscles of lightning rapidity, and the large elevated eyes situated like watch-towers at the highest possible point, to the strong back legs adapted for jumping and swimming, the toad is fitted to cope with all situations. The power to jump is likely to be a great advantage in the world of animals, for such a sudden movement from an unexpected quarter will startle the enemy just enough to allow escape.

The toad is fitted for his place in life by what he does, as well as by what he is. Let an enemy seize him roughly, and he is a dead toad. "Playing dead" saves him many a time. He will lie on his back with scarcely any perceptible motion for minutes at a time. (See Figs. 79 and 80.) Even the breathing movements seem to be suspended. Suddenly one leg is thrust out, then another, the eyes open wide, and in an instant more, the toad has turned over and is ready for new emergencies. Whether this habit is a protective instinct, or whether the toad really is insen-

87

sible from fright during the time that it "plays dead," the resulting protection is the same, for, as a rule, animals that feed upon living food associate motion with life so firmly that they pay no attention to a motionless creature.

One of the greatest protections afforded the toad is given by his habit of burrowing. Under stone or board or shrubbery, he makes his snug house all of soft earth — floor, walls and roof. His method of making it is very unexpected. Perhaps it would not be so if we remembered the appearance of his hind feet. They are greatly hardened and thus especially fitted for digging and each bears a conspicuous spur. (Fig. 44.) The toad makes his house and enters it at the same time — a great advantage, it would seem. But he must back in, which must have its disadvantages, since he cannot be certain until he is thoroughly and snugly in that he is going to have a house at all; he may bump against a stone, or take a long tumble into a cellar, or, worse still, into a well.

Each morning he backs into his old burrow, or perhaps kicks into a new one; and rests with his nose and bright eyes at the open doorway. If an enemy comes, he shuts the door in the intruder's face by forcibly backing his way farther in until the earth caves down over his head.

This is just what he does when cold autumn days come. And here he lies, with his toes drawn under him and his head bent downward, all secure in his closely shut house. He sleeps—and the days grow colder — and winter is here. Still he sleeps, with his house yet more protected, perhaps, by coverings of leaves and snow. The winds blow, but he does not feel them. He is cold; we should call him frozen perhaps, he is so stiff and cold. But if the heart, the stronghold of his life, is not frozen, he wakes up some warm spring day when the ferns are unrolling and the cold is gone, and scarcely knows that he has slept more than a day.

What a change in him! The long sleep, the warm, moist air, all the instincts of his being, tend to fill him with physical joy. It is such a pleasure to eat; it is so delightful to move; it is such a satisfaction to soak in the water of the spring rains.

He is converted into a social creature and finds himself going with many other toads to the pond where he spent his own early days. And now at the pond and in the water (Fig. 63) he can contain himself no longer, but bursts into that spring song, beautiful to himself and to his companions.

88

PLATE XXIII

FIG. 63.—Toads go to their native ponds immediately after their winter hibernation.

PLATE XXIV

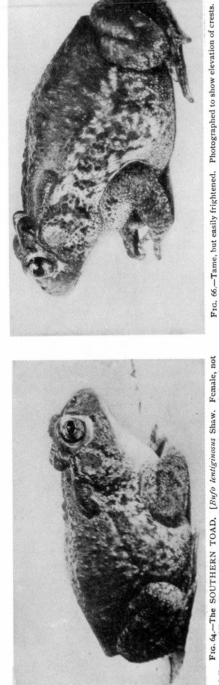

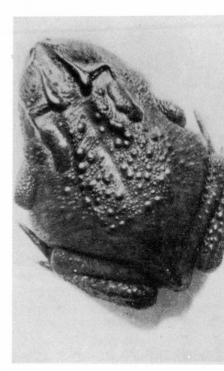

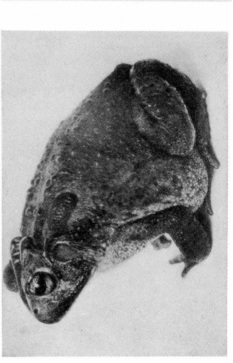

FIG. 64.—The SOUTHERN TOAD. [*Bufo lentiginosus* Shaw. Female, not full-grown. Mimmsville, Ga.] Photographed to show structural characteristics—i. e., size of eye, ear and parotoid glands, and outline of head.

FIG. 66.—Tame, but easily frightened. Photographed to show elevation of crests.

FIG. 65.—The SOUTHERN TOAD. Very meek.

FIG. 67.—Photographed to show arrangement of bony crests of head.

We also find the toad's song one of the most beautiful sounds in nature. The effect of a " chorus " of toads is most harmonious indeed — a crooning sound that seems a fit companion for amorous spring air, bursting flower buds, and the feeling of new life in our own hearts.

THE SOUTHERN TOAD

Bufo lentiginosus Shaw

IDENTIFICATION CHARACTERISTICS

Colour: Variable, often bright red-brown, with or without darker spots, a light vertebral stripe or a broader light band on the sides. The male may be nearly black. The young toads (one to three years old) may show much bright orange in the colouration. (For one phase of colouration, see Colour Plate IV.)

Measurements: Size of *Bufo americanus*, i.e. male 2½ to 3 inches; female much larger. Head relatively long, its length contained only 3½ to 4 times in total length. (Fig. 64.)

Structure: Parotoid glands relatively small and narrow. Crests of the head remarkably conspicuous, because of the elevation, posteriorly, of the divergent straight crests which lie on top of the head between the eyes. These are not only greatly elevated, but also are swollen into large knobs at their ends. Meeting each of these ridges just in front of the knob and behind the eye is a second ridge, which extends at right angles to the first downward to a point above the ear. A third ridge on each side passes backward from this point to the parotoid gland. (See Figs. 64 to 67, and compare with Figs. 48, 70, and 84.)

Range: The Southern States east of Texas.

This Southern toad, which is so like the American toad, its near relative at the North, is a valuable and interesting ally to man. It is very common, and may be seen in large numbers about houses and gardens in late afternoon and at dusk. During the daytime it hides in burrows of its own making, or in moist places under boards and stones.

It is probably of this toad that the following incident is told. The story illustrates the rapidity with which food is seized and swallowed, and the small part played in the process by the sense of taste. Among its other insect food the Southern toad finds fireflies very palatable. So small boys feed the toad with the burning ends of matches, and it is said that only after several have been swallowed does the toad find out its mistake and object to the heat.

The male is very much smaller than the female and is much duskier in colouring. The general colour may vary from light reddish or greenish brown to black. There is usually a light stripe along the middle of the back and a broader one lengthwise along each side. The underparts are dirty white. The upper surface is warty, but much less strongly so than is the corresponding surface in the American toad. (Compare Figs. 67 and 48.) The parotoid glands are somewhat kidney-shaped and are relatively narrow. The eye is unusually large and beautiful, with an elongated black oval pupil and a golden iris. The ear is large (though smaller than the eye) and is vertically oval.

The foot is smaller and more slender than that of the American toad, and the foot tubercles are correspondingly smaller. The mouth has a conspicuous indentation in the upper jaw and a hooklike extension of the lower jaw to fit into this indentation.

This toad is one of the meekest and gentlest looking creatures that ever lived a lowly life on the ground. (Fig. 65.) Although it becomes very tame in captivity, so that it will take food from one's fingers, or eat sitting in the hand, it still remains very timid, and is startled by any rapid or unexpected movement. (Fig. 66.) While in captivity, toads of this species ate earthworms and insects of various sorts. Among the latter were large polyphemus caterpillars, hairy caterpillars (such as yellow bear and woolly bear), various sphinx caterpillars, red-legged locusts, and in fact all insects offered, except a large staghorn beetle. This beetle was swallowed, but was almost immediately disgorged, and the toad showed evident signs of discomfort long after. *Bufo lentiginosus*, like many other toads, shows, when excited, curious, nervous movements of the toes. These movements are especially conspicuous when the toad is watching a moving worm or insect just before seizing it.

After having been kept in a dry place for a few days, this toad — as well as *Bufo l. woodhousei* from Arizona, and other toads from southern North America — displays an interesting relation to water and interesting movements in it. When released in proximity to water, the toad hops eagerly towards it and squats in a place where it is shallow. After sitting quietly for a few moments, he turns around once or twice, then puts the water up on his eyes and the top of his head by means of his hands, using first one and then the other. This is not surprising, for we have seen the front feet used as hands in a similar movement during moulting or eating. However, there follows a most unusual movement, showing that the hind legs can be put to uses other than those of burrowing and locomotion. The wet feet are lifted one at a time, and their under surfaces are rubbed very dexterously over the toad's back and sides until all is wet. Finally, the hind legs are stretched backward and rubbed together in the water in a fashion that reminds us of the similar movement of the hind legs of a fly.

The throat of the male is black, and expands into a rounded resonating sac when the toad gives its call. This call consists of a single tone, which is vibrated, and which lasts several seconds. It is high-pitched and extremely sweet; in fact, it would take a practiced ear to distinguish the call from that of the American toad.

Bufo lentiginosus and *Bufo americanus* do not show a series of intergrading forms in a district intermediate in position to their respective southern and northern centres of distribution. Instead, they seem to be distinct species occupying the same localities where their ranges overlap.

THE ROCKY MOUNTAIN TOAD

Bufo lentiginosus woodhousei Girard

IDENTIFICATION CHARACTERISTICS

Colour: Usually dingy greyish or yellowish brown, with much yellow on the lower sides and on the concealed portion of the femur. The toad may be conspicuously spotted with dark (Figs. 71 and 73), or unspotted, the rounded warts alone being dark-coloured. There is a light vertebral streak. Underparts light yellowish, unspotted, except for aggregations of small black spots on the breast. (Figs. 69 and 73.) Eye metallic yellow. Throat of male black. Tips of fingers and toes dark-coloured. (For one phase of colouration, see Colour Plate IV.)

Measurements: Size unusually large, i.e. male 3½ to 4 inches.

female 4 to 5½ inches. Head short, its length contained in total length nearly five times. (Fig. 68.) A toad having a length of head seven-eighths inch has a width 1¾ inch. The length of the leg to the heel equals the length of the body forward to some point between the eye and the end of the muzzle. Tibia but little longer than femur. (Fig. 70.)

Structure: Skin rough, with rounded warts. Eyelids warty. (Fig. 70.) Parotoids long and oval, not reniform in shape and not descending greatly on the shoulders. Ear a distinct vertical oval, variable in size from a diameter half that of the eye to one which in the case of old specimens almost equals it. The top of the head is usually lifted above the neck region behind. (Figs. 73 and 74.) There are two conspicuous bony ridges parallel between the eyes. These may have a groove between them, and may have their edges crenated along this groove (Fig. 70), or they may be obscured by having the groove quite filled up between them. (Figs. 72, 73 and 74.) At right angles behind the eyes these ridges meet two other ridges, each of which extends outward and downward between the eye and the parotoid to the ear on its respective side. Muzzle not projecting greatly beyond the lip. Palm with one large tubercle (Fig. 69), and a smaller one at the inner base of the first finger. Sole of foot rough, with small tubercles. Web of foot relatively short. Inner tubercle usually large, with free cutting edge. Outer tubercle large, but flat, without cutting edge. (Fig. 71.)

Range: This is the common toad of the Rocky Mountain region. It is reported from Montana, Nevada, Utah, Colorado, Nebraska, Kansas, Arizona, New Mexico, and Texas.

The Rocky Mountain toad is usually dingy in colour. Just after a moult, its colouration becomes brighter and richer in tone, with sharp contrast between the spots and the background. It has great power of change of colour from light to dark.

It is related to the American toad (*Bufo americanus*), and still more closely to the Southern toad (*Bufo lentiginosus*), but attains a greater size than either of these. The male of this toad is about the size of the female of the American toad. The relative length of the head and the shape of the cranial crests will always

FIG. 68.—The ROCKY MOUNTAIN TOAD. (*Bufo l. woodhousei* Gird) Phœnix, Arizona. (For coloration see Colour Plate IV.) A large rough-skinned toad with an unusually short head.

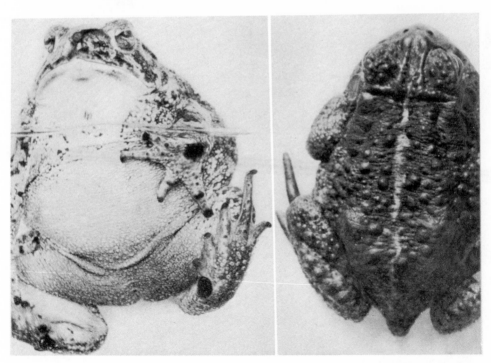

FIG. 69.—*Bufo l. woodhousei* Gird. Ft. Worth, Texas. Structure study of the under parts (in water).

FIG. 70.—*Bufo l. woodhousei* Gird. Phœnix, Ariz. Structure study of the bony crests of the head and of the texture of the skin of the upper surface.

PLATE XXVI

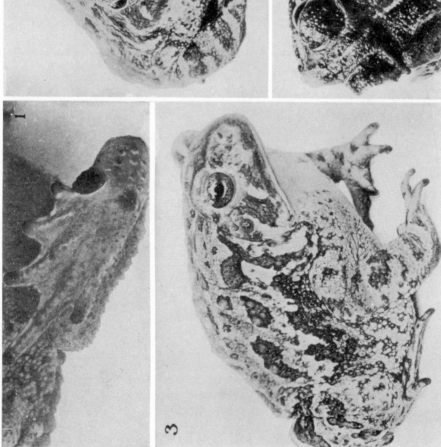

FIG. 71 (1).—Structure study of foot of the ROCKY MOUNTAIN TOAD. (Phœnix, Ariz.)

FIG. 73 (3).—The ROCKY MOUNTAIN TOAD may be bright-coloured with sharp contrast between the spots and the background of colour. (Ft. Worth, Texas.)

FIG. 72 (2).—A toad with determined ideas regarding his own actions. He can easily be deceived but will resist open coercion until he is thoroughly exhausted. (Ft. Worth, Texas.)

FIG. 74 (4).—The region of the top of the head between the parallel bony crests is quite filled in. The top of the head is elevated above the neck region behind. See also (2) and (3).

suffice to distinguish it from *Bufo lentiginosus*. However, its characteristics are so like those of *Bufo americanus* that in some specimens it is almost impossible to make the distinction, and it would then seem that *Bufo l. woodhousei* is *Bufo americanus* with only the variation to be expected from a different geographical distribution. The three toads mentioned are alike not only in general appearance, but in each case the male has a wrinkled black throat, and can extend a rounded vocal throat-pouch. In each case, also, the call given is a vibrated note of high pitch and sweet quality. These calls are difficult to distinguish one from the other, and prove a common ancestor.

This toad is often confused with *Bufo cognatus*, which is found in many of the same localities. The confusion arises, however, on superficial examination only, as the two toads are very different indeed. The cranial ridges of *Bufo cognatus* are not parallel, but diverge backward from a prominent bony elevation between the nostrils. (See Figs. 70 and 89.) The voices of the two are different, and could never be confused after once hearing. That of *Bufo woodhousei* is sweet and musical, while the other is emphatically the opposite. The vocal pouch of *Bufo woodhousei* is a rounded sac extending from the margin of the lower jaw to the line on the breast somewhat below the arm insertions and from one angle of the jaw to the other. That of *Bufo cognatus* is a bladder sent out from the base of the throat in the midline between the arm insertions. (See Fig. 100.)

There are many minor differences between the two, such as the following: The foot of *Bufo cognatus* is relatively much longer than that of *Bufo woodhousei* (compare Figs. 70 and 91); the parotoids of *Bufo cognatus* extend obliquely down on the shoulder, while those of *Bufo woodhousei* are almost parallel. (See Figs. 68 and 91.)

FOWLER'S TOAD

Bufo fowleri Putnam

IDENTIFICATION CHARACTERISTICS

Colour: General colour light or dark grey (or dull brown), which may be greenish or yellowish in tone, very rarely reddish. Sometimes dark or dingy and unspotted; more often spotted and striped with dull brown or black. A prominent light vertebral streak and spots margined with light. (See Figs. 77, 78, 80, and 84.) Spots unusually distinct, and seldom deviating from a typical arrangement. This arrangement is as follows: six pairs along the vertebral streak — first pair, elongated spots placed obliquely on the eyelids and top of the head; second pair, rounded and small, between the anterior ends of the parotoids; third pair, greatly elongated, more or less pear-shaped, situated on the anterior part of the back; fourth, fifth, and sixth pairs irregular, the last often obscure. There is an irregular band of light colour on the side bounded below by dark. Between the anterior part of the eye and the jaw there is a dark band, and back of this, extending from the eye and lower border of the parotoid, there are three or four dark bands, more or less parallel to this one. The warts situated on the dark spots are usually lighter or brighter than the spots. Iris bright metallic yellow, with tracery of black veining. Throat of male black. Throat of female light, with perhaps a few spots on the jaw. Underparts light, unspotted. (See Figs. 75 and 79.) There may be much yellow reticulated with black on the posterior lower sides and on the anterior and posterior faces of the femur.

Measurements: Size medium, i.e. male $2\frac{1}{2}$ inches, female slightly larger. Head relatively short; length of head contained in total length about four times. Legs relatively long, i.e. length of leg to heel equals length of body forward to some point anterior to the eye in the female and to the muzzle or beyond in the male. Tibia longer than femur.

Structure: Skin everywhere finely warty on the upper parts. Groups of somewhat larger warts on the dark spots of the back. (See Fig. 84 and Colour Plate IV.) Underparts granulated. Parotoids long, narrow, parallel ovals. (Fig. 84.) The top of the head may be higher than the neck region behind. The two bony crests of the top of the head are variable in their characteristics. They are usually near each other, considerably elevated, parallel, and grown together at their posterior ends. Conspicuous ridges behind the eyes meet these parallel ridges at right angles. Ear a vertical oval, two-thirds the size of the eye. The muzzle projects beyond the upper lip. The nostrils, which open upward, are situated half-way between the eye and the jaw on a vertical line with the upper lip. Fingers slender, prominent tubercles under

PLATE XXVII

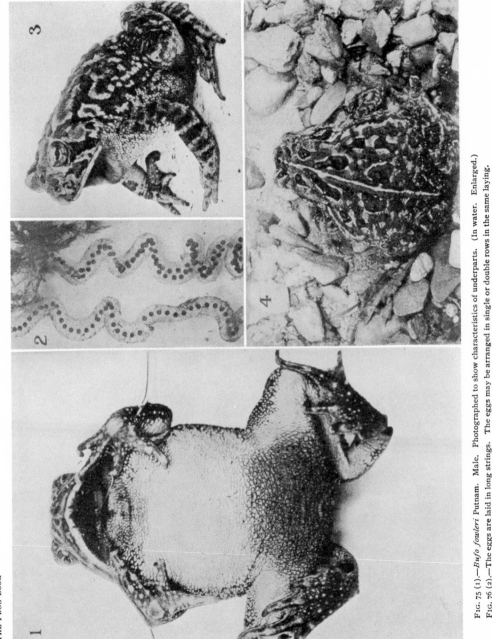

FIG. 75 (1).—*Bufo fowleri* Putnam. Male. Photographed to show characteristics of underparts. (In water. Enlarged.)

FIG. 76 (2).—The eggs are laid in long strings. The eggs may be arranged in single or double rows in the same laying.

FIGS. 77 and 78 (3 and 4).—To show the spotted character of the toad: (For one phase of coloration see Colour Plate IV.)

PLATE XXVIII

FIG. 81.—To show protective resemblance of FOWLER'S TOAD.

FIG. 79.—When roughly handled the toad "plays dead." Even the breathing movements are suspended. (*Bufo fowleri*, female. Providence, R. I.)

FIG. 80.—Suddenly the toad turns over and is ready for new emergencies.

finger-joints; one large palm tubercle; order of lengths of fingers from the shortest to the longest, second, fourth, first, third. Toes slender; web deeply indented; inner sole tubercle well developed; outer sole tubercle small (See Figs. 79 and 82.)

Range: Danvers, Woods Hole, and Cuttyhunk Island, Massachusetts. Common throughout Rhode Island. Probably common in other parts of Massachusetts, and perhaps in still other New England States.[1] Specimens are in the American Museum of Natural History, in a collection representing the Batrachia of the vicinity of New York City.

Fowler's toad comes from its hibernation later in the spring than the American toad. On warm evenings in late April and early May, it is the latter only that we hear at the ponds. In late May and in June the toad chorus in Rhode Island consists mainly of the voices of Fowler's toad, with only an occasional sweet note from the American toad. In July it is rarely that we hear any voice but that of the Fowler's toad.

The call of the Fowler's toad is a metallic droning sound, not conspicuously vibrated. The pitch of the call may be as high as that of *Bufo americanus*, but descends in doleful fashion through several intervals before the close. Its carrying power is unusually great. The quality is indescribable; on the whole, the call is weird and mournful and not especially agreeable to our ears.

The small black-throated males sit for hours in the shallow water of the pond margin or of the marshy edge of some brook, and send forth woeful answering calls, inflating their throat-pouches enormously at each emission of sound. (Fig. 83.) We can discover them by means of these inflated throats if we approach their haunt with a lantern or on a moonlight night. The swollen throats look like great light-coloured transparent spheres — like large white bubbles — among the dark grass or above the black water. That these spheres are transparent, thin-walled, and empty, except for air, is interestingly proved by looking at them from the side opposite the lantern.

A few of these toads may be heard calling from park lagoons,

---

[1] G. M. Allen describes the song of the Fowler's toad heard in New Hampshire, but attributes this song to the American toad. "Notes on the Reptiles and Batrachians of Intervale, N. H." Proc. Bost. Soc. Nat. Hist., 29: 63-75.

river margins, and ponds at any time during the late spring and the summer months. Occasionally, however, in some shallow country pond, there will be, for a few nights, so many hundreds of these toads that it would seem that all the Fowler's toads had assembled for miles around. The males outnumber the females to an astonishing extent. Out of eighty toads captured on such an occasion, only seven were females. The loud, weird chorus made by such an assembly of Fowler's Toads is described as a " terrible squawking" by some who have heard it. Others have compared it to the persistent whooping of a party of Indians.

The eggs are laid in long tangled strings, like those of the American toad. (See Fig. 76.) The eggs are slightly smaller than those of *Bufo americanus*, and may be arranged in one or in two rows in the same laying. The development of this species is rapid. Owing to the length of the breeding season, we may find young Fowler's toads of many different sizes during the summer and autumn. They show the cranial crests and the characteristic spots within three or four weeks after the tail is lost.

The adult *Bufo fowleri* is delicately moulded and is more slender than most North American toads. It is also better developed for leaping, the legs being unusually long. (See Fig. 84.)

The habit of the toad is what would be expected from its structure — it is as agile as a frog, and difficult to catch. After the breeding season, the remainder of the summer and the autumn are spent in a toad's ordinary haunts. We may see the Fowler's spotted back at the sides of country roads, in parks and gardens, and in waste fields and pastures, where insects are numerous. There is marked uniformity in size and colour among the adult toads, much more so than in *Bufo americanus*.

Few people, if any, living in Massachusetts and Rhode Island, realise that there are two kinds of toads in these states. *Bufo fowleri* differs from *Bufo americanus* distinctly and fundamentally as follows:

It is always yellowish or greenish grey, never taking on the rich yellow, orange, and red browns of the American toad. It is uniformly more spotted and striped in colouration. The underparts are never spotted as they are in the other toad. It is usually less fat and squat, and is much more agile. The muzzle projects farther beyond the jaw. The parotoids are narrower and are never kidney-shaped. The skin is somewhat less rough, and never has the large warts so conspicuous in the *Bufo americanus*. The head is less broad, the whole form more delicately moulded. The foot is less broad and thick; the toes more slender. The voices are wholly different, and could never be confused after being heard with even small attention. The time of breeding is different, *Bufo fowleri* not being able to endure as low a temperature as does *Bufo americanus*. Two to four weeks after *Bufo americanus* has appeared in the ponds, and, in fact, after the greater number of this species has returned to land life, *Bufo fowleri* comes from hibernation. Moreover, the eggs of the latter toad are often arranged in double rows. They never are, as far as reported, in the case of *Bufo americanus*. There should be no trouble in distinguishing the two toads. The confusion arises in regard to the cranial crests. Those of *Bufo americanus* are usually like the type for that species (see Fig. 48), but *Bufo fowleri* varies most remarkably in this structure. The head crests may be parallel or may diverge; may lie close together or far apart; may be considerably elevated and sharp-edged, or low rounded ridges; may be on a raised occiput or not; and may be fused at their posterior ends, or separated by a groove as in *Bufo americanus*. The great variation in the cranial crests of *Bufo fowleri*, *Bufo l. woodhousei*, *Bufo quercicus*, and other toads would seem to indicate that this structure cannot perhaps be made so fundamental in classification as has been thought.

Since *Bufo fowleri* differs fundamentally from *Bufo americanus*, and occupies the same localities, it must be granted full specific rank.[1]

---

[1]The closer relationship that must have existed between these two toads in previous ages is shown in the fact that the tadpoles are almost identical in structure. The mouth of the tadpole of B. fowleri is more delicate, the delicacy especially noticeable in the papillae. The tadpoles differ in colour. (M. H. Hinckley, "On Some Differences in the Mouth Structure of Tadpoles." Proc. Bost. Soc. Nat. Hist., Vol. XXI, pp. 307-314).

BUFO HEMIOPHRYS, COPE

Identification Characteristics

Colour: Brown, with medium-sized dark spots on each side of a light vertebral streak. The tubercles set in the spots are reddish in colour. There are brown spots on the upper lip, below the ear and between the parotoid gland and shoulder. An irregular brown band extends backward along the side. Sides below this band reticulated with dark. Legs (even the feet) banded with dark. Posterior surface of the femur coarsely reticulated with dark. Underparts (except the throat) spotted.

Measurements: Length $2\frac{1}{4}$ inches. Length of head (to end of cranial crests) enters the total length about $4\frac{1}{2}$ times. Length of leg to heel equals the length of the body forward to the eye.

Structure: Skin tubercular; tubercles small but prominent, often set in rows on the back and tibia. Smaller granulations of the skin conspicuous everywhere, especially on the sides. Parotoid narrow, oval. Head rounded; muzzle vertical in front; nostrils terminal. Ear a vertical oval, two-thirds the diameter of the eye. Cranial crests as follows: Parallel ridges between the eyes, elongated and united behind in a transverse ridge above the nape. These ridges of the top of the head turn outward at their posterior ends, as if to form ridges back of the eyes to the ears, but extend only a short distance, and end abruptly. Foot webbed extensively, but webs deeply indented. Inner sole tubercle unusually large, outer small; both of these tubercles have free cutting edges.

Range: "Northern boundary of the United States." Type specimens in the National Museum show northeastern Dakota (Turtle Mountains) to be the type locality. Specimens are re-reported also from Manitoba, Canada.

Bufo hemiophrys, of which the type specimens — seven in number — were found in 1874, is to be looked for in Dakota and Manitoba, instead of in Montana, as stated by Cope. Owing to the misstatement in " Batrachia of North America," diligent search was made for this toad in northern Montana throughout the spring and summer of 1905 by several collectors, but no specimens came to light.

FIG. 82.—Structure study of hand and foot of FOWLER'S TOAD.   (In water.   Enlarged.)

FIG. 83.—FOWLER S TOAD sits in the grass at the pond margin or in the shallow water and sings. The rounded vocal pouch is inflated and acts as a resonator.   The mouth is kept closed.

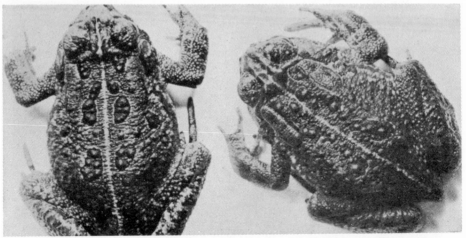

FIG. 84.—Structure study to show the texture of the skin, the parotoids and the cranial crests of FOWLER'S TOAD.

PLATE XXX

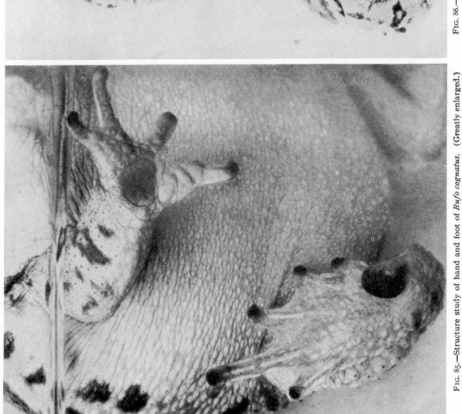

FIG. 86.—(Upper toad.) Defensive.
FIG. 87.—Ready for emergencies.

FIG. 85.—Structure study of hand and foot of *Bufo cognatus*. (Greatly enlarged.)

This toad differs from the species of the Pacific Slope (*Bufo boreas*) in the possession of bony ridges on the head, while it is like them in skin structure and arrangement of warts. It differs from the species of the Rocky Mountains and Western plains (*Bufo l. woodhousei* and *Bufo cognatus*) in having the underparts conspicuously spotted and in the arrangement of the cranial crests, but agrees in certain features, such as the foot structure. The species bears a superficial resemblance to *Bufo fowleri*.

BUFO COGNATUS, SAY

IDENTIFICATION CHARACTERISTICS

Colour: General colour may be brown, of light or dark shade; grey; or green, dull or brighter. There is a light vertebral streak. The toad may appear striped or spotted, depending on whether the dark spots or the light borders of the spots are more conspicuous at the time. Specimens from Arizona tend to have the spots more emphatic; specimens from Colorado more often appear striped. (Compare Figs. 89 and 90, also 91 and 92. For one phase of colouration, see Colour Plate V.)

The arrangement of the spots may be as follows: One obliquely set above each eye; one on the back, just within the parotoid gland on each side; three oval spots set obliquely and ranging along each side of the vertebral streak. Two similar spots back of and in line with the parotoid gland, and two or three others on the upper sides. Other more obscure spots may be present. Underparts light, unspotted; yellow posteriorly. Much yellow (especially in the case of young toads) on palm, sole, and on concealed surface of femur. Ends of fingers and toes dark-coloured.

Measurements: Size large, i.e. length 3 to 4½ inches. Head short, wide; small for the size of the toad. The length of the head is contained in the total length about five times. A toad 4¼ inches long has a length of head of ⅞ inch only. Legs very short, femur scarcely visible outside of the skin of the body. (See Figs. 88 and 89.) Tibia somewhat longer than femur. Foot extends considerably beyond the knee when the leg is folded. (Fig. 91.)

Structure: Whole upper surface, including the eyelids, set rather closely with warts, some medium-sized and some small. Often the larger of these warts are set in wreaths around the inner

99

margins of the large spots. (See Fig. 89.) Distinct line of slightly larger warts from posterior end of parotoid backward. Muzzle very steep, both on the sides and in front. (Fig. 91.) There is a hard, bony elevation above the nostrils and between the eyes in front. This elevation fills up what in other species of toads is a groove between the two lines of the canthus rostralis. (Figs. 87 and 89.) There are two rounded bony ridges extending obliquely backward from this median bony elevation. Back of the eyes, these two ridges meet two similar ridges, each of which extends between the eye and the parotoid gland outward and downward to the ear of its respective side. (See Figs. 86 and 89.) The nostrils open upward and are situated just half-way between the top of this bony elevation and the jaw below. (Fig. 86.) The ear is a conspicuous vertical oval. It varies in size, but is usually less than half the diameter of the eye. The parotoid glands are short elevated ovals extending obliquely down on the shoulders. (Figs. 89 and 91.)

Hand with one large palm tubercle; the remainder of the palm set with crowded small tubercles. (See Fig. 85.) Foot thick, with tarsal ridge. Toes slender, fourth toe much longer than the others. Web deeply indented. Sole tubercles large, both with cutting edge; the inner is at least three times as large as the outer. The tubercles under the toe-joints may be double. (Figs. 85 and 88.)

Range: Bufo cognatus Say, has been reported from Nebraska, Colorado, Kansas, Arkansas, and Arizona. It is probably found in other states of the Western plains, as well as in others of the Rocky Mountain region.

Bufo cognatus, common toad of the Western plains, is one of our largest North American species. It is a toad very distinctive in its characteristics, notwithstanding the fact that in localities where it is found with *Bufo l. woodhousei,* the two toads are usually confused.[1] It can always be recognized by the bony elevation in front, above the nostrils and between the eyes anteriorly; by the large outer sole tubercle with its cutting edge; by the short femur and long foot.

[1]See p. 93.

PLATE XXXI

FIG. 89.—*Bufo cognatus* Say. To show identification characteristics of bony crests of head, of parotoids, etc. (For one phase of coloration see Colour Plate V.)

FIG. 88.—*Bufo cognatus* Say. Female. Phœnix, Ariz. Photographed (in water) to show the structural characteristics of the under surfaces.

PLATE XXXII

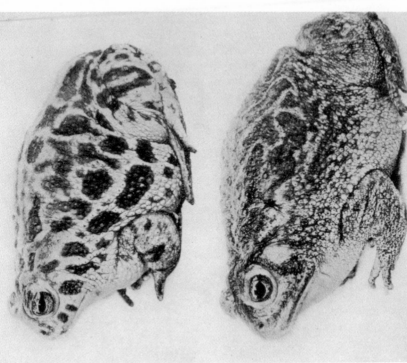

FIG. 91.—*Bufo cognatus* from Phoenix, Arizona. (Upper toad.) To show short head, steep descent of muzzle, length of foot, etc.

FIG. 92.—*Bufo cognatus*, Denver, Col. (Lower toad.) This species of toad may appear striped or spotted (compare with Fig. 91).

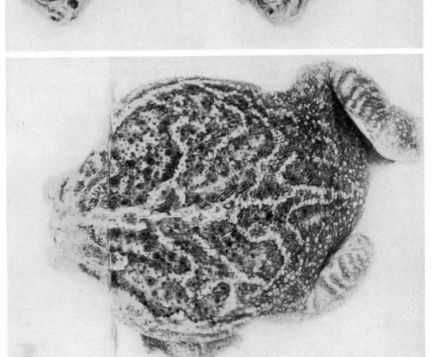

FIG. 90.—*Bufo cognatus* Say. Female. Denver, Col. Photographed (in water) to show intricate pattern of lines on the back.

Judging from the series of decidedly different sizes of this toad found in the spring, at least five years must be required for full growth to be attained.

The female *Bufo cognatus* seldom makes any sound. When taken in the hand, it shakes with wrath, but usually remains silent. The male however, "talks" in a voice resembling the squawk of a toy doll. This squawk of the *Bufo cognatus* is much like the sound produced by *Bufo halophilus* of California. The harsh note is given over and over again at brief intervals until the cause of annoyance is removed. The pitch of the note is low, ranging from B to A below middle C. In the midst of the harsh low-pitched notes, the toad sometimes surprises one by giving a cry pitched about two octaves above (usually A).

At the base of the throat of the male is a wrinkled black and purplish spot, which at first sight, one might judge the result of an injury. This is thin skin, lying fold upon fold, and can be extended into a vocal bladder of enormous size. (See Fig. 100.)

Bufo cognatus is not nearly related to the American Toad or to *Bufo lentiginosus*, but is closely connected with *Bufo compactilis* of the Southwest and *Bufo quercicus* of Georgia and Florida. The relationship shows itself not only in various technical details, but in visible external features. They each show the reduced femur and short leg, the short head and broad depressed body, diverging parotoid glands that descend on the shoulders, well-developed sole tubercles, deeply indented webs, and a vocal bladder at the base of the throat. The cranial ridges mark a point of variance among the three. The variation in size also is notable. *Bufo quercicus* is the smallest known toad in the world, measuring only an inch and a quarter in length. *Bufo compactilis* is medium in size, and *Bufo cognatus* is one of the largest toads in North America.

Bufo cognatus is peculiarly alert and active. When annoyed, it inflates the lungs, thus greatly increasing the size of the body, and lowers the head in a defensive attitude. It is incapable, however, of any defense beyond this, and stealthily creeps away, keeping the flattened body close to the ground.

A curious incident occurred when *Bufo cognatus* was being kept in captivity for study—an incident probably illustrative of the way in which stories have arisen regarding toads found in stones and buried in impossible places. A large fat specimen of

Bujo cognatus escaped one morning from its moss-garden in a building in Rhode Island. That day repairs had been begun on a cement floor in the basement of the building. In the afternoon of the day, while workmen were continuing to remove the cement floor — which had been put down seven years before — they came upon a fat toad just fitting a burrow under the floor. Excitement followed, with many stories of toads found in similar situations where they had been for more than seven years. If the toad had not turned out to be the lost *Bujo cognatus* from Colorado, and had been a native of Rhode Island, there would have existed no proof that it had not been there seven years instead of a few hours.

BUFO COMPACTILIS, WIEGM

IDENTIFICATION CHARACTERISTICS

Colour: Greenish-grey or brown, generally light in tone. No vertebral light streak. Spotted irregularly with dark, or without spots. Small warts everywhere may be tipped with red. There may be large dark spots on the lower sides and on the legs and arms. Hands and feet light-coloured. Large tubercles of the foot black. Toes tipped with black. Iris yellowish. Underparts light, unspotted. Throat of male dark. (See Figs. 93 to 95.)

Measurements: Size medium, i. e. length $2\frac{1}{2}$ to $3\frac{1}{2}$ inches. Head short. Head anterior to eyes rounded and remarkably short. The legs are short, the femur scarcely showing at all outside of the skin of the body. The length of the leg to the heel is shorter than that of the body forward to the ear.

Structure: Body unusually fat and squat. Whole surface evenly and closely covered with small rounded warts. These closely placed warts are also on the top of the head and on the eyelids. (Fig. 95.) Crown of head flat, without bony ridges (although there may be slight traces of ridges inside of and behind the eyes). Ear a small vertical oval. (Fig. 93.) Parotoid glands are short ovals, extending obliquely outward and downward. (Fig. 95.) Hands and feet small and delicate. One extremely large tubercle with cutting edge on the palm. Two sole tubercles, each unusually large and each with cutting edge. (Fig. 94.) Webs medium in development.

PLATE XXXIII

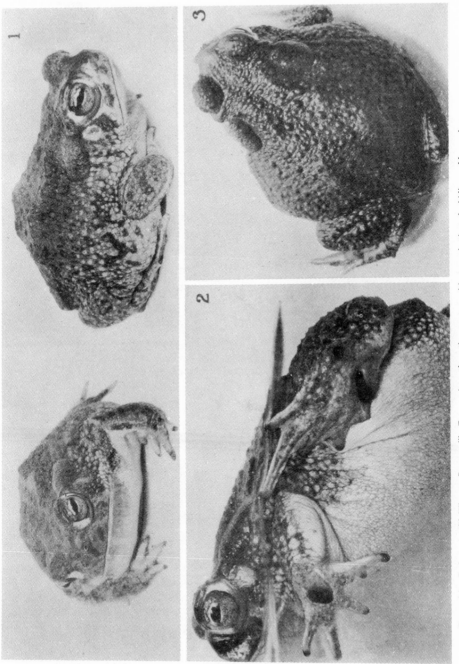

FIG. 93 (1).—*Bufo compactilis* Wiegm. Brownsville, Texas. A gentle, active creature with strong instincts for hiding and burrowing.

FIG. 94 (2).—Structure study of hand and foot.

FIG. 95 (3).—The paratoid glands extend downward on the shoulders. The whole upper surface is thickly set with small rounded warts.

PLATE XXXIV

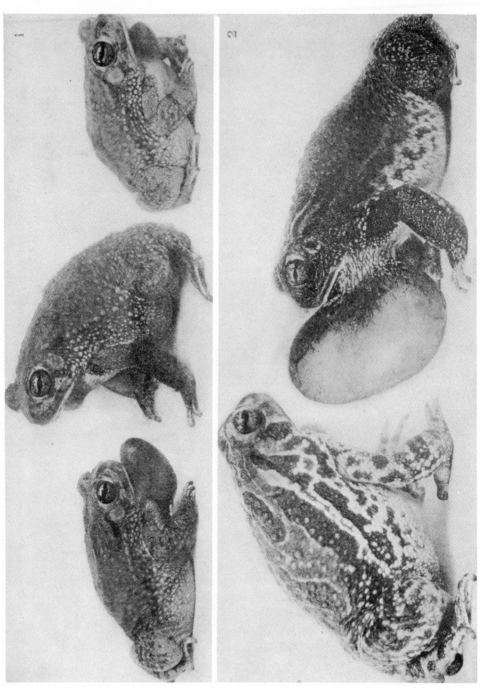

FIGS. 96 to 98 (1).—Studies of *Bufo compactilis* Wiegm. Brownsville, Texas.

FIGS. 99 to 100 (2).—*Bufo cognatus* Say. Phoenix, Arizona. (The vocal bladder can be inflated through the nostrils artificially by means of a blow pipe.)

Range: Bufo compactilis is reported from New Mexico, Texas, and Kansas.

Bufo compactilis bears, at first sight, a striking resemblance to the burrowing Spadefoot Toads. It is like *Scaphiopus hammondii* and *Scaphiopus couchii* in fact, in the shape and proportions of body and legs, the size and disposition of the warts, and in the unusual development of the foot for burrowing. The resemblance is only superficial, however, as the horizontal pupil tells us at once. *Bufo compactilis* is a true toad, closely related to *Bufo cognatus*.

This toad has strong instincts for hiding and burrowing. When kept in captivity in moss-gardens with other toads, it is always found under the moss and leaves, while the others may be on top. If it does happen to be out in search of food and an enemy approaches, it flattens and spreads itself on the ground until it looks like a circular pebbly surface elevated an inch or less.

The young toads, when examined closely, sometimes show a beautiful colouration. The soft grey-brown of the background is enlivened by the bright red tips of the warts, and enriched by a few black spots and many irregularly placed moss-green patches.

The eye is bright and intelligent looking, and indicates the alertness and activity which make this toad no exception in its group.

When annoyed, it gives repeatedly a note that has somewhat the quality of the quack of a duck. But its musical powers do not stop here, as we would know if we examined the throat region. There is a wrinkled sac at the middle point of the throat, on a line with the angles of the jaws. It consists of fold upon fold of thin skin, confined to a spot of not more than one-half inch in diameter. These folds are released one after another as the sac is inflated until there is produced a large blind tube looking like the bladder of a fish. (Figs. 96 to 98.) The toad may sit very erect while singing, and the bladder extends forward and upward to a considerable distance above the head. The call is very loud and penetrating, and is harsh in quality. The calls are repeated continually, about one per second, with a short pause between each two. The bladder remains inflated during the calling but decreases somewhat in size between the notes. The pitch in the specimens observed was about two octaves above middle C (D). The notes were kept

103

at this pitch for some minutes, when suddenly there would be a distinct drop, followed almost immediately by a sudden rise again to the original pitch.

The life history and habits of *Bufo compactilis* are not on record.

THE OAK TOAD

Bufo quercicus Holbrook

IDENTIFICATION CHARACTERISTICS

Colour: Rich dark brown or grey-brown, with a distinct white or yellow vertebral streak extending forward to the margin of the upper jaw. The warts along this light line may be tipped with vivid red and orange, as are also those on the posterior part of the eyelid and on the sides of the body. Four pairs of black spots — irregular, elongated, white-edged — lie along the vertebral line. The first spots are on the top of the head. Underparts grayish white, unspotted. Throat of male dusky. Light band from end of parotoid gland backward. A broad black band on the side of the body is made conspicuous by this white above and the white of the underparts. Bright orange on palms of hands and soles of feet; also some orange on under surface of femur. Sole tubercles black. Legs irregularly spotted or banded with black. (Fig. 101.)

Measurements: Size small, i. e. length of adult 1¼ inches. Head short, its length contained in total length four times. Legs extremely short; length to heel not equalling length of body forward to the arm insertion. Femur almost concealed in the skin of the body, tibia not much longer. (Figs. 101 and 106.)

Structure: Exposed surface everywhere thickly set with warts of varying degrees of minuteness. These warts cover the head and eyelids, back, sides, legs, and arms. Those on the forearm and tarsus are spinous. The palms of the hands and soles of the feet are finely tubercular. Underparts everywhere granulated, even the throat. (Fig. 106.) The parotoid glands are oval and long (three times length of eye), extending down on the sides. (Fig. 103.) The bony crests of the head are parallel and widely separated. They extend backward close to the inner edges of the orbits; their ends bend abruptly inward, a little beyond the anterior ends of the parotoid glands. The ridges back of the

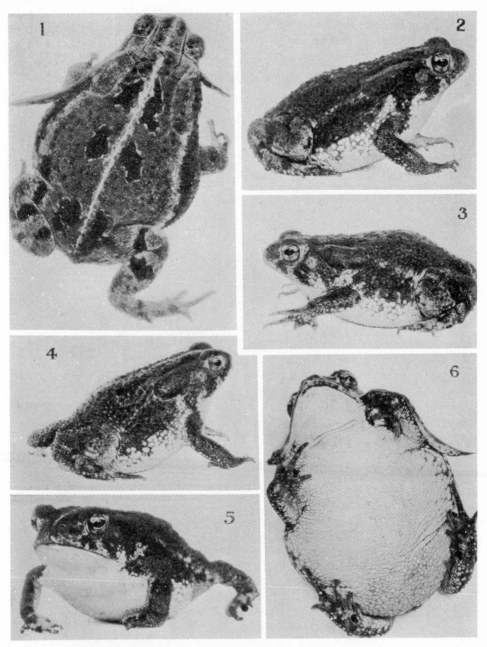

FIG. 101 (1).—The OAK TOAD (*Bufo quercicus* Holbrook). Ozona, Florida. Nat. size 1¼ in. Photographed (in water) to show bony crests of the head, and the arrangement of light and dark colour on the upper parts.

FIGS. 102 to 104 (2–4).—The OAK TOAD is closely covered with small warts which are spinous on legs and arms

FIG. 105 (5).—*Bufo quercicus* is a most alert toad.

FIG. 106 (6).—To show structure of the underparts.

FIGS. 107 to 109.—*Bufo alvarius* Girard. Phœnix, Arizona. Photographed to show skin texture, parotoid glands, cranial crests and other identification points. Actual length 5 in. (For coloration see Colour Plate V.)

eyes and those extending backward to the parotoid glands are well marked. (Fig. 101.) The inner sole tubercle is fairly large, considering the diminutive size of the foot. The outer tubercle is small. The webs are very short. (Fig. 106.)

Range: Bufo quercicus has been reported from North Carolina, South Carolina, Georgia, and Florida.[1]

This is said to be the smallest known toad. It is a little, dusky, hopping creature, which has probably been mistaken many times for the young of *Bufo lentiginosus*, the Southern toad. It is so small that we need a lens in order even to make out many of the details of its appearance. This is especially true of the crests of the head. They are obscure not only because of their small size, but also because of their dusky colour and the warty condition of the surrounding surface.

The eye has a shining golden iris. Its expression indicates much alertness. The ear is round and conspicuous, although it is much smaller than the eye.

It is said[2] that this toad may be seen in all kinds of places and at all times of day; that it is out during the brighest sunshine as well as at dusk and after rains. It was first found in sandy places, where there were low growths of oak — hence its name, " Oak Toad."

After heavy rains, Oak Toads resort in large numbers to shallow pools. They are difficult to see, but give notice of their presence by an ear-splitting chorus of high-pitched sounds.[3] The individual call is like that of a young chicken in distress, but considerably louder. The male alone gives the call, and while producing it seems to have in his mouth a transparent bladder about the size of a man's thumb. The fact is that this toad has a large vocal bladder that can be extended from the midline of the lower throat region. This structure relates it to *Bufo compactilis* and *Bufo cognatus* of the Southwest. (See Figs. 97 and 100.)

---

[1] Beaufort and Kinston, N. C.; Charleston, S. C.; Green Cove springs, Little Sarasota Bay, Arlington, Milton, Oakland, Ozona, and Kissimee, Fla.

[2] Loennberg. Notes on Reptiles and Batrachians collected in Florida in 1892 and 1893. Proc. U. S. Nat. Museum, vol. XVII, pp. 317, 339.

[3] C. B Lungren, collector. Ozona, Fla.

When taken in the hand, the Oak Toad gives a rather musical chirping sound, like that of a young bird.

BUFO ALVARIUS, GIRARD

IDENTIFICATION CHARACTERISTICS

Colour: Greyish or brownish green, of either light or dark shade. The sparsely scattered small warts are orange in colour, sometimes rimmed with dark. Underparts light. (Fig. 110.) The throat and breast of the female are mottled with grey. Iris light or dark metallic yellow, with a prominent veining of red. The iris is dark in front of and behind the oval black pupil. Fingers and toes tipped with black or red-brown. (For colouration, see Colour Plate V.)

Measurements: Size large, i. e. length 5 inches or more. The head is short. Its length is contained $3\frac{1}{2}$ to 4 times in the total length. Legs relatively short; the length of the leg to the heel is not equal to the length of the body forward to the ear. Femur very short. Tibia somewhat longer than femur. Foot very little longer than tibia. (Fig. 111.)

Structure: Skin leathery and smooth. Head rounded in front. (Fig. 108.) The ear is a very distinct vertical oval. The bony crests of the head are conspicuous, curved ridges. There is one on each side, which follows the upper border of the eye and curves outward and downward to the ear. (Fig. 109.) The parotoids are long and oval, greatly elevated, and very wide apart at their posterior ends. (Fig. 109.) They are separated from the eye by the width of the crest only. Small, flat, rounded warts are scattered over the whole upper surface. There is a large oval wart on the femur and a long one — or a line of shorter ones — on the tibia (along the margin that is nearest the femur when the leg is folded). (Fig. 109.) These glands are considerably elevated, and are very conspicuous. There may be a gland similar to these on the forearm. There are one or more round or oval white warts behind the angle of the jaw. (Figs. 107 and 108.) The foot is thick and has a conspicuous ridge along the inner edge of the tarsus. Both inner and outer sole tubercles are present. (Fig. 111.) The web is short and thick; it extends to the tips of the toes, but is deeply indented. There are two very large palm tubercles. (Fig. 110.)

Plate XXXVII

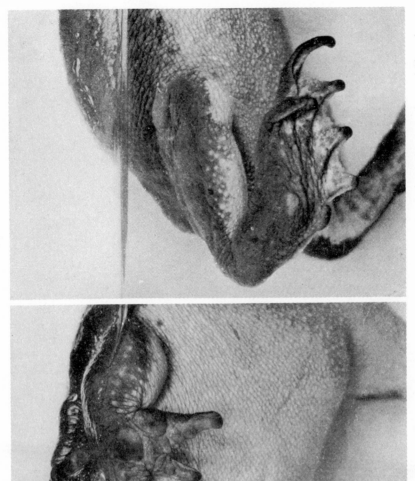

Fig. 110.—*Bufo atvarius* Girard. The palm has two large rounded tubercles.

Fig. 111.—The foot has a thick short web, a tarsal ridge and two sole tubercles.

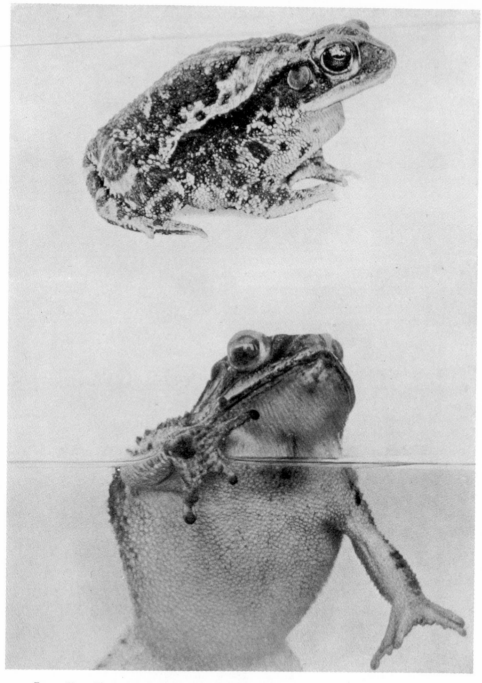

FIG. 112 (Upper Figure).—*Bufo valliceps.* Hitchcock, Texas. This species of toad is alert, but less wild than most North American forms. (For one phase of coloration, see colour Plate V.)

FIG. 113.—Photographed (in water) to show outline of jaw, texture of skin of underparts, and structure of hand. [Enlarged.]

Range: Bufo alvarius is reported from southern California (Fort Yuma) and Arizona (Phœnix).

There would never be any possibility of confusing this toad with any other. Its green colouration and its smooth skin identify it at once. It is peculiar, also, in attaining a size greater than that of any other North American species. In addition to these, the toad has the following other distinctive characteristics: the conspicuous glands on the legs, the peculiar white warts at the angle of the jaw, the curving crests of the head, and the greatly diverging parotoid glands.

The parotoid glands, beginning immediately back of the eye, are so long and descend on the shoulder so much that when they are only three-fourths of an inch apart at their anterior ends, they may be separated at their posterior ends by a distance more than twice as great. The parotoids are about the same width throughout their length. The elevated shoulder-blades show plainly on the back between them.

The bony crests of the head are smooth and rounded. Although not greatly elevated, they are very conspicuous, because of the smoothness and even colour of the surrounding surface. The crests extend backward from the nostrils in front, diverge and encircle the eyes. There is a crest under each eye in front, and another short one passes forward over the ear, on each side. The skin between the crests on the top of the head is thin and adheres to the bone underneath.

The ear is unusually conspicuous. It is placed immediately back of the eye, under the anterior part of the parotoid gland, and is surrounded by a prominent ridge. The eye is large and gentle in its expression. The iris is peculiar in having its metallic yellow thickly set with a tracery of bright red veins. There are two curious elevations in the gold of the iris; they are situated in the midline of the eye at the margin of the iris, immediately above and immediately below the pupil. The eyelid is smooth, but is thickened, and presents a prominent angle at each extremity.

The upper jaw projects beyond the lower so that the nostrils are set anterior to the vertical line of the mouth-opening. The oval nostrils are large; they open upwards and backwards. The inner finger of the male is thickened at the base, and the brown inner and upper surfaces of the first and second fingers are hard and horny.

When it is held in the hand, this toad jerks spasmodically, and vibrates the whole body, as if about to explode with wrath. The only sound, however, produced in protest is a gentle chirping note, less loud and emphatic than that of the American toad.

Most curious are these large, uncouth creatures, with their great strength of body, their protective rhinoceros-like skins, and their greatly contrasting meek appearance and gentle voice and manner. The question of their survival in contest with other races is a very interesting one.

Bufo alvarius is said to have habits similar to those of our most common toads.

BUFO VALLICEPS, WIEGM

IDENTIFICATION CHARACTERISTICS

Colour: Variable; often rich brown, with three broad bands of cream colour or yellowish grey extending from the head to the posterior end of the body. The central band is straight; the others are curved, extending from the eyes backward over the parotoids, then downward on the sides, following the lateral outlines of the body. (Figs. 112 and 114.) The eye varies between gold and bright coppery red. Light colour along the jaw and over the shoulder. (Fig. 112.) There may be a few irregularly placed black or bright orange spots on the back. Usually, a long and narrow, yellow-bordered spot transversely placed back of the eyes between the bony ridges. Legs and arms may be banded or spotted. Underparts light or dark, unspotted. (Fig. 113.) (For possible colouration, see Colour Plate V.)

Measurements: Size large i. e. length 3½ to 5 inches. Head relatively long; a toad 3½ inches long has a length of head of 1⅛ inches. Legs short; the length of the leg to the heel scarcely equalling the length of the body forward to the eye. Tibia only slightly longer than the femur. (Fig. 114.) Foot short.

Structure: Skin set closely above and below with small tubercles. (Figs. 113 and 114.) The arms and legs are conspicuously tubercular. Even the palms and soles are set close with tubercles.

(Figs. 113 and 115.) No large warts. The light-coloured tubercles behind the angle of the jaw and in a row along the lower margin of the light lateral band are somewhat longer than the others. (Fig. 114.) Head rounded, acute in front. (Fig. 113.) Jaws hard and bony. Upper jaw deeply indented in midline. An elevated bony ridge usually parallel to the upper jaw extends from in front of the eye to the angle of the jaw. Ear conspicuous because of its smoothness; half to two-thirds size of eye. (Fig. 112.) The many bony ridges of the head are much elevated, thin, and sharp-edged, except the short one extending over the ear backward to the parotoid. The head ridges are as follows: A short median one from jaw to nostrils; two starting at the upper end of this diverge backward to a point just behind the eyes, there converging slightly to points just within the anterior ends of the prominences made by the scapulars; one each side connecting at obtuse angles with the long ridges of the top of the head and lying close behind the eye; a shorter, thicker ridge between this ridge and the parotoid of each side. There are also short ridges in front of the eye and between the eye and the ear. (See Fig. 114.) The parotoids are short, and may be oval or triangular in shape. The nostrils open upward, are close together and are placed nearer to the jaw than to the eye. The shoulder-blades are two curved prominences between the parotoids. (Fig. 114.) Hand small; one large and one small palm tubercle. (Fig. 113.) Foot small; inner and outer tubercles both present, but insignificant; webs short. (Fig. 115.)

Range: Bufo valliceps Wiegm is a Mexican toad found commonly in Texas. It is reported also from Louisiana.

Bufo valliceps is unusual among North American batrachia in the appearance of its head. The head is broad and shallow, and except for the bright eyes, seems wholly made up of high bony crests separating variously shaped bony concavities.

This toad is variable in colour and has much power to change colour. It may be black with touches of rich orange and yellow-brown, so that it looks like a piece of burned wood. With such colouring, the underparts may be as dark as the upper surface. Such colouration may change within half an hour to delicate fawn-colour or dove-grey, with the light bands and spots cream white.

At such a time the underparts are white also. Among the medium shades, changes take place rapidly between greys, warm browns, and olive-greens. In each case the light colour of the lengthwise bands harmonizes with the background, so that a pleasing colour effect is produced. Young specimens may have the throat bright yellow.

The crests of the head are usually black, even when the head itself is light, but they also may become light in colour on a long enough exposure to sunshine.

Bufo valliceps is alert and active, but is less wild than most North American species. It is evidently less used to burrowing — as we should judge from its foot structure — and so does not become alarmed when finding itself in a place where there is nothing under which to hide. When annoyed, it gives high-pitched, bird-like notes. There is no appearance of a vocal pouch.

BUFO PUNCTATUS, BAIRD AND GIRARD

IDENTIFICATION CHARACTERISTICS

Colour: Greyish or reddish brown. Warts tipped with red, and sometimes encircled by black at their bases. Underparts light. Throat of male dusky. Much orange on under surfaces of hands and feet. (For possible colouration, see Colour Plate V.)

Measurements: Size medium, i.e. length 2 to 3 inches. Length of head enters total length three and a third to three and a half times. Legs short, heels widely separated behind, when toad is in sitting position. Femur largely buried in the skin of the body. Length of leg to heel equals length of body forward to ear or sometimes to eye.

Structure: Upper parts (head, eyelids, back, and legs) closely set with small tubercles. Head broad, flat, not thick through. Very flat between the eyes, and sharply angled along the canthus rostralis. No bony ridges on top of head (or slight traces of any). A short bony ridge between ear and eye. Nostrils terminal. Eyes set wide apart; eyelids broad, i.e. eye strictly vertical in position. Parotoid gland considerably elevated, but very short (not much longer than eye), rounded or somewhat triangular. Ear distinct, round, half the diameter of the eye. The head is rough, with small granulations. These granulations are promi-

PLATE XXXIX

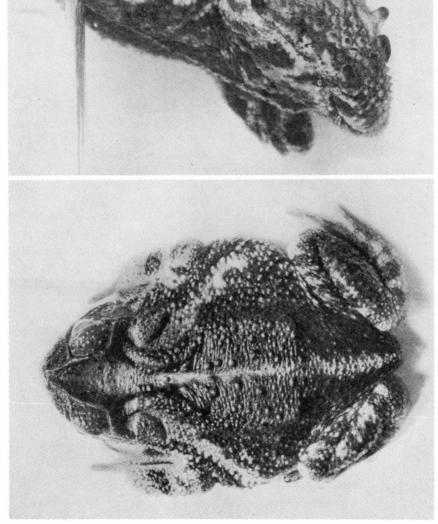

FIG. 114.—*Bufo valliceps* Wiegm. Brownsville, Texas. Structure study of upper surface.

FIG. 115.—Structure study of foot of *Bufo valliceps*. (Enlarged.) The foot is small, the web short, the sole tubercles insignificant. The toad is not greatly adapted for either swimming or burrowing.

FIGS. 116 to 120.—*Bufo punctatus* Bd. and Gird.   Dallas, Texas.   Length 2½ in.   (For coloration see Colour Plate VI.

nent on the end of the muzzle, margin of the upper jaw, canthus rostralis, eyelid, parotoid gland, and bony ridge between the eye and ear. Sole tubercles both present and both small. Tubercles under the joints of the toes scarcely discernible. Tarsus and foot covered with spine-like tubercles. Webs short, but toes narrowly margined beyond. Tarsal fold broad and rounded. (For structure, see Figs. 116 to 120.)

Range: *Bufo punctatus* is reported from Texas, Arizona, and Lower California. It is found in Texas from as far north as Fort Concho and as far south as San Antonio. Its range extends along the boundary line between the United States and Mexico to the Pacific Ocean and up the Colorado River to the Grand Cañon and beyond. In Lower California it has been reported from the extremity of the peninsula.

Bufo punctatus is one of our most easily distinguished toads. It has not the usual fat squat form of the toads, but is more slender, and is rather delicately moulded, in fact. The hands and feet are peculiarly small and delicate. The shape of the head and its granular roughness are very distinctive features. Adult specimens may be so small that they do not exceed *Hyla versicolor* in size, or *Hyla arenicolor*, their companion in the ponds in May. On the other hand, specimens from Lower California may be large (3 inches) and may differ not only in size, but also in showing a pattern of spots and stripes. The species is apparently closely related to *Bufo debilis* and *Bufo valliceps*.

Dr. Stejneger gives the following colour description of specimens collected in 1889 at the bottom of the Grand Cañon.[1] "Above 'malachite-green,' densely speckled with small dots of bright vermilion; limbs paler, dotted with vermilion and also with minute black specks, which likewise occur on the flanks; region surrounding nostrils black; upper lip and whole under surface bluish white, irregularly speckled with black; posterior part of belly and underside of thighs dark brownish flesh-colour; soles dull orange."

In captivity these toads make small burrows in moss or soft

[1] These specimens are similar to those collected in the region of the Little Colorado River by Möllhausen.

earth, and sit patiently hour after hour with just the bright eyes showing at the doors of their burrows. When taken in the hand, the male gives a faint bird-like note. Its dusky throat can extend into a large rounded vocal pouch. The habits and life history of *Bufo punctatus* are not recorded.

BUFO DEBILIS, GIRARD

IDENTIFICATION CHARACTERISTICS

Colour: Ashy brown, with small black tubercles. Eyelids and parotoids may be crossed by black lines. Legs may be broadly banded with black; these bands may have their outlines strongest, so as to give the appearance of narrow black cross-lines. Underparts and concealed surfaces light, unspotted.

Measurements: Size small, i. e. length $1\frac{1}{2}$ to 2 inches. Head short, its length contained in total length of head and body four times or more. Leg short; its total length just equals the total length of head and body.

Structure: Skin rough, with small warts and granulations. Underparts finely granular. Head wide and flat; space between the eyes greater than width of eyelid. Parotoids divergent and very large, each extending backward to a point beyond the shoulder; their upper margins are nearly straight, their lower obtusely angled. The foot has webs of medium size; the sole tubercles are insignificant.

Range: Bufo debilis is reported from the following places in Texas: Upper Wichita River, Nueces River, Lower Rio Grande, and the Brazos (Waco).

Bufo debilis is a small burrowing toad with an appearance and range remarkably like those of *Bufo punctatus*. It can always be distinguished from the latter, however, by its smaller size, **its** shorter legs, and its unusually large parotoid glands.

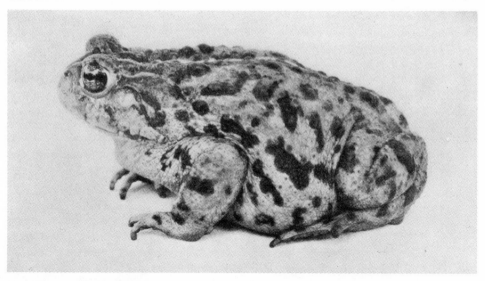

FIG. 121.—The CALIFORNIA TOAD (*Bufo halophilus* Baird. Female. Carmel, Cal.) In bright light the California Toad becomes clay colour or light olive with a pronounced spotting of black. The large warts set in the spots have brownish red centres.

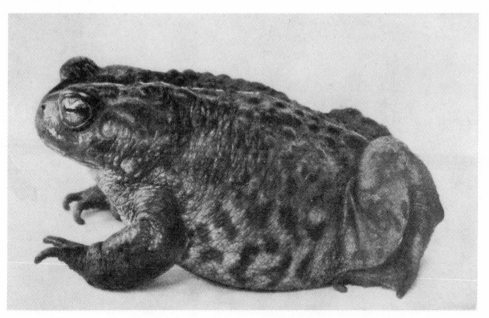

FIG. 122.—The CALIFORNIA TOAD just from its burrow, or on a dark day, is dusky with spots on the lower sides and under-surface only. Photographed to show structural characteristics of head.

FIG. 123 (1).—*Bufo halophilus* Baird. Carmel, Cal. Male (in aquarium of water) showing light, spotted underparts.

FIG. 124 (2).—Male. To show web of foot, and sole tubercles.

FIG. 125 (3).—Female. To show vertebral streak, rounded warts, extremely short legs and glandular elevations of the tibia.

FIG. 126 (4).—Male. The arm is long and muscular. The leg is relatively longer than that of the female.

THE CALIFORNIA TOAD

Bufo halophilus Baird

IDENTIFICATION CHARACTERISTICS

Colour: Dusky and unspotted above, or light and conspicuously spotted (even on hands and feet). (Figs. 121 and 122.) When light, the colour may be yellow, grey or green, in tone. Eye bright metallic yellow. There is a vertebral streak. (Fig. 125.) The larger warts are coloured like the background, have red-brown centres, and are set in the black spots. Legs spotted or barred. Toes tipped with brown. Underparts dingy white, spotted with black. (Fig. 123.) Male may be nearly black on the underparts.

Measurements: Size large, i.e. length 4 to 5 inches; female larger than male. Head relatively short, about quarter the total length. Legs short, those of the female shorter relatively than those of the male. The femur scarcely shows outside the skin of the body. Length of leg to heel equals length of body forward to the ear. Fingers do not vary greatly in length. Fifth toe slightly shorter than third.

Structure: Skin with scattered low rounded warts of medium or large size, skin smooth and shining between the warts. Warts distributed everywhere, on legs and feet, on head and eyelids. Large glandular elevations on the tibia. (Fig. 125.) Outline of jaw rounded. (Fig. 123.) Length of head in front of eye not greater than the long diameter of the eye. Descent of muzzle steep in front and under eye. Upper jaw indented in the midline. Muzzle projects slightly beyond the jaw. Nostrils on a vertical line with the jaw. No bony crests on the head. Space between the eyes greater than the width of the eyelid. Eye large. Ear round, small (one-third to one-half diameter of eye.) Arms of male very muscular. Palm with one large and one smaller tubercle; also closely set with many small tubercles. The tubercles under some of the finger-joints are prominent, i. e., first and second fingers have one each, third and fourth, two each. First, second and third fingers of male black and horny on their inner margins. Foot thick and broad; tarsal fold from heel to base of inner toe. Toes broadly webbed, webs variable in their amount of indentation. Both outer and inner sole tubercles large.

Range; Type locality, Benicia, California. Reported from San

113

Francisco, southern California, and Lower California. It has been found east of the Sierras also.

Bufo halophilus is a very large, tame-looking toad. On dark, cool days, it is so dark a dull grey or olive that the spots are wholly obliterated—only the low rounded warts show. The colour below becomes dark to correspond with that above. The parotoids and the glands on the tibia are more distinct in this dark phase of colouration than in the light. On bright warm days the toad is a very different-looking creature. It is clay-colour or light yellowish green, with a pronounced spotting of black or dark brown, and the warts are brownish-red centred.

When hunting its insect food, this toad often walks instead of hopping. We should expect this habit, because of the unwieldy size of the body and the shortness of the legs. When frightened and trying to escape an enemy, it flattens its body and creeps along stealthily and alertly. In fact, of all the strong, alert toads of North America, this is perhaps the strongest and most alert. Nothing seems to exhaust or cool its ardour, not even physical injury, if it once becomes alarmed and tries to escape. When this toad is active and excited, its skin constantly sends out a secretion, so that it looks and feels slimy. This secretion has a peculiar oily odour, not especially disagreeable.

It is much dependent on being under the protection of some cover, even in high temperatures. It makes a shallow burrow for the day and a deeper one for the winter months.

After having been deprived of water for some time, this toad shows interesting movements, aimed at getting all parts of the absorbing skin wet. He squats in shallow water, flattening the body as much as possible. He moves about slowly, keeping the body depressed, then puts the water on the top of his head by means of his hands, and wets his back with his feet. These movements are always unexpected and interesting.

The female is apparently voiceless; the male gives rapidly a series of high-pitched notes, like the harsh sounds produced by a squawking toy doll.

Bufo halophilus has a subspecies representing it at the north; namely, *Bufo halophilus columbiensis* (*Bufo microscaphus* Cope) with the Columbia River the type locality.

PLATE XLIII

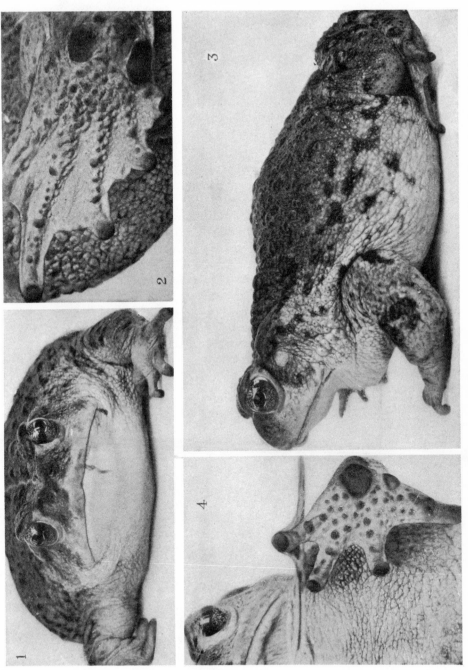

FIGS. 127 to 130 (1 to 4).—*Bufo halophilus* Bd. and Gird., from San Diego, California. Female. Photographed (2 and 4 in water) to show skin texture, outline of head, size of ear and parotoid, structure of hand and foot and other identification characteristics.

PLATE XLIV

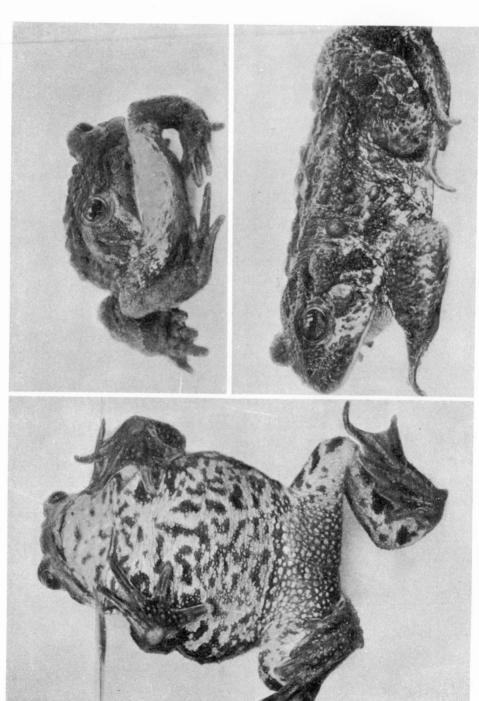

FIG. 131.—*Bufo boreas* Bd. and Gird. Friday Harbor, Puget Sound. (Enlarged.) Not full grown, actual length 2⅝ in. May attain length of 4 to 5 in. Photographed (in water) to show structure of concealed surfaces.

FIGS. 132 and 133.—*Bufo boreas* Bd. and Gird. Photographed to show various characteristics of identification.

Much study needs to be done on the California toads. One of the puzzling points concerning *Bufo halophilus* is the marked difference between living specimens from southern California (San Diego) and those from the type locality (near San Francisco). The same discrepancy is observable in the specimens of the National Museum. The Southern toads have a rougher skin, a more extended muzzle, a smaller ear as well as parotoid, a larger and more extended inner sole tubercle, and a proportion of head and body one to four and a half instead of one to four. A study of the life history and habits of this Southern toad would settle at once the question of its relation to the Northern *Bufo halophilus*. (See Figs. 127 to 130 and compare with Figs. 121 to 126.)

BUFO BOREAS, BAIRD AND GIRARD

IDENTIFICATION CHARACTERISTICS

Colour: Variable; dull or warm browns, greys or greens. There is a wide vertebral streak, also a conspicuous patch of light colour under the eye, passing obliquely to the jaw. (Fig. 133.) Touches of light or bright colour may be found in the following places: on the parotoids and warts, on the sides of the toad, at the angles of the jaw, and on the forearm and tibia. This light colour varies with the background; it may be orange (or reddish), greenish, white, or yellow. Eye bright orange-yellow. There may be a light band from parotoid backward. Underparts closely spotted, with black everywhere, even on throat and under-surfaces of arms and legs. (Fig. 131.) Tubercles of feet black. Fingers and toes tipped with black or red-brown.

Measurements: Size large, i. e. length $2\frac{1}{2}$ to 5 inches. Head short, its length contained about four times in the total length. Space between the eyes greater than width of eyelid. Head relatively long in front of eyes. Arms long; forearm conspicuously longer than the hand. (Fig. 132.) Length of leg to heel equals length of body forward to parotoid or eye. Tibia not greatly longer than femur.

Structure: Skin very warty, and tubercular between the warts. Warts relatively large, round, often set in short rows running lengthwise along the back. (Fig. 133.) Large, light-coloured warts at the angle of the jaw. No head crests. (Fig. 132.) Top of head flat, warty.; eyelids warty. Tibia with one or more larger warts or glandular elevations resembling the parotoids. Even the buttocks and posterior surfaces of the femurs are covered with large tubercles. Head rounded in front. Muzzle not projecting beyond jaw, but sloping gradually downward, both in front and under the eyes. (Fig. 133.) Upper jaw indented in the midline. Eyes set wide apart. Ear round, one-half to two-thirds the diameter of the eye: set under anterior end of parotoid and separated from the eye by a narrow bony crest. Parotoid a short oval, with a narrow neck leading to the eye. (Fig. 133.) Hand with one large and one small palm tubercle. (Fig. 131.) Each finger may have the joint nearest the palm marked with a conspicuous double tubercle. Foot thick, with a strong tarsal ridge, and with two prominent sole tubercles. Sole very thickly covered with depressed warts. Toes webbed to their tips, but webs deeply indented.

Range: Type locality Columbia River and Puget Sound. Reported from Portland, Oregon, and Friday Harbor, Washington.

This toad, the common toad of Oregon and Washington, has a representative in the southern part of the Pacific Slope, *Bufo boreas nelsoni* Stejneger. The type specimen was found in 1891 at Oasis Valley, Nevada. It is similar to *Bufo boreas*, except that the skin is smoother between the warts, the toad has a longer, more pointed muzzle, and the longer legs have a less-indented web and a smoother sole. *Bufo b. nelsoni* is found east of the Sierras, in the high altitudes of southeastern California and western Nevada.

COLOR PLATE I

THE COMMON TREE FROG [*Hyla versicolor* LeConte].
In and about the ponds in May. Jack-in-the pulpit means to him
convenient shade and a comfortable seat.

COLOR PLATE II

Fig. 1.—*Hypopachus cuneus* Cope. Brownsville, Texas. May be gray or warm shades of brown. There is much red on the concealed anterior surface of the femur.

Fig. 2.—*Engystoma carolinense* Holbrook. Raleigh, N. C.

Fig. 3.—*Lithodytes latrans* Cope. Helotes, Texas.

Fig. 4.—*Scaphiopus holbrookii* Harlan. Providence, R. I.

Fig. 5.—*Scaphiopus couchii* Baird. Brownsville, Texas. This spadefoot may be gray, green or brown.

Fig. 6.—*Rana onca* Cope. Las Vegas, Nevada. The spots are evanescent in character; they may be outlined with light or not.

Fig. 7.—*Rana boylii* Bd. and Gird. Mill Valley, Cal. This is the Yellow-legged Frog of California.

Refer to Index to locate descriptions.

COLOR PLATE III

THE AMERICAN TOAD [*Bufo americanus* Le Conte.
Providence, R. I.]

Figs. 1 and 3 represent male toads; 2 and 4, females.

Fig. 1.—So surprised by the suddenness with which they were removed from their respective places and set down before the camera, that they retain unnatural positions and subdued expressions for some minutes. The toad at the left just from its dark burrow (note small pupil); the one at the right from bright sunlight.

Fig. 2.—Delicate coloration possessed just after moulting the skin.

Fig. 3.—Coloration perhaps most often seen.

Fig. 4.—Bright color often assumed by female when active on a warm, sunny day.

COLOR PLATE IV

The upper figure shows one phase of coloration of the Southern Toad. [*Bufo lentiginosus* Shaw. Female. Mimmsville, Ga.]

The second figure represents the Rocky Mountain Toad. [*Bufo l. woodhousei* Bd. and Gird. Female. Phoenix, Arizona.]

The remaining two are male and female of Fowler's Toad. [*Bufo fowleri* Putnam. Providence, R. I.]

COLOR PLATE V

To show coloration of four toads of Southwestern North
America.

    (1) *Bufo punctatus* Bd. and Gird.   Tucson, Ariz.
    (2) *Bufo cognatus* Say.   Phoenix, Ariz.
    (3) *Bufo valliceps* Wiegm.   Brownsville, Texas.
    (4) *Bufo alvarius* Girard.   Phoenix, Ariz.

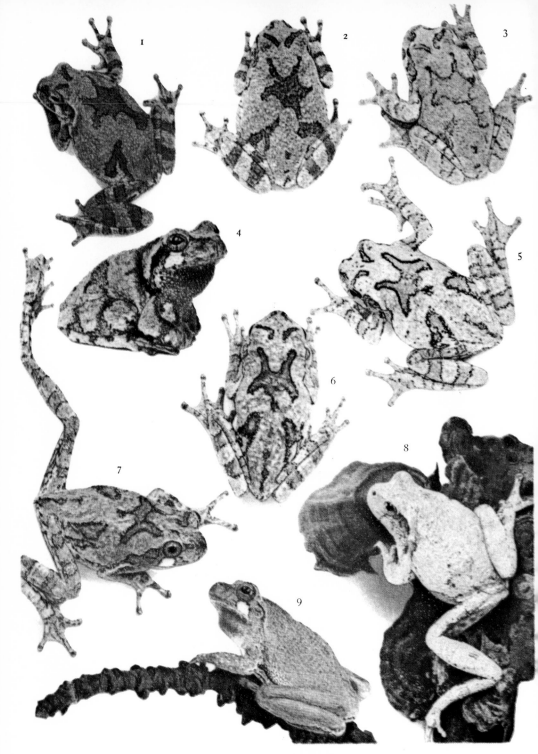

COLOR PLATE VI

THE COMMON TREE FROG. [*Hyla versicolor* LeConte.]
Any individual of this species passes through the color changes
indicated. The change from unspotted dark (not shown on plate)
to plain white or green is always through an intermediate spotted
phase. The frog of the upper three figures is from Staten Island,
N. Y.; the plain green one below from White Bear Lake, Minn.
the other figures represent a frog from Providence, R. I.

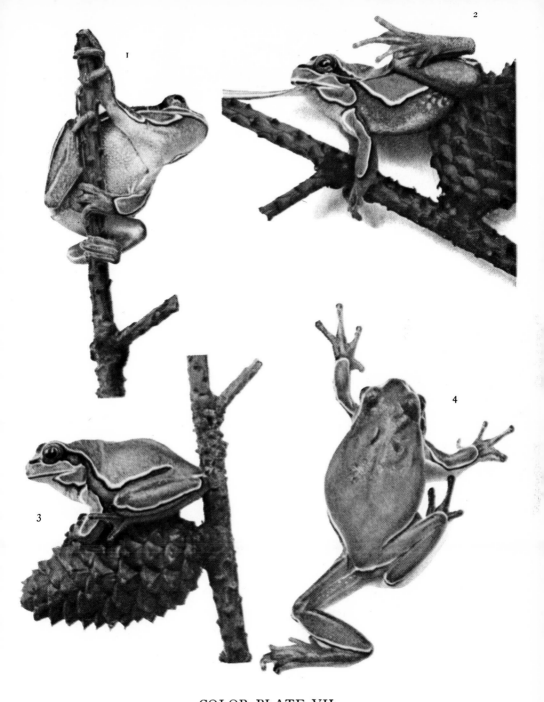

COLOR PLATE VII

Hyla Andersonii Baird. Female. Lakehurst, N. J. Photographed to show exact coloration.

    Fig. 1.—Ready to leap. Photographed to show underparts.

    Fig. 2.—In water. Photographed to show spots concealed under arm and leg; also foot structure.

    Fig. 3.—Side view on pine cone.

    Fig. 4.—To show body proportions; also coloring of hand and foot.

COLOR PLATE VIII

THE TREE FROG OF THE WESTERN COAST REGION [*Hyla regilla* Bd. and Gird. Males, except for the two in the center]. To show variation in color and pattern.

COLOR PLATE IX

Hyla Regilla Bd. and Gird. Carmel, Cal.
Figs. 1, 3 and 5 are photographs of the same male frog (all
three photographs taken within ten minutes). Figs. 2, 4
and 6 are a similar series of a female.

Hyla regilla may change rapidly from a dark unspotted to a
light unspotted condition, or the reverse order, through a
vividly spotted phase of coloration.

COLOR PLATE XI

THE LEOPARD FROG [*Rana pipiens* Shreber]. Male
(left) and female (right). Ithaca, N. Y. The Leopard Frog may be
green or brown. It has rounded dark spots outlined with light.

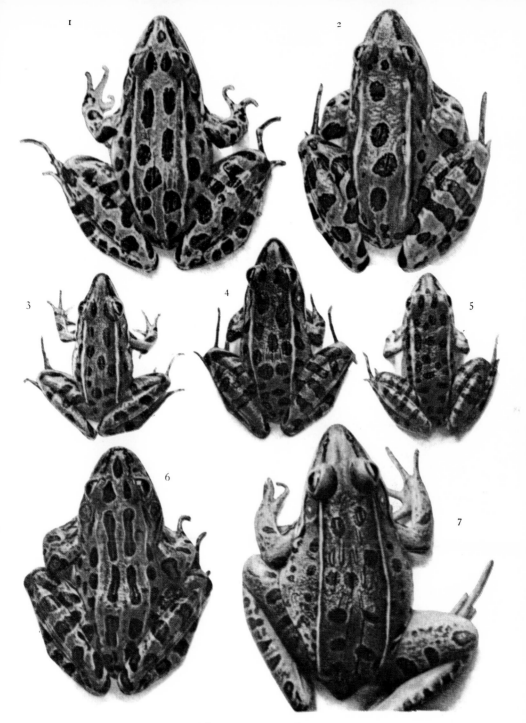

COLOR PLATE XII

To show the coloration of some spotted frogs of North America.

Figs. 1 and 2.—THE COMMON LEOPARD FROG [*Rana pipiens* Shreber, Rhode Island]. Typical pattern of coloration and great divergence from it.

Figs. 3 and 4.—THE SOUTHERN LEOPARD FROG [*Rana sphenocephala* Cope. Immature. Seven Oaks, Florida.]

Fig. 5.—Immature *Rana pipiens*. Helotes, Texas.

Fig. 6.—*Rana pipiens*. Ithaca, New York.

Fig. 7.—Female *Rana sphenocephala*. Hitchcock, Texas.

Refer to Index to locate descriptions.

COLOR PLATE XIII

Fig. 1.—GREEN FROGS. Male and Female. [*Rana clamitans* Latreille. Rhode Island.] The male can be distinguished by the larger ear and the yellow throat.

Fig. 2.—THE PICKEREL FROG. Female. [*Rana palustris* Le Conte. Rhode Island.] Distinguished from the Leopard Frog by the squarish shape of the spots. Compare with color plates 11 and 12.

Fig. 3.—THE STRIPED FROG. Male. [*Rana virgatipes* Cope. Lakehurst, N. J.] The underparts are spotted and striped with irridescent yellow. The upper parts are rich brown with four stripes of brighter color running lengthwise along the body.

Refer to Index to locate descriptions.

COLOR PLATE XIV

To show change of color in three North American frogs.

(1) THE EASTERN WOOD FROG [*Rana sylvatica* Le Conte. Providence, R. I.] Any individual frog may be brown of so dark a shade that it is nearly black or so light that it is flesh color; the intermediate phases of coloration may be red, yellow or ashy in tone.

(2) *Rana aurora* Bd. and Gird. Seattle, Washington. The different sizes represent frogs one year old, two years old, and three or more years old.

(3) THE GOPHER FROG [*Rana æsopus* Cope. Orlando, Florida.] The spots are always dark brown or black. The background may change from creamy white to dark brown (gray, yellow or purple in tone).

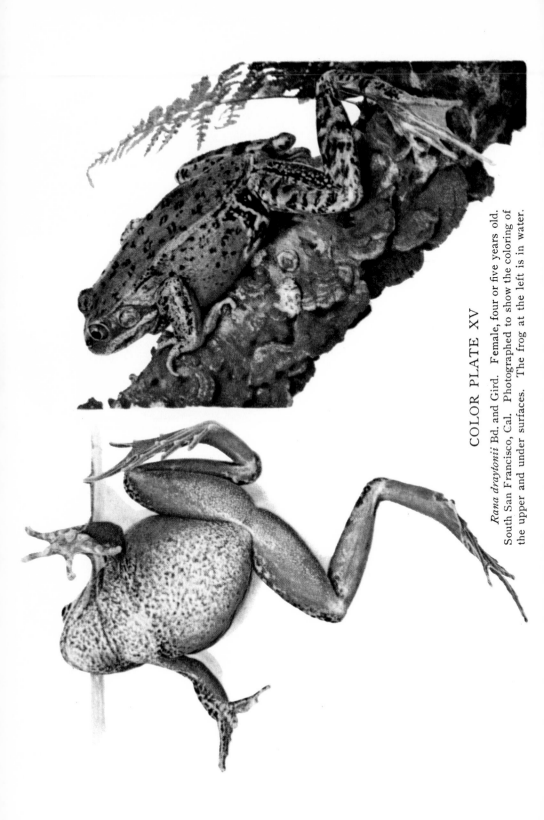

COLOR PLATE XV

Rana draytonii Bd. and Gird. Female, four or five years old. South San Francisco, Cal. Photographed to show the coloring of the upper and under surfaces. The frog at the left is in water.

COLOR PLATE XVI

THE WESTERN FROG [*Rana pretiosa* Bd. and Gird. Female. Seattle, Washington.] Photographed (in water) to show the coloring of the upper and under surfaces.

COLOR PLATE X (*facing*)

To show possible coloration of some N. A. Hylas. In all cases not only is there great power of change, but any pattern of spots or bands on the top of the head and on the back is evanescent in character.

Fig. 1.—THE SPRING PEEPER [*Hyla pickeringii* Storer. Providence, R. I.] Varies through many shades of ashy or yellow brown.

Figs. 2 and 3.—THE GREEN TREE FROG [*Hyla cinerea* Daudin. Ft. Myers, Florida]. May be green or brown, but is always known by the light bands.

Fig. 4.—THE SOUTHERN TREE FROG [*Hyla squirella* Bosc. Hitchcock, Texas].

Figs. 5 and 6.—THE SOUTHERN TREE FROG. Havelock, N. C. These tree frogs vary through all shades of green, gray and brown, and may be spotted or not.

Fig. 7.—THE FLORIDA TREE FROG [*Hyla gratiosa* LeConte. Orlando, Fla.]. May be green or brown, spotted or not. It is often found with the change from green to brown in process, in which case the frog is green conspicuously spotted, but with brown gradually replacing the green on the back.

Fig. 8.—THE ARIZONA TREE FROG [*Hyla arenicolor* Cope. Tucson, Arizona]. Can change from flesh color through many shades of gray and brown, and may be spotted or not.

Refer to Index to locate descriptions.

FAMILY IV. HYLIDÆ: THE TREE FROGS [1]

THE COMMON TREE FROG

Hyla versicolor Le Conte

IDENTIFICATION CHARACTERISTICS

Colour: Varying through many shades of green, brown, or grey. An oblique dark band on the top of the head, above each eye; a large dusky patch on the upper back, often star-shaped. The arms and legs are transversely barred. All of the dark markings may be indistinct or lacking. (See Plate XX, also Frontispiece.) A light spot below the posterior half of eye. Underparts light, bright orange-yellow posteriorly. Concealed leg surfaces vermiculated with brown.

Measurements: Length 2 inches. Head short and broad; body stout. Ear two-thirds size of eye. The leg to the heel measures the length of the body forward to the eye.

Structure: Skin covered with relatively coarse tubercles. Undersurfaces granulated, less conspicuously on the throat. Prominent fold of skin across breast. The disks on fingers and toes are large. Web of hind foot well-developed. Fingers slightly webbed. (See Figs. 134 to 142.)

Range: Throughout eastern North America west to Kansas, northward into Canada, and southward into Texas.

Probably more familiar than any other member of the batrachian group, if we except the common toad, is this entertaining little acrobat of the frog world. (Figs. 134 to 137.) Some June morning when we are admiring the blue flowers of the clematis that climbs the porch, we see what looks like a yellowish white oval of putty plastered against the white pillar shaded by the vine. It is our Common Tree Frog (or Tree Toad, as it is called) sound asleep.

Late some July afternoon we sit reading by the porch window. Something seems to fly from the vines to the window. With

[1] Refer to pp. 7, 9 and 46.

sprawling legs, our tree frog climbs the smooth glass, to snuggle in the corner of a window-pane, his toes tucked well under him and pressed closely against the glass. The moist under surface of his body seems also to do its share of the work of holding him securely in this upright position. Now he awakes and wildly dashes for a fly, but only bangs his nose, because the fly is on the other side of the glass. If we catch the fly and carry it out to him, he takes it from our fingers into his cavernous pink mouth.

In August, we look for ripening grapes on the vine that covers the low stone smoke-house. On the mossy ledge of the roof, in the shade of a leaf, is a clump of grey lichen that comes to life when touched. Again it is our tree frog. He takes a flying leap, catches a slender stem by one sticky front foot and hangs swinging in air with outstretched legs. We are certain he will fall. Instead, he deliberately draws himself up to the swaying support and from it makes a second spring to a place of concealment.

We stand at the old-fashioned gate, and on the top of one of the white-painted posts there is something that looks like a flattened mass of smooth green wax. Even on looking closely, it is hard to distinguish the folds of the legs, so successfully are the adjoining skin surfaces blended. It is our sleepy tree frog, who may be slow to awake until we take him into our hands. Even then he clings confidingly to our finger, perfectly willing to remain on so comfortable a perch. In fact, it is not easy to get rid of his cool sticky toes. If we reverse the position of our finger so that his head is down, he turns clumsily until his head is uppermost again. His bright eyes, his confiding way, all his diminutive self, make a genuine appeal to our liking.

In September, when we climb the apple tree to get more perfect apples than those which have fallen to the ground, we put our hand on a lichen-covered branch only to find it soft and alive under our touch. We go hazel-nutting along the country road, and the first cluster of nuts that we pull from under its umbrella of leaves has a green tree frog on it.

And so we know this tree frog well. We learn to expect him in the orchard and about the house in early summer and to miss him again early in September, when he disappears for his long winter's sleep in some cozy hollow among tree roots or in a tree trunk.

We know his voice also, though perhaps we have never actu-

The COMMON TREE FROG (*Hyla versicolor*) makes his home in the trees along forest paths as well as in those about the house and in the orchard.

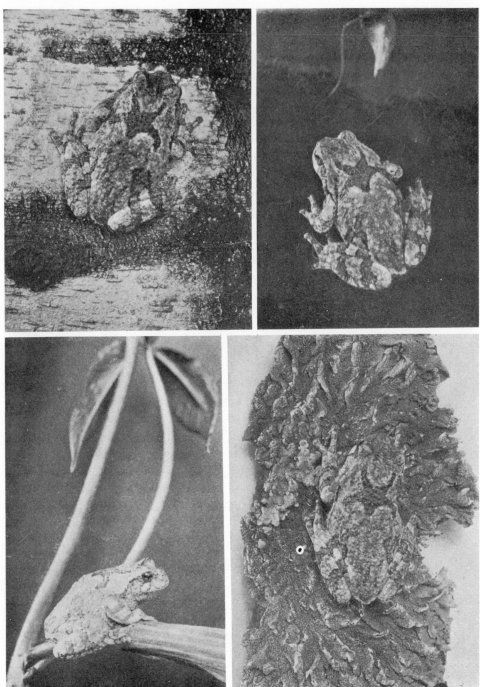

FIGS. 134 to 137.—The COMMON TREE FROG (*Hyla versicolor* Le Conte). Rhode Island. The conspicuous markings are the two bars on each leg and the irregular star on the upper part of the back. This Hyla is well concealed when resting on the gray birch or on a lichen-covered tree or stone.

ally watched him sing.   At dusk or on rainy days a loud resonant trill comes from the trees and vines.   The sound has the charm of contentment in it; in fact it is much like the purring of a cat, only louder.   At a distance it sounds something like the bleating of a lamb.   The pitch is uniform, but may vary with the individual, from G above middle C to E above.   It continues for two or three seconds at a time, then ends abruptly.   It may be given several times in rather close succession.   If we see the tree frog trilling, we are surprised that the whole body is so greatly agitated and that the throat extends into so large a sac.   The size of the sac decreases between each two trills and at the end collapses, leaving a very wrinkled throat.

The fact that the tree frog calls during damp weather, and therefore often before storms, has made him accepted as a weather prophet; however, he can scarcely be called a reliable one.

The Common Tree Frog measures about two inches in length. The head is broad and blunt, the body is fat and squat.   The skin is granular and has the appearance of being much too large for the frog.   The tree frog is like the frogs in having teeth on the upper jaw.   The eye is large; the ear is inconspicuous.   The fingers and toes have their ends extended into broad disks that secrete a sticky substance on their lower surfaces.   The toes are webbed as far as the disks; the fingers are webbed nearly one-third of their length.   The male and female are more nearly alike than is usual among tree frogs.   They may not differ in size or color, except that the throat of the male is dark.   They can be distinguished from one another by the ears, which are always smaller in the female than in the male.

The colour varies greatly at different times and in different conditions.   (See Colour Plate VI)   In bright light and high temperature it may be yellowish white with no markings.   In a dark, moist or cool place, it may be a deep stone-grey or brown.   Most often, perhaps, it is bright grey with dark markings.   The most conspicuous of the markings are the two bands on each leg and each arm, and the irregular star on the upper part of the back. There is usually a conspicuous lighter spot just below the posterior half of the eye.   This tree frog can always be distinguished from tree frogs resembling it by the vermiculations of brown and yellow on the concealed leg surfaces.   (See Colour Plate VI.)

However, we have not exhausted this tree frog's possible

change of dress when we have considered all gradations between white and stone-grey or brown. There is almost as wide a range between white and green. When the background of colour is green, his characteristic markings may or may not appear. Also, there may be various combinations of the green and the grey. One of the most attractive of his suits is bright grey, with dark grey markings broadly bordered with bright green.

The underparts are light. There is much orange-yellow on the body and legs where they fold against one another. This colour is very conspicuous when the tree frog leaps.

The changes in colour are not rapid, an hour at least seeming necessary to create any radical difference. But it is usually true that the given dress — whatever it may be — harmonizes so perfectly with the surroundings — whatever they may be — that the tree frog is as invisible as though he were Perseus in his charmed helmet. Whether his resting-place be a green leaf or a plant stem, the bark of a grey birch or a lichen-covered oak, (Figs. 134 to 137), his dress and his ability to keep perfectly still for hours at a time form an excellent protection. Chance may bring him to our hands many times in a summer, but he is very difficult to find if we make definite search.

In the different parts of its range, this *Hyla* shows considerable variation. The variation displays itself mainly in the changed

In May when apple trees are in bloom the Common Tree Frog is at the ponds.

shapes of the dark markings of head and back and in the varying amount of dark mottling on the undersides of the legs. Cope describes a brown spotted form from Mount Carmel, Illinois, giving it the rank of a variety (*Hyla versicolor phæocrypta* Cope).

In May, when apple trees are loaded with flowers and give out their delicate fragrance, and the low hum of honey-bees, we may know that our tree frogs have put aside their sleepy tendencies for the time and are joyously paddling about in the water of some pond. The painted-cup and golden ragwort are giving colour to the marsh nearby. Probably the jack-in-the-pulpit means only convenient shade and a comfortable seat to the frogs. (Frontispiece.) Very likely they do not even

notice at dusk the near voices
of the redwings or the more
remote one of the wood-thrush.
However this may be, it is certain
that they do hear the voices of
their companion tree frogs, and
that they feel the warmth of the
spring air and of the shallow
sun-warmed water.

The eggs are attached in
small groups, and also singly,
to grasses or plant stems at the
surface of the water. They are
not easily found unless the grasses
are separated and examined
minutely. The eggs are very
light in colour, grey above, white
below. They hatch on the second or third day, at a very early
stage in the development. The
tadpoles are then about one-

When Jack-in-the-pulpit appears
we may expect to hear the trilling of
Hyla versicolor from pond and
river margins.

fourth inch long and of a light yellow colour. After the hatching,
the development proceeds very rapidly, so that in three weeks
from the date of egg-laying, the tadpoles[1] not only are fully formed,
but have the hind legs budded. They have much gold-colour in
the skin, and the widely separated eyes are flame-colour. The
whole surface of the tadpole shows a brilliant metallic sheen, and
sometimes the tail is almost red in colour. The brightly coloured
creatures are very timid indeed, and move with the rapidity of
young fishes. This rapid movement saves them many a time
from the clutches of a great diving-beetle or some other enemy.
In early July, near the end of the seventh week after the eggs are
laid, the tadpoles complete the metamorphosis and leave the
water. It seems that the green dress is the one in which the
young frogs begin their life on land, but they may very soon change
to grey or some combination of the two colours. When they are
green in colour, they can be recognized by the white spot under the

---

[1] The mouth structure of the tadpole of *Hyla versicolor* is as follows: The upper lip bears one
row of teeth, the lower has three. The upper lip curves downward at each side of the beak. The
border of the lower lip is not doubled in at the corners of the mouth.

eye. The yellow colouring of the body and legs does not appear until after they have left the water.[1] The young frogs are over one-half inch long when they leave the water, and by October are one inch in length. They are known to feed upon spiders, flies, and plant-lice.

Hyla versicolor has a relatively keen sense of locality, sometimes remaining in one place for weeks or more at a time. It is said that these tree frogs may stay in one tree for weeks and months. In such a situation they would certainly find themselves surrounded by supplies for their every demand — food, shelter, and moisture. A tree frog is so small that a tree with its many branches and leaves is like a palace for him. There are sunny rooms which flies and beetles visit. There are darker ones where ants and plant-lice, beetles and tree crickets are to be found. There are rooms on the north side of the tree, where the large branches join the trunk. These are cool and moist on the hottest summer day.

The Common Tree Frog is most active at dusk and in the night. It is then that he wanders over his great palace. His bright eyes see every moving caterpillar and beetle, and his sticky tongue snaps them up greedily. He sees moving objects at two or more feet distance, and makes aerial leaps to get them. He is almost sure to catch the insect, and what becomes of himself does not trouble him, since he is certain to touch some leaf or twig with at least one of his four sets of sticky toes. A bit of frantic acrobatwork does the rest, and places him securely on some perch where he can enjoy his meal at leisure.

HYLA ARENICOLOR, COPE

IDENTIFICATION CHARACTERISTICS

Colour: Sand-colour, light or dark grey, or olive. Three or four irregular rows of rounded dark spots on the back, or fewer large blotches. For colouration, see Colour Plate X. A curved band of dark colour between the eyes; this band may be broken in the midline, as it is in *Hyla versicolor.* Two or three bands of dark colour on the leg. (Fig. 144.) Eyes metallic yellow, or grey. Ear

---

[1] The most of the facts regarding the development are from M. H. Hinckley's account. Proc. Bos. Soc. Nat. Hist., XXI, 1883, p. 104.

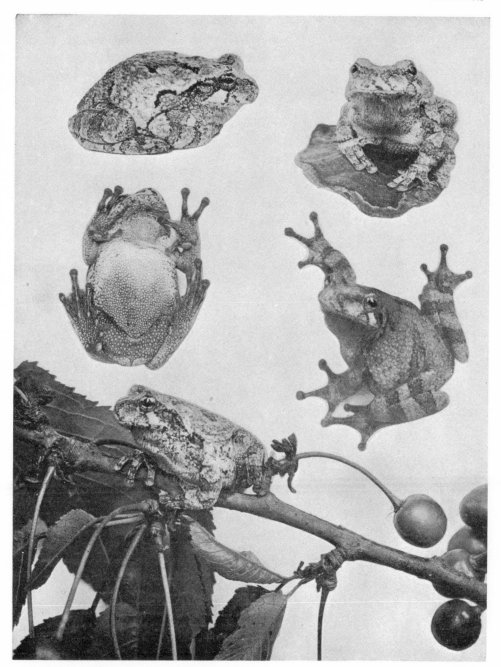

FIGS. 138 to 142.—Studies of the COMMON TREE FROG (*Hyla versicolor* Le Conte). Male. Staten Island, N. Y.

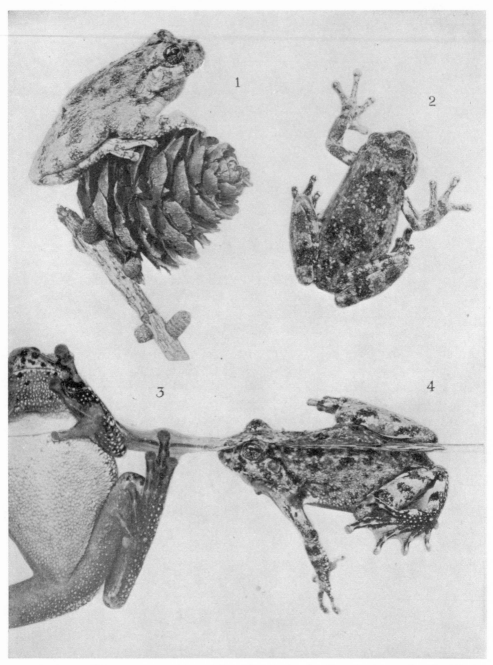

FIG. 143 (1).—*Hyla arenicolor* Cope. Tucson, Arizona. Length 1½ to 2 in. (For coloration see colour Plate X.) A gentle tree frog of slow tendencies. Photographed to show outline of head, size of ear, and texture of skin.

FIG. 144 (2).—The dark colour may be in large blotches on the back (compare with Colour Plate X).

FIG. 145 (3).—Enlarged to show rough character of skin of the underparts (even the throat) and of the undersurfaces of hands and feet.

FIG. 146 (4).—To show web and sole tubercles.

bronze. Many minute yellow spots on and between the large dark spots. (Fig. 144.) A white spot under the eye. Orange-yellow at the arm insertion, and on those parts of the femur and tibia that fold against each other. This orange is not spotted or marbled with dark. Underparts light. (Fig. 145.)

Measurements: Length 1½ inches to 2 inches. Head short. Leg to heel measure as long as that of the body forward to the anterior border of the eye. Tibia longer than femur.

Structure: Skin rough, with small tubercles. (Fig. 143.) Head broad, flat, rounded in front. (Fig. 144.) Throat and underparts granular. (Fig. 145.) Nostrils terminal. Eyes small. Ear two-thirds the diameter of the eye. (Fig. 143.) A fold across the breast and another at the base of the throat. Disk on fingers and toes well developed. No webs between fingers. Web of foot medium in size; two joints of fourth toe free. Inner and outer tubercles present, small (Fig. 146): a prominent tarsal fold.

Range: *Hyla arenicolor* is a Mexican form, found also across the border in the United States. It is reported from southern California, New Mexico, Utah, and Arizona.[1]

Hyla arenicolor resembles the Common Tree Frog (*Hyla versicolor*) in general appearance and colouring, but is less attractive. The frog is more clumsy, the outlines less delicate, the eyes are smaller, and the colouring is duller. It is somewhat more active than *Hyla versicolor* and leaps greater distances, as we should expect from the greater length of its legs.

Its call consists of a series of short notes resembling the bleating of a goat. The throat-sac of the male, inflated during the calling, is dark coloured and large. The throat of the female is white, with spots of dark. Both male and female give a sharp high-pitched cry when taken in the hand.

The colour is rapidly changeable from grey or brown so dark that it is nearly black, through distinctly spotted phases, to a pinkish or greyish unspotted white.

---

[1] Tucson, White River Cañon, Arizona; Santa Fé, Fort Wingate, New Mexico; Upper Colorado River.

THE FLORIDA TREE FROG

Hyla gratiosa Le Conte

IDENTIFICATION CHARACTERISTICS

Colour: Green or brown of various shades, usually with all upper surfaces distinctly spotted. Sometimes unspotted bright yellow-green. Spots many, more or less rounded, either large or small. Spots may be brown or green of even shade, or light green or brown encircled with darker colour. Legs and arms irregularly banded with dark. Pin spots of bright yellow irregularly placed on the larger spots or between them. Ear brown. Eye bright reddish bronze. Jaw dark, bordered above by white or yellow. (Fig. 147.) This light colour may be continued to the shoulder and sometimes beyond. White or yellow bordered by purplish brown on posterior margin of arm and hand and along posterior edge of foot. Sides may be reticulated with bright yellow. Throat may be purplish brown (female) or bright yellow or green (male). Underparts light, yellowish. (Fig. 147.) For colouration, see Colour Plate X.

Measurements: Large for a tree frog, i.e. Length 2 to $2\frac{1}{2}$ inches. Head short; $\frac{5}{8}$ inch in a frog $2\frac{1}{4}$ inches long. Width between eyes greater than width of eyelid. Ear one-half to two-thirds the diameter of the eye. (Fig. 150.) Legs relatively short; leg to heel equals length of body forward to eye. Tibia shorter than femur. (Fig. 149.)

Structure: Skin thick and leathery, granulated over the whole upper surface as well as on the lower. (Figs. 148 and 149.) Head unusually thick through (Fig. 153), very short and obtuse anterior to the eyes. A fold of skin over the ear from eye to shoulder (Fig. 150); another fold across the breast and one at the base of the throat. (Fig. 147.) Ear round. Hand large; disks on fingers unusually large. Outer fingers slightly webbed. Foot webbed half length of fourth toe. Inner sole tubercle prominent. (Fig. 147.) There is a tarsal fold.

Range: Reported from Georgia, Florida, and Mississippi only.[1]

Unfortunately, this tree frog has an unusually limited range.

[1] Riceborough, Ga.; Bay St. Louis, Miss.; Green Cove Springs, Tarpon Springs, Micanopy, St. Augustine, Orlando, and Georgiana, Fla.

FIG. 147 (1).—The FLORIDA TREE FROG (*Hyla gratiosa* Le Conte). Orlando, Florida. Length 2¼ in. Structure study of underparts. (In water.)

FIG. 148, 149 and 150 (2, 3 and 4).—Structure studies of the upper surface. The upper parts are granulated, as are the underparts. (For coloration see colour Plate X.)

FIGS. 151 to 153.—The FLORIDA TREE FROG (*Hyla gratiosa*). With throat pouch partially extended (Orlando, Florida), and sound asleep (Green Cove Springs, Florida).

It has very rarely been found outside of Florida. It is the largest tree frog of North America, and probably very valuable in the work of destroying noxious insects.

Hyla gratiosa presents a peculiar appearance because of the even granulation of the upper parts. In this characteristic of the skin it differs from all other North American *Hylas.* All others present a surface either smooth and fine in texture, as in the case of the Green Tree Frog (*Hyla cinerea,* Figs. 154 to 160), or one rough with fine warts, as in the Common Tree Frog (*Hyla versicolor,* Figs. 134 to 137).

The Florida Tree Frog has colour changes as marvellous as those possessed by most of the *Hylas.* It may be plain bright green and remain so for months, in fact, one in this phase of colouration was kept for over two years and during this time there was no tendency to become spotted or to turn brown. Also, the brown-spotted phase may likewise endure for months without change. On the other hand, the changes may be very rapid indeed. The tendency for rapid colour change, here as elsewhere among the Hylidæ, seems to be at its height when the animals are well-fed, and in the season of greatest activity, that is, in the spring and summer months. At this time the greatest variation in colour may be seen in an individual during the twenty-four hours. It may be bright green with vivid spots, dark at their edges and light in their centres. Gradually (within the space of ten minutes) the spots become more and more obscure until the frog is plain green, very light in tone. Again, within the half-hour the spots reappear, become more distinct, darkening in their centres. The ground colour becomes ashy in the middle of the back; this colour darkens into a mulberry, which colour spreads, obscuring the green. Meanwhile the spots continue to darken until the whole frog is rich brown prominently marked with darker brown spots.

The throat-pouch of the male is very large and is bright yellow or vivid green in colour. When the tree frog is taken suddenly into the hand, this sac is likely to be inflated and the frog gives a harsh-sounding squawk. The voice is unusually harsh and low-pitched.

This *Hyla* is a curiously artificial-looking frog. If it did not move, we might well think some one's fancy had moulded it out of wax. When it is angry or startled, it fills the lungs, expanding the body until it is nearly as broad as long. It has the slow tendencies of some of the other large tree frogs. It shows a marked desire to cling to one's finger and will not leave, even when the finger is constantly turned so that the tree frog is head down. It will each time clumsily turn around to bring its head uppermost, tuck its toes well under, and settle for a period of contentment and rest.

THE GREEN TREE FROG

Hyla cinerea Daudin

IDENTIFICATION CHARACTERISTICS

Colour: Dark brownish green, bright pea-green, or light greenish yellow. A band of white or metallic yellow extends from the most anterior point of the jaw, widens backward along the jaw, continues under the ear and along the sides, sometimes to the thigh, sometimes only half the length of the body. A dark band from the posterior border of the eye and through the ear extends as a border above this light band of the sides. Jaw dark below the light band. A similar light-coloured metallic band extends along the posterior margin of the tibia and is bordered by dusky colour below. Narrower light bands also on anterior margin of tibia, and on posterior margin of tarsus and of the arm. Ear bronze. Eye golden or bronze. Underparts light, unspotted. Green on sides of throat. Throat pale yellow. (See Colour Plate X, also Figs. 154 to 160.)

Measurements: One of our largest tree frogs, i. e. length $1\frac{3}{4}$ to $2\frac{1}{2}$ inches. Head $\frac{1}{2}$ inch long in specimen of $1\frac{3}{4}$ inches length. Legs very long; length of leg to heel equals length of body forward to the end of the muzzle. Tibia much longer than femur. The whole leg is one and a half times length of head and body.

Structure: Skin of upper parts fine and smooth in texture. Underparts granulated. Head very pointed; flat and broad between the eyes. Eyes large; not greatly elevated, but extending far at right and left; pupil elongated. Ear situated half its diameter from the eye, round, small (about half the diameter of the eye). A fold of skin over the ear to the shoulder. Legs extremely slender. Webs very short. Disks on fingers and toes well developed. Inner sole tubercle small.

Range: Hyla cinerea is found in the southern United States

FIGS. 154 to 160.—The GREEN TREE FROG (*Hyla cinerea* Daudin). From Ft. Myers, Florida, except the lower right hand frog, which is from Hitchcock, Texas. (For coloration see Colour Plate X.) This tree frog is alternately dignified and ludicrous in appearance. It is green, with bands of white or gold. There may be a few orange spots on the back.

FIGS. 161 to 164.—*Hyla evittata* Miller. Washington, D. C. Length 1⅞ in. A smooth-skinned, plain green tree frog closely related to *Hyla cinerea*. (Compare with Figures 154 to 160) to see difference in color pattern and outline of head.) Photographs made from two *Hylas* that had been in captivity more than a year. (Courtesy of Dr. Paul Bartsch, Smithsonian Institute.)

both east and west of the Mississippi. It is reported from North Carolina, South Carolina, Georgia, Florida, Louisiana, Mississippi, Missouri, and Texas. It is also found in southern Illinois.

———————

The Green Tree Frog is perhaps the most beautiful tree frog of North America. Its slender form and smooth fine coat of green and gold certainly give it an air of distinction. It is more slender than any other North American tree frog. The slenderness is accentuated also by the lengthwise stripes of metallic white or yellow.

As to colouration, this tree frog has great ability to change from light to dark. The colour may be nearly black, or it may be so light a greenish yellow that the stripes can scarcely be distinguished. There is some variation in colour pattern; that is, the light bands on the legs may be narrowed or obsolete, the light band of the side may extend no farther than half-way instead of quite to the posterior end of the body, and the dark bands bordering the light ones may be distinct or wholly lacking. One tree frog[1] found at Bay St. Louis, Mississippi, wholly lacked the stripes of the sides. This *Hyla* sometimes has a few small orange, black-rimmed spots on the back.

The legs are so long that, except when it is leaping or resting, the frog seems very awkward. In fact, it very often loses its dignified air and becomes extremely ludicrous in appearance. It is gentle and not easily frightened. In this it is like *Hyla versicolor* and *Hyla gratiosa* and radically different from some of the smaller North American *Hylas*, such as *squirella, pickeringii*, and *regilla*. When aroused, however, it becomes as active as any tree frog.

The Green Tree Frog is most interesting when kept in captivity. It lives high among the ferns and vines of its moss-garden, and is especially fond of flies. It will see a fly at a distance of three or four feet, and will catch it, making but one leap over the intervening distance. It is said that this tree frog can leap a distance of eight to ten feet. When the call is given, the throat-pouch is inflated and the body over the lungs swells and relaxes forcibly.

These tree frogs live at the margins of bodies of water, on the

———————

[1] In possession of G. S. Miller, U. S. Nat. Museum.

broad-leaved aquatic plants. They are abundant in southern gardens also.[1] They are commonly seen resting on wellhouse or fence, or on the leaves of the okra or other plants of the garden.

In southern Illinois, *Hyla cinerea* is said to be found likewise on lily-pads and other aquatic vegetation at the edges of lakes, as well as in gardens and corn-fields.[2] The chorus as heard in Illinois is described as follows: " Its note resembles the tone of a cow-bell heard at a distance. Where abundant about water, the frogs are very noisy just before dusk, the chorus being broken, however, by longer or shorter intervals of silence. A single note is first heard, and, as if that were a signal, it is taken up and repeated by a dozen noisy throats till the air is resonant with sound. After a time it ceases as suddenly as it began, to be again resumed after a period of quiet.''

HYLA EVITTATA, MILLER

IDENTIFICATION CHARACTERISTICS

Colour: Olive-brown, or green of yellow or blue tone. There is no conspicuous pattern of stripes or spots; there may be few or many inconspicuous, orange-yellow flecks of colour on the back. The vivid colour of the back extends on the sides of the throat under the jaw. The dark colour of the upper parts meets the white of the underparts abruptly instead of blending into it. Ear may be brown, with green centre. The large eyes show golden or bronze reticulations. The nostrils, which are not pigmented, appear red. Underparts white, sometimes yellowish on breast, throat, and sides.

Measurements: Length $1\frac{1}{2}$ to 2 inches. Head $\frac{1}{2}$ inch (in frog $1\frac{3}{4}$ inches) long. Length of leg to heel equals or exceeds length of frog forward to the eye. Tibia but slightly longer than femur.

Structure: Skin unusually smooth. Underparts granulated, except throat region. Outline of head rounded, less pointed than in *Hyla cinerea* Daudin. Muzzle projecting slightly beyond jaw. Head relatively thick through, compared with *Hyla cinerea*. Distance between the eyes greater than width of eyelid. Nostrils nearer to the end of the muzzle than to the eyes; they are farther from each other and somewhat nearer the eyes than in *Hyla*

[1] Bay St. Louis, Miss. C. S. Brimley.
[2] H. Garman Bulletin Illinois State Lab. Nat. Hist., 1892.

cinerea. Ear medium in size, a distinct fold of skin over it from eye to shoulder. A fold across the breast. Proportions and characteristics of extremities like those of *Hyla cinerea.* (See Figs. 154 to 160, and p. 126. Compare Figs. 161 to 164 with Figs. 154 to 160.)

Range: Hyla evittata has been reported only from the region about Washington, D. C., but is likely to be found also from Long Island Sound to Chesapeake Bay in regions near the coast.

The type specimens of *Hyla evittata* Miller were found in 1898 at Four Mile Run, Virginia. Before that date, the species, when found, had been supposed identical with the well-known *Hyla cinerea.* The resemblance of the two tree frogs is remarkable. The distinction can always be made without difficulty, however, since *Hyla evittata* lacks the outlining bands of white and has a thicker and less pointed head. Moreover, the skin of *Hyla evittata* is smoother than that of *Hyla cinerea* and has the appearance of being even smoother than it is, because this tree frog always has a shining, wet-looking surface. This characteristic of the skin makes the frog look as though it were moulded from smooth green wax. Again *Hyla evittata* has a marked tendency to display blue-green shades in its dress, while *Hyla cinerea* tends decidedly toward the yellow-greens.

It is unusual to see any creature displaying everywhere so even a colour. The colour may be a little deeper or a little more blue along the middle of the back, on the head, and on the tibia, but otherwise there is likely to be no variation. The flecks of orange set in the vivid green make a brilliant display under a lens, but they are too small to make any impression on the naked eye. There are no colour lines for the canthus rostralis, none for the line of the jaw or for the fold over the ear; in fact, every feature so familiar in the colour patterns of other frogs is lacking here. No other tree frog in North America shows so conspicuously the dividing line between the vividly coloured parts exposed to light and the white or colourless parts concealed in resting position. There are not only the abrupt dividing lines on the sides and along the margins of each joint of arms and legs, but on the throat and hands and feet, also, the lines are conspicuous. The white extends

V-shaped in the midline of the throat to the chin; it is against this white that the hands are snugly folded. The inner margin of the tarsus and the inner toes, the inner finger and a part of the second are white; even the webs that fold between the toes lack the green. It is interesting to watch *Hyla evittata* take the resting position, hugging the arms and legs close to the sides, tucking the hands and feet well under, and resting the head on the hands until no trace of light colour is visible.

This tree frog is an alert and active one. It shows an interesting protective instinct, reminding one of the meadow grasshopper (*Orchelimum*). When it is on a branch, if an enemy approaches, it swings round to the back of the branch. Here it will continue for some time to remain invisible by moving around the limb, to the right when the enemy moves to the left, to the left when the movement of the enemy is to the right, and so on. When it is finally grasped, it may open the mouth and give a high-pitched cry.

The power for colour change is pronounced, as it is in all members of the Hylidæ. In bright light, as when hunting for insects among the pond-lilies and pickerel-weed of its haunt, it is brilliant yellow-green. On darker days and in captivity it tends to a dress of myrtle-green. It is like *Hyla cinerea*, in that in hibernation it may take on its lightest shades.

"Very little is known about the habits of *Hyla evittata*. In June and July the animals are to be found in the rank vegetation of the tide marshes. Here they remain quiet during the day, but as evening approaches they become active and noisy. Their food at the time consists chiefly of a small beetle that is found on the leaves of the pond-lilies. The note is like that of *Hyla pickeringii* in form, but in quality it is comparatively harsh and reedy, with a suggestion of distant guinea-fowl chatter, and scarcely a trace of the peculiar freshness so characteristic of the song of the smaller species. The song period continues through June and July. Later in the season the frogs leave the low marsh vegetation. As they are then perfectly silent, they are difficult to find, though occasionally one may be seen in a bush or small tree, but never far from water.

It is thought that the eggs are laid during June and July. They are small, loose masses, attached to the stems of pond-lily leaves.

ANDERSON'S HYLA

Hyla andersonii Baird

IDENTIFICATION CHARACTERISTICS

Colour: Unspotted pea-green over all upper parts, except hands and feet. The green is edged with white everywhere, except on the posterior and anterior borders of the femur and on the anterior margin of the tibia. The edge of white is everywhere set off by a line of black below it. A purplish brown band extends from the nostril, through the eye, to the shoulder, including the ear. Iris dark or bright bronze. The lower sides are violet-grey, spotted posteriorly with yellow or orange. The exposed surfaces (when the frog is in sitting position) of hands and feet are purplish grey; the concealed parts of these and of the legs are yellow spotted with orange; i. e. the yellow is found on the first finger and along the inner side of the arm, under the arm at its attachment, on the inner two toes and the inner half of the tarsus, and on parts of the body, femur, and tibia, where they touch one another when the leg is folded. The green of the upper arm extends in a scallop on the breast. The green of the face extends across the jaw to form a broad scallop on the side of the throat. (For colouration, see Colour Plate VII.)

Measurements: Size small, i. e. 1¾ inches or under. Head broad, obtuse in front. Length of head enters total length three and a quarter times. Femur and tibia equal in length, and together slightly shorter than length of head and body.

Structure: Skin smooth. A fold across breast. Eye large. Ear about one-third size of eye. Inner sole tubercle distinct; outer tubercle not present. The disks on fingers and toes are medium in size. The webs of the toes are short.

Range: As far as discovered, only from Lakehurst, New Jersey, south to Anderson, South Carolina.

―――――――――

Only six times has this very distinctive *Hyla* come under observation. The first specimen is the type specimen found at Anderson, South Carolina, by Baird in 1854, and named and described by him. The second specimen was found in 1863 by Dr.

131

Leidy at Jackson, New Jersey. The third was found hy Dr. J. A. Peters at May's Landing, New Jersey, in 1888. In 1889, Dr. J. Percy Moore captured two specimens, both males, at Pleasant Mills, New Jersey. In 1901 a specimen was found at Clementon, New Jersey, and was presented to the Philadelphia Academy of Science by Witmer Stone. Finally, in September, 1904, for the sixth time, *Hyla andersonii* came to light. It was found by Mr. William T. Davis at Lakehurst, New Jersey. It was shaken from a low oak tree during a hunt for insects.

The photographs of the colour plate are from the last-named specimen, which was kindly loaned for the purpose by Mr. Davis.

In appearance this tree frog is one of the most interesting representatives of its kind. It is nearly as large as the common tree frog, *Hyla versicolor*, and has a most unusual pattern of dress. The vivid green, with its bounding lines of white and black, gives the appearance of a tailor-made coat from which hands and feet protrude. A somewhat harlequin effect is produced by the lengthwise colour division of the hand and foot. This tree frog looks rather bizarre in side view because of the prominent scallops of colour extending to the throat and breast. Although in its green and white lines it bears a superficial resemblance to *Hyla cinerea* (see Figs. 154 to 160), on close inspection there is no possibility of confusing it with any other North American tree frog. It resembles somewhat the common tree frog of Europe. (*Hyla arborea*.)

The creature has a very gentle and alert expression. It is, in fact, one of the most alert and timid of our tree frogs. In captivity it is seldom content until it finds some moist hiding-place in moss and ferns or under wet decaying pieces of wood. When such a place is found, the *Hyla* backs into it with the burrowing movements common among the Salientia. Here, with flattened body and closed eyes, it remains sleeping away the days and nights. The sleeping position is interesting, in that the long delicately-coloured toes are lifted to the green of the sides, and rest pressed close to the body, just above the shoulder.

This *Hyla* is relatively hardy. The tree frog found June 1, 1888, was still alive and well in January, 1889. How much longer it lived is not recorded. The specimen caught in September, 1904, is in plump condition now in June, 1905.

The specimen photographed moulted the skin February 10th. For several hours before the moult the skin was very dry and lustreless, and the frog kept rubbing one hand and then the other over the head and eyes, as if in discomfort. The skin was thin and white. It was shed in one piece and swallowed as it was shed, in just the manner described for the similar process in the toad and frog.

This *Hyla* differs conspicuously from *Hyla versicolor* and *Hyla regilla*, in fact from most of its nearest relatives in North America, by the fact that it has apparently but a limited power to change colour. The green may pale or deepen, it may even take on a tinge of brown; the lavender tints of hand and foot may be extremely light, or so dark that they become a deep purplish brown. But when we compare this with the radical and rapid changes in *Hyla regilla* and others, the limitation is very evident. As far as observed, the pattern of dress is never obscured.

Hyla andersonii is an agile climber, but ascends largely by clasping the hands and feet around the support. The adhesive power of the disks is relatively not great, and the under-surface of the body does not seem to aid them as much in climbing as it does many tree frogs. On a relatively smooth vertical surface up which *Hyla cinera, versicolor, pickeringii, regilla*, and many others will climb rapidly and with confidence, Anderson's *Hyla* holds itself with great difficulty, even for the space of a few seconds.

The call of the specimen that was found June, 1888, is described as made up of a shrill note repeated three of four times in succession. Those discovered in June, 1889, were found during and preceding a thunder storm, clinging to the under sides of pine twigs in a swampy thicket. Their throats were swollen in the manner characteristic of the *Hylas*, and before the disturbance came, their voices made part of a chorus that emanated from all parts of the swamp. The single note was compared to that of a guinea-fowl, or of the rail.

Hyla andersonii is certainly rare, and, as far as discovered, has an unusually limited distribution. However, it is probable that the apparent limit of range, and the seeming scarcity within this range, are due, in part at least, to the retiring habits of the tree frog, and in part to the inaccessible character of its chosen haunts.

THE PACIFIC TREE FROG

Hyla regilla Baird and Girard

IDENTIFICATION CHARACTERISTICS

Colour: Extremely variable. Any shade of grey, brown, or green; occasionally distinctly red. A narrow black or dark brown band extends from the nostril (or from the muzzle) to the eye, and, widening behind the eye, continues through the ear to the shoulder. This dark band is bordered below by a band of light colour. The immediate line of the jaw is dark. (Fig. 166.) The dark band which passes through the ear may be continued along the sides of the frog in a series of black spots. There may or may not be a V-shaped mark between the eyes, extending well up on the eyelids, and elongated dark spots placed lengthwise along the back and upper sides. Underparts dark or light. Throat of male always darker than remainder of underparts. (Fig. 169.) The undersurface has much orange colour posteriorly. (See Colour Plates VIII and IX.)

Measurements: Size small, i. e. length $1\frac{1}{4}$ to $1\frac{3}{4}$ inches. Leg long; length of tibia equal to length of femur, and equal to half total length of frog.

Structure: Skin finely tubercular above, granulated below, except for the throat region. (Fig. 169.) *Canthus rostralis* very distinct. (Fig. 165.) Ear distinct, less than half the diameter of the eye. Head obtuse in front. Disks on fingers and toes relatively small. Fingers long, not webbed. Toes webbed half their lengths. (Figs. 169.)

Range: Hyla regilla has been reported from Washington, Oregon, California, Nevada, Lower California, and from Cerros and Santa Cruz islands, which are twenty miles from the Californian mainland. This makes its range cover an area from Vancouver Island on the north to Cape St. Lucas at the south, and from the islands of the coast to the eastern base of the Cascades and Sierra Nevada. In the region of Washington and Oregon, its range extends well into the desert part of the Great Basin, following the streams of the country. In Death Valley it is found at isolated springs and wells, more than half-way across the Great Basin. There is no authentic report of its occurring in Texas. "Moreover, it may be noticed that in altitude *Hyla regilla* ranges from sea-level to 10,000 feet in the vicinity of Mount Whitney. Thus it occurs from the Lower Sonoran well up into the Boreal Zone, equal to the difference in latitude between Florida and Labrador, and the extension of its range is thus second to that of no other *Hyla* in North America."[1]

If we capture several specimens of *Hyla regilla*, we are almost immediately impressed by three facts: first, their great alertness and activity; second, their great variation in colour and colour pattern; and third, their rapid and marked colour changes.

They are not quite as active and impossible to manage as *Hyla squirella* of the Southern States; they compare more favourably in activity with *Hyla pickeringii* of eastern North America. These frogs are small, with bodies relatively slender and legs unusually long, so we are not surprised at the number of the leaps made and the distance covered with each movement. They show little tendency to climb, and will remain at the bottom of an uncovered moss-garden for days at a time without any attempt at escape.

Their variation in colour is great. They may be any shade of grey, green, or brown, and sometimes are more or less vividly marked with red. It is not to be wondered at that one not familiar with the fact that colour is seldom a specific characteristic should think that the lot contained several kinds of frogs. Most of the frogs present only one colour or shade, but there are likely to be several in a given lot that will combine two shades or two colours. The back may be brown while the sides are green, the head and shoulders may be red while the body posteriorly is green, and so on. (See Colour Plate VIII.)

Not only does the background of colour vary thus greatly, but the colour pattern is so variable that at first sight it may be difficult to see what are the elements of the common pattern. This common pattern consists of a triangular patch between the eyes and lengthwise bands on the back. There may be small spots placed irregularly between the bands, and on the sides of the frog below the bands. But there is what seems to be nearly every possible disguise of the pattern. The triangle between the eyes

---

[1] F. C. Test. " A Contribution to the Knowledge of the Variations of the Tree Frog Hyla Regilla." Proc. U. S. Nat. Museum, vol. XXI, pp. 477–492.

may be very large, extending well up on the eyelids, and sending a point far back on the neck, or it may be decidedly small. It may be of solid colour, or only in outline. It may be separate or connected with the band in the midline of the back, or it may be broken into two or occasionally three spots. The longitudinal bands of the back may be distinct broad bands, two, three, or occasionally five in number, or they may be broken into spots rounded or elongated, regular or irregular in shape. The bands may have parallel sides, or may be fantastic in shape. They may be broad and conspicuous, and if there are spots instead of bands, these may be many and crowded, or bands and spots may be so reduced that they are scarcely noticeable.

Judging from the one hundred fifty specimens examined from regions about San Diego and San Francisco, California, and Seattle, Washington, those from the south are more likely to have the dark colour in lines or bands with few spots between and on the sides, and those from the north to have broken bands and crowded spots showing much more dark colour. The specimens from the north, besides having more dark colour, measure considerably larger than those at the south.

Hyla regilla has the power to change colour rapidly. Let us isolate two and observe them. They have been in wet moss in a dark place, and are nearly black in colour. When looked at more closely, one is seen to be a very dark green, and the other a rich dark brown. There is no trace of spots; only the light band above the jaw shows. On exposure to bright light, the colour immediately lightens; one becomes decidedly green, the other decidedly brown. Soon a pattern of spots and bands shows obscurely on their backs. This pattern becomes more and more distinct as the background grows lighter. When the medium shade of green or brown is at its brightest, the pattern shows most vividly. However, if they still continue to remain in bright light, we could scarcely find time to draw the pattern while it is vivid, for as the background continues to grow light, the spots begin to be dulled. They become less and less distinct, the background becomes still more light in tone, and the pattern wholly fades, and leaves one frog metallic fawn colour with golden reflections, and the other yellowish green of a very light tone. This change from a colour so dark that there are no spots to a light unspotted colouration may take place within eight or ten minutes.

(See Colour Plate IX.) Putting the frogs into a dark situation again, they reverse the change, become vividly spotted, and finally dark and unspotted.

Any given collection of these tree frogs taken from the pond will contain spotted specimens, unspotted dark and unspotted light ones, and many in which the pattern shows obscurely. But all will develop the typical pattern vividly if they are put under the right conditions. Of the one hundred fifty specimens examined, no frog was found in which the pattern was wholly lacking, though three out of the number had the pattern so reduced that it consisted of a very small triangular patch between the eyes and mere dashes of colour on the back. (See frogs in lower right-hand corner of Colour Plate VIII.)

The dark band through the ear and its continuation in dark spots on the sides are constant factors in the colouration. The only time that they are not visible is when the background is as dark as the markings.

Hyla regilla lives low, hopping about on the ground among the blackberry vines and other vegetation, as does *Hyla pickeringii* of eastern North America. It is found especially about springs, ponds, and moist places of all sorts. It calls from some place of concealment in these situations on dark or rainy days and at dusk. It may be heard occasionally throughout the winter, even. In spring, it is to be found in great numbers in shallow pools. The frogs then sing in chorus (especially at night), and a small number of them can produce a noise so great that it sounds as though made by thousands.

The eggs are laid in February [1] and later. They are small (1 mm. diameter) and are in clusters of from twenty to fifty. The clusters are attached to grasses and leaves in the shallow water. (Fig. 167.) The tree frogs themselves may be found either in the water or under stones and leaves nearby, depending on the temperature of the day.

Hyla regilla breeds in shallow ponds at Seattle, Washington, in late February, at the same time that *Rana pretiosa* is laying its eggs. The breeding-time begins earlier in southern California; the metamorphosis may be completed in April. The young tree frogs are small ($\frac{1}{2}$ inch long), but show the typical pattern on the

---

[1] Feb. 12th, Carmel, Cal. L. S. Slevin, collector.

head and back as well as the dark and light parallel bands on the sides of the head.

This tree frog is hardy. In captivity it hides during the greater part of the time, under moss or leaves. It eats small earthworms and beetle larvæ from acorns and chestnuts, with the usual eagerness displayed by members of the group.

It frequently sings in captivity, usually from under cover of moss or ferns. The call reminds one of that of *Hyla pickeringii*, in that it consists of a series of short untrilled notes. It differs in pitch and quality from that of Pickering's frog. The pitch is relatively low, about G of the second line; the quality is harsh, often grating. The throat-pouch is yellowish brown when distended; it is much broader than deep, and when fully inflated is at least three times as large as the frog's head. This *Hyla* very often sits with the vocal pouch partially distended, the small bag palpitating with the breathing movements. Sometimes, when taken in the hand, the frog will swell the throat and give the call which sounds like the harsh sound made by various mechanical toys. When greatly annoyed or when injured, this tree frog, like *Hyla versicolor*, gives out a milky secretion from the skin of the upper surface of the body.

Hyla regilla is an attractive little frog. It is delicately formed and beautifully coloured. Besides the colouring already described, it shows much iridescence. Various parts shine with gold and bronze; the iridescence is marked in the region below the eye and on the shoulder and upper arm.

THE SPRING PEEPER

Hyla pickeringii Holbrook

IDENTIFICATION CHARACTERISTICS

Colour: Varies from light fawn colour to dark brown, and may be yellow, red, or ashy in tone. There is a V-shaped dark mark between the eyes, an oblique cross on the back, and bars on the legs. (Figs. 170 to 172.) The underparts are light in colour, yellowish posteriorly. The throat of the male is brown. (For colouration, see Colour Plate X.)

Measurements: This is the smallest representative of the genus *Hyla* in North America. Male, $\frac{3}{4}$ to 1 inch; female, 1 to $1\frac{1}{4}$ inches.

FIGS. 165 to 169 (1–5).—*Hyla regilla* Bd. and Gird., and its eggs. All of the frogs represented are males. (1), (4) and (5) are from Carmel, Cal., (2) is from Seattle, Washington. (For coloration see Colour Plates VIII and IX.)

FIGS. 165 and 166 (1–2).—Very alert. *Hyla regilla* may appear spotted or unspotted, light or dark, smooth or rough.

FIG. 167 (3).—The eggs are laid in clusters attached to grasses.

FIG. 168 (4).—The vocal pouch is broader than deep. It is yellowish-brown in colour. It may be inflated to a size three times that of the head.

FIG. 169 (5).—The throat of the male is black and wrinkled. There is a fold of skin across the breast.

Most of the SPRING PEEPERS live on the ground in the woods throughout the year except for a few weeks in early spring, when they are to be found in the ponds and the marshes adjacent.

Structure: Head pointed, sharply angled along the lines from nostrils to eyes. The muzzle extends beyond the upper lip. The ear is visible, but is smaller than the eye. The disks on fingers and toes are prominent. The feet are only moderately webbed.

Range: Eastern North America. It has been reported from the following states: Maine, Vermont, New Hampshire, Massachusetts, Rhode Island, Connecticut, New York, Pennsylvania, Maryland, North Carolina, South Carolina, Ohio, Illinois, and Michigan. It is reported also from Canada (New Brunswick to Manitoba).

There are few people in the eastern United States who do not know the voices of the Spring Peepers, although they may only guess who these singers may be. If they recognize the singers as frogs, they are likely to judge from the size of the voices that the frogs are large, and sometimes they are loath to accept the statement that Peeping Frogs are tiny things an inch or less long. (Fig. 171).

We expect pussy-willows to usher in the spring. We listen for the kong-quer-ree of the red-winged blackbird. We do not have to look or listen to know that the Peepers have spring in their hearts. The chorus of voices greets us when we leave our suburban car. We drive from one suburb to another and scarcely leave one singing company behind us before the voices of a second greet us in front. We go by rail from city to city, and from the marshy regions along the track their voices sound above the roar and rattle of the train.

The call comes from low marshy ground in the open, or from pools and marshy land in the woods; from water wholly exposed to the sun's rays, or from the depths of dark forest swamps. It can be heard with distinctness at least a quarter of a mile away. As we approach, it sometimes reminds us of a loud jangle of musical sleigh-bells. It is somewhat difficult to isolate a single voice from the chorus. If we do so, we find that it is high pitched, loud, penetrating, and usually not trilled. Occasionally an especially enthusiastic call is strongly trilled. It is not exactly a whistle, nor is it flute-like; but it is more like the thin, sweet sound from a pipe. Each prolonged call seems to be made up of two tones, the first lower and sliding into the second. The first is pitched

March first. Spring Peepers begin calling when the pussy willows are gray.

somewhere between B and E, two octaves above C, and the second is not more than an interval above. As we listen longer to the chorus, we perceive that the pitch varies greatly with the individual, and that the different tones are not always in harmony. Occasionally there is a distinct rhythm in the chorus, the calls are given together, and the pauses occur together. More often, however, the calls alternate irregularly.

After we have heard the chorus every spring for years, the Peeper is still merely a voice to us. Let us solve the mystery. It is a morning in the first week of March, with the temperature at 58° F. We are tempted to a country walk. Here is a wooded strip of land between a marsh black with alders and an open pond. The Peepers should be here. The redwings are making a great noise in the alders. A few sprays of pussy-willow gleam silver against the background of the alders. On the other side, the pond is still largely covered with ice. But the woods between are very beautiful, and full of life and the promise of life. The dark trunks and branches of oak and pine are relieved here and there by clusters of slender grey birches. Low stumps and hillocks are covered with moss — spots of vivid green in sharp contrast to the surrounding brown. Two partridges fly up from the path ahead with a startling whirr of wings. We hear in the distance what must be the low croaking of a green frog, but, on following the sound, find it is made by a downy woodpecker drumming on a resonant sycamore.

There is a Peeper! The thin, sweet " Pe-ep, pe-ep, pe-ep, pe-ep, " sounding much like a bird's call-note, comes from the moss and leaves at the water's edge.

140

After the four calls, there is silence. Then the call comes again, and is repeated several times before the pause.

We search among the leaves and moss. No amount of looking reveals the shelter of this atom of a frog so eager for spring. The Peeper is still but a voice.

In two weeks we go again. It is afternoon, and the temperature is at 65° F. The pussy-willows are no longer grey; they have developed into spikes of golden or green flowers, and are surrounded by early bees and flies. The sound of a chorus of frogs reaches us before we leave the car, although the marsh is more than a quarter of a mile distant. As we approach, and the individual voices become distinct, we are astonished that they are so loud and penetrating compared with the isolated calls we heard in early March. The combination of sounds is almost ear-splitting. The largest company seems to be in the connected pools about the roots of a tangle of grey birches and swamp-maples. It is easy to penetrate here. We step from tree root to tree root or from log to log over shallow pools of black water filled with brown leaves, grasses, and sticks. A slow painted-turtle walks through the shallow water, now in the shadow a black movement only, now showing distinctly as it comes into a spot of sunlight. But where are the frogs? The voices are all about us. There is one particularly loud one at our very feet. We look; we scrutinize every leaf and stick and bit of grass. It is maddening that we cannot see the singer. With our slightest movement the sound ceases. And so again and again. We finally retreat, with the Peeper still a mysterious piping voice.

Late March. Spring Peepers are singing both day and night when the pussy-willows are in blossom.

141

The middle of April. When pussy willow seed pods are ripening, Spring Peepers are calling only during the late afternoon and night.

Once more we try. It is the middle of April. The yellow flowers of the pussy-willows have disappeared. The green ones have developed into caterpillar-like clusters of green seed-pods. The Peepers are still singing in the marshes, but only during the late afternoon and at night. Let us try an open marsh where there will be light enough for the search. Here is a boggy piece of land that must be pasture in midsummer. It stretches into meadow on all sides. There is no difficulty in getting to the very centre of it by stepping from one grass hillock to another. We heard the chorus at a distance of many blocks, and it has continued as we approached; but as we step onto our first hillock it becomes quiet all about us; the quiet spreads, and now the whole bog is silent. We penetrate a little farther and then stand still. After what seems a long time, one Peeper calls far to the right. The call is taken up by frogs nearer and nearer, until we are surrounded by sound. This time our search is rewarded. We see one frog. He is so small, that, instead of its seeming strange that we had not found them before, we think it a miracle that we have discovered one now. He swims vigorously from a clump of grass to a floating twig, which to him is a log, climbs upon it, and is in full view for a moment; then plunges into the water again, and swims to another clump of grass and leaves almost at our feet. Instantly he begins singing, and although he is partially concealed by a projecting leaf, we can see his swollen throat gleam like a great white bubble under the level

142

rays of the late afternoon sun. The transparent inflated throat is one-half as large as the frog's head and body together. It does not greatly change size between the calls, but collapses at the end. The frog's mouth is kept closed during the calling.

For some time we watch him as he sings. We try to capture him, and get only a handful of mud for our pains. Silence begins again, and spreads rapidly, till not one frog is peeping. We suddenly feel the dreariness of the place, the wind blows cold and it is getting dark. We retreat with the congratulatory remark, " At any rate, we have seen a Peeper!"

After we have seen one Pickering's *Hyla* at the marsh, it is not difficult to see others, especially if we take active measures and push apart the floating leaves and sticks of the shallow water. More than one tiny yellow or brown frog will swim out from among the leaves. Most of them will be males, since they far outnumber the females.

One of the best times to capture Pickering's tree frogs is at night. During the day time they usually call from the cover of moss and leaves. If we go to the marsh at night, they do not seem to see or hear us, and it is not as difficult as might be supposed to locate them by means of their inflated white throats.

If we do capture them, and keep them under glass for a few days or weeks, we shall find them very interesting. They are small, measuring one inch or less. They are very slender and delicate, and unusually alert looking. The rhythmic throat movement is rapid, more rapid than that of even the land Wood Frog. The elevated eyes have the usual golden rim, whose iridescent color may be so deep as to seem almost orange in tone. The body is flexible; there seems to be much more movement in the neck region than is usual among the frogs. The skin is soft and moist and closely granular underneath. The disks on the fingers and toes are distinct, but not conspicuously large as in the Common Tree Frog. The webs of the hind feet extend less than half the length of the toes.

The colour is usually light yellowish brown, but there is a great range for variation, and the changes are relatively rapid. Within an hour, frogs that were pale greyish yellow may become dark wood-brown. Sometimes the brown is reddish or salmon in tone. There are definite markings, which can be distinguished unless the background is extremely dark. These are, first and

Early May. The chorus of Spring Peepers closes as the pussy-willow is scattering feathery seeds.

foremost, an oblique cross on the back, and transverse bars on the hind legs. There is also a V-shaped mark between the eyes, a similar mark, reversed, on the back posterior to the cross, and a short line extending lengthwise at each side of the cross. The underparts are yellowish white, more or less mottled with brown. The undersurfaces of the legs may be yellow. The male is likely to be considerably smaller than the female, and is usually darker in colour.

Pickering's Tree Frogs thrive well in a small moss-garden. They may be kept successfully, even all winter. They rest or sleep much of the day under the moss, or, perhaps, exposed on some plant. (Fig. 171.) They sing often, especially in the late afternoons and on rainy days, but usually from under cover of moss and leaves. (Fig. 172.) They eat small worms and flies greedily. They climb up the glass sides of their houses, alternating several rapid steps with relatively long pauses. They never seem to climb downward; jumping is easier. They never attempt to escape; their small garden with food and companions is a whole world to them.

The time of the chorus of Spring Peepers extends from early March until May, and often until the second or third week of May. It may have brief interruptions, due to snow and severe cold, although Pickering's *Hyla* often sings when the temperature is below 50° F. The chorus begins when the pussy-willows are grey and the blue violets of the marsh are just opening. It ends when the pussy-willows are scattering feathery seeds and the violets have long-stemmed leaves and flowers strugling for light through surrounding rank growths of fern, hellebore, and skunk-cabbage.

The season of their chorus closes at about the time that the Common Tree Frog chorus begins. Sometimes for two weeks or more we may hear their voices together from the same or adjacent swamps.

The season of the chorus begins in February or March; not many of the eggs are laid [1] until April. The eggs are generally fastened singly to plants in the water, although they sometimes lie free at the bottom, and are sometimes in small masses (4 to 10). They may be laid singly or in small groups by frogs in captivity. They are exceedingly small (1-12 inch in diameter), so small that they look like tiny plant seeds. Each is surrounded by a viscid substance and a distinct outer membrane. The egg is deep brown above and cream-white below when first laid, but becomes light grey in the early stages of development.

---

[1] May 15, 1892. *Hyla pickeringii*. O. P. Hay, Irvington, Ind.

April 6, April 17. *Hyla pickeringii*. F. W. Putnam, Cambridge, Mass.

April 25, 1904. *Hyla pickeringii*. M. C. Dickerson, Providence, R. I.

March 9, 10, 13, and April 5, 1890. *Hyla pickeringii*. T. H. Morgan, Baltimore, Md.

The chorus of Spring Peepers begins when the blue violets of the marsh are first opening, and closes when these violets are struggling for light among rank growths of fern and hellebore.

The tadpoles hatch in from six to twelve days, depending on the temperature. In less than a week after hatching, the gills are covered and the usual "pollywog" form is assumed. In seven or eight weeks from the time that the eggs are laid, the tadpoles [1] are full-grown. They are small and delicate. Each measures one inch long, including the tail, which is twice the length of head and body together. The undersurface of the body is reddish bronze, shining with metallic lustre. The characteristics of the head of the adult frog can be seen in the tadpole even before the front legs appear; that is, the eyes are set extremely wide apart, the lines between the eyes and the nostrils are sharply angled, and the upper jaw projects beyond the lower. The toes of the back legs are provided with distinct pads before the front legs appear. The cross on the back often shows before the tail begins to be absorbed.

As soon as the front legs break through their coverings, the creatures are eager to leave the water. They may be found some distance from the water while the tail is still long. They are certain to climb the grasess and sedges and to sit on floating leaves and twigs before the metamorphosis is completed.

In June they may be found in hundreds among the brown leaves and green moss of the bank. They are little, dark-coloured, leaping objects, which from their small size we might mistake for young toads, if we did not examine them closely. They have not yet gone very far from their pond or marsh, but their diligent search for gnats, mosquitoes, and ants has already begun.

When we stand on the sphagnum border of the marsh and look into the water, we see so many enemies of these tadpoles, that the wisdom of their early escape to land life appeals to us. There are water-beetles and bugs, leeches, diving-spiders, and the larvæ of dragon-flies and caddis-flies. There are always newts to devour them. There are Leopard frogs perhaps, and certainly Green frogs, that eat the adult Pickerings as well as the tadpoles.

Very often the marsh or pool dries up before the development is completed. The water recedes, to leave a small pool measured only in feet, and perhaps only in inches, where enemies and tadpoles are crowded together.[2] If the evaporation proceeds too

[1] The mouth structure of the tadpole of the Pickering's *Hyla* is like that of the tadpoles of *Hyla versicolor* (see footnote, p. 121), except that the lower lip has only two rows of teeth, instead of three.

[2] It is said by M. H. Hinckley that birds, such as the crow, the heron, and the woodcock, take advantage of such conditions, and make feeding-places of these reduced pools, as is proved by the tracks and borings in the mud adjacent.

rapidly, all the tadpoles may perish and leave only blackened stains on the mud to show where they have been; but if it is more slow, or comes but a short time previous to their final change, this change may be hastened by the conditions and the young Pickerings will leave the water earlier — and smaller — than is their wont.[1]

Pickering's Tree Frogs are likely to be silent and in hiding during July, but from the close of July until December they may be found not only in the woods, but in all sorts of unexpected places. Their main interest in life lies in hunting small insects. The chase may take them to the trees of the orchard, to the low growths of the vegetable garden, or to the shrubs and vines of the flower-garden. They have been found even in green-houses, apparently attracted there by the moisture and food supply.

We may find them on tree trunks, in the tops of alder and huckleberry, or on tall ferns. But the greater number of them remain on the ground, in the woods or about the marsh. Like the young Wood Frogs, they hide and leap and hunt among the trailing dewberry, the wintergreen, and the partridge-berry.

We may hear them and find them in November even, when the sun shines down between the bare trees to the yellow and red

Pickering's Hyla is still calling in the woods, when the witch-hazel's yellow flowers appear.

---

[1] This characteristic of adaptability, possessed by all of the Bactrachia, is more pronounced among the Salamanders where the larval stage may be greatly shortened, or prolonged for months or years.

147

leaves, the patches of russet fern, and the clusters of jack-in-the-pulpit's red berries on the ground.   All remind us of the approach of winter. We know that to-morrow, if not to-day, the cold wind will blow and the snow will fall.   But to-day the sun is bright on the witch-hazel's yellow flowers, and there is good courage in the shrill piping voice of this little *Hyla*.

Pickering's *Hyla* sleeps during December and January, nestled under moss and leaves, but wakes in icy February to herald the spring with the same shrill piping voice of good cheer that we heard in the November woods.

THE SOUTHERN TREE FROG
Hyla squirella Bosc

IDENTIFICATION CHARACTERISTICS

Colour: Green or brown; bright or dull, of light or dark shade. There is a dark patch from the eye to the shoulder, including the ear; a dark line from the nostril to the eye; a light line along the jaw from under the eye to the shoulder. This light line may be continued along the sides half-way or all of the way to the posterior part of the body, and may be margined below by dusky colour. There may be a V-shaped dark mark between the eyes and round or elongated spots on the back. There may be much orange-yellow on the throat, under the arm at the place of its insertion, on the two inner fingers, and posteriorly on the concealed parts of the body, femur, tibia, and tarsus (parts concealed when frog is in resting position). Eye bright orange-yellow or bronze. Ear brown, metallic. Legs irregularly barred or not. The concealed leg surfaces are not spotted nor vermiculated. (Distinctions from *Hyla femoralis* and *Hyla versicolor*.) (See Colour Plate X.)

Measurements: Size small, i. e. length 1 inch to 1⅔ inches. Length of head contained three and a half times in total length. Length of leg to heel equals length of frog forward to end of muzzle. Tibia and femur of equal lengths. The knee touches the elbow when the arm and leg are pressed against the body.

Structure: Skin smooth and fine in texture. Head somewhat acute, rounded in front. Canthus rostralis prominent. Nostril nearer to end of muzzle than to the eye. Ear two-thirds size of eye. Eyes widely separated. A fold of skin across breast.

FIGS. 170 to 172 (1 to 3).—*Hyla pickeringii* Storer. Providence, R. I. Length 1 in. (For coloration see colour Plate X.)

FIG. 170 (1).—The tiny atoms of tree frogs leave the water before their tails are absorbed.

FIG. 171 (2).—Asleep on pitcher plant leaf.

FIG. 172 (3).—In captivity *Hyla pickeringii* becomes very tame. It swells its throat and sings on all occasions—one of these occasions being when touched by some companion tree frog (*Hyla regilla*) wandering through the moss of the vivarium.

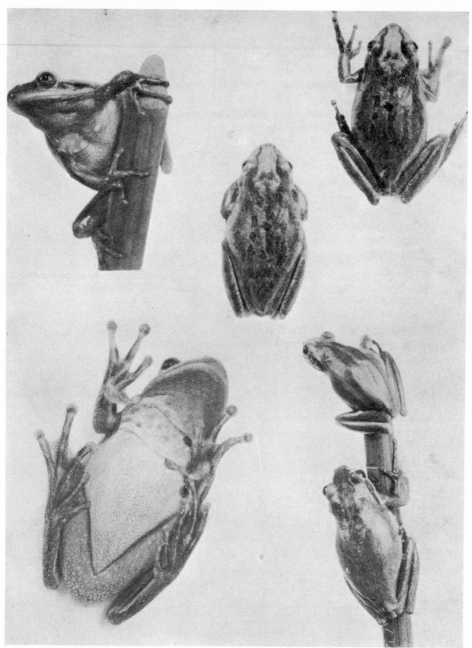

FIGS. 173 to 177.—The SOUTHERN TREE FROG (*Hyla squirella* Bosc). This is a delicate, smooth-skinned little tree frog, one of the most active in North America. (Enlarged.) Nat. size 1½ in. Havelock, N. C. (For coloration see Colour Plate X.)

Disks on fingers and toes well developed. Inner sole tubercle small; no outer sole tubercle. Tubercles under joints of toes somewhat prominent. Webs short. (See Figs. 173 to 177.)

Range: *Hyla squirella* Bosc is found in the southern part of North America, its range extending well up the Mississippi. It is reported from North Carolina, South Carolina, Georgia, Florida, Louisiana, Mississippi, Texas, and southern Indiana.

Hyla squirella is a delicate, smooth-skinned, little tree frog, and is one of the most active in North America. It is a most difficult frog to catch, giving leap after leap in rapid succession and in changing directions. If we do succeed in catching a half a dozen and carry them home in a pail or box, there are few chances but that we shall lose most of them the moment they are uncovered. They do not wait to be lifted out; they do not climb onto one's finger and cling confidingly; they jump simultaneously with the opening of the box, all in different directions.

Of all the tree frogs of North America, this one has perhaps the greatest power for rapid colour change, and during these changes presents the greatest variety of colours and shades of colour. At any given moment *Hyla squirella* may wear any one of the following costumes: unspotted dark chocolate brown or dark brownish olive; light purplish brown with dark brown spots; light yellowish or greyish brown without spots; any medium shade of brown with green spots; olive green unspotted; light yellow green spotted with brown; unspotted light pea-green; light greenish gray; light fawn colour, or still lighter shades ranging down to flesh colour.

Most curious is the fact that although these changes take place under the influence of various stimuli, such as light, moisture, and heat, they may go on without these stimuli. Frogs shut in a dark pail with no change of conditions will not appear twice alike when the pail is opened at intervals during the space of several hours. Some may be green and others brown; some spotted, others not; some light while others are dark. And at any given time of observation those that were dull and spotted before may be bright unspotted green, the ones that were light may be dark, and so on. The light line along the jaw undergoes great changes

149

also. This tree frog furnishes a most interesting case for the study of metachrosis.

Hyla squirella lives on either low or tall vegetation. It may be found on the vines and shrubs of the garden or the river and lake margins, or it may climb into the trees of similar localities. It conceals itself under the decaying bark of trees or under dead logs. It is said to hibernate in old logs.

THE HYLA OF THE PINE WOODS
Hyla femoralis Latreille

IDENTIFICATION CHARACTERISTICS

Colour: Brown or grey above, dull white underneath. A triangular dark spot between the eyes. A large blotch on the anterior back, sending two short branches forward (which may unite with the spot between the eyes) and two larger ones outwards and backwards. There may be several spots irregular in shape and position on the posterior back. A dark line extends from the end of the muzzle along the canthus rostralis through eye and ear, continuing along the sides of the frog to the thighs The immediate margin of the jaw is usually dark, perhaps relieved by a lighter colour above (never a distinct line or band). Arms and legs may have dark cross-bars. The posterior surface of the femur is brown, spotted with white or yellow. Posterior lines of tibia and tarsus margined with dark, which is in turn edged with light above.

Measurements: Size small, i. e. length 1¼ to 1¾ inches. Head short, much broader than long. Body short and broad. Leg short; length to heel equals length of body forward to ear or eye.

Structure: Skin nearly smooth above. Underparts granular, even in the throat-region. Muzzle rounded, slightly projecting beyond jaw. Nostrils terminal. Canthus rostralis angular. Ear small. A fold of skin across the breast. Fingers long. Disks on fingers and toes well developed. Foot provided with a tarsal ridge, small inner sole tubercle, and web of medium size. The fingers show slight webs.

Range: Hyla femoralis is reported from Florida (Arlington, Micanopy, Green Cove Springs), Georgia (Allapaha, Riceborough,

Nashville), South Carolina (Goose Creek), North Carolina (Wilmington), and Texas (Dallas).

Hyla femoralis is a tree frog that, as far as known, lives high in the pine trees of the Southern States. It is not as large as the Common Tree Frog (*Hyla versicolor*), but bears a somewhat close resemblance to it in body proportions, in colour, and in markings. It can always be known by certain definite points, as follows: It is distinguished from *Hyla versicolor* by the dark line through the ear and by the lack of a white spot under the eye. Also, the posterior surface of the femur is brown, spotted with light colour, not reticulated as in *Hyla versicolor*. This spotting on the posterior femur will always distinguish it also from *Hyla squirella*, the common tree frog at the South.

Nothing is on record regarding its life history or habits.

SMILISCA BAUDINII, D. AND B.

Identification Characteristics

Colour: Changeable from a colour so dark that it is nearly black, to delicate shades of green, grey, or fawn colour. When the medium shades are most intense, there is a pronounced colour pattern, which is obscure or lacking when the shade is light or dark. (Figs. 178 to 180.) This pattern consists of a band between the eyes, connected with a cross-shaped mark on the back, various irregular spots placed laterally and posteriorly to the cross, transverse bars on the arms and hands, and three of four transverse bars on the legs. In addition, there is a permanent colour pattern as follows: a light spot under the gold or bronze eye; a light line along the jaw, extending back to the shoulder (the immediate edge of the jaw is dark); a dark line from the eye backward to the shoulder, terminating in a prominent black patch of colour over the arm insertion; and a distinct white spot above and encircling arm insertion. (Fig. 182.) The belly is light, unspotted. Breast and throat (female) obscurely or distinctly spotted with dark. (Fig. 183.) Posterior surface of thigh somewhat spotted, not reticulated. Sides light, spotted with dark (perhaps reticulated); yellowish posteriorly.

151

Measurements: Size large for a tree frog, i. e. length 2⅛ inches or more. Head short compared with total length (⅝ inches in frog of 2⅛ inches.) Leg measurement to heel equals length of body forward to the eye (female).

Structure: Skin of upper parts relatively smooth, set everywhere with very fine tubercles. Underparts granulated, even on throat. (Fig. 183.) Eyes widely separated. Canthus rostralis unusually prominent, nostrils near their terminal point. Ear round, nearly as large as the eye. (Fig. 182.) Distinct fold of skin over the ear from eye to shoulder. A prominent fold across the breast. Disks of fingers and toes large. Webs of toes medium in size. Fingers slightly webbed. (Fig. 181.) Inner sole tubercle small; outer lacking. Tubercles under joints of fingers and toes fairly prominent. (Fig. 183.) A conspicuous tarsal fold.

Range: Smilisca baudinii is typical of Mexico and Central America. In Texas, it has been reported from Brownsville and Helotes.

This tree frog is one of the largest found in North America. It bears a superficial resemblance to *Hyla versicolor*, the Common Tree Frog, (see Figs. 134 to 142), but can always be recognized by definite characteristics, as follows: The head is more deeply angled along the line of the canthus rostralis. The body is relatively longer, the head narrower; the skin is less tubercular. The ear is much larger. The black patch on the shoulder and the white one encircling the arm at its insertion are peculiar to this species, while, on the other hand, this frog lacks the reticulations on the posterior surface of the femur characteristic of *Hyla versicolor*.

Smilisca baudinii is like *Hyla versicolor*, also, in its sluggish tendencies. When it is aroused, it is a powerful leaper.

Its colour changes are no less remarkable than is usual among the members of the Hylidæ. It may change rapidly from a dark unspotted condition to a light unspotted condition, through medium shades displaying a conspicuous colour pattern. (Figs. 178 to 180.) For instance, we remove it from its hiding-place under moss and leaves, and find it nearly black. Put it in bright light and watch. Slowly the colour becomes less dusky and the pattern begins to appear. It is most conspicuous in its outlines, which

FIGS. 178 to 180 (1-3).—*Smilisca baudinii* (D and B).   Brownsville, Texas.   Length 2⅛ in.   This tree frog change from nearly black (1) to delicate light green or fawn colour (3) through phases of coloration in which the colour pattern is conspicuous (2).

FIG. 181 (4).—Very alert. Body flexible. Fingers with slight webs.

FIG. 182 (5). *Smilisca baudinii* can be distinguished by the black spot on the shoulder and the white spot at the base of the arm.

FIG. 183 (6). Structure study of underparts. (Enlarged.)

FIG. 184.—Studies of the CRICKET FROG (*Acris gryllus* Le Conte). The upper surfaces (frogs from Raleigh, N. C.) are tubercular and may be green or brown. The undersurfaces (frog from Hitchcock, Texas) are relatively smooth. When frightened this frog " plays dead " in water floating about (in the position indicated) like a stick or leaf.

FIG. 185.—Studies of the SWAMP TREE FROG (*Chorophilus n. feriarum* baird.) Raleigh, N. C. Color gray or brown with or without longitudinal stripes or series of spots. The SWAMP TREE FROG does little climbing because of the small size of the disks on fingers and toes; also it is a poor swimmer because of the lack of large webs.

gradually become bright green lines. As the brown of the background lightens, it seems to get an admixture of green not seen unless the frog is looked at closely. The green becomes more prominent, seeming to spread outward from the vivid green of the lines bounding the pattern of spots and bars, until the whole upper surface of the frog is green. The dark colour pattern becomes lighter and lighter, the green continues to lighten until the frog is most beautiful in a dress of light yellow green with spots of gold or fawn colour. Within a few minutes more, the spots have wholly disappeared leaving the frog plain green.

At other times the change from dark to light shows no green colour, but warm tones of brown instead. In this case the frog becomes a delicate unspotted fawn colour as the last stage in the series. Or the change may be effected displaying only soft shades of grey. In all dresses, the frog is an unusually attractive one in its colouration. In the change from dark to light, or the reverse, the ear and eye respond also to the given stimuli. The spot under the eye shows a considerable range of colouring; it may be white, or some shade of yellow or green. When light-coloured, the frog displays metallic reflections, especially on the forearms and tibiæ. In this light dress, all spots and marks are obliterated, except the heavy black blotch over the arm, the white spots under the eye and around the base of the arm, and a few black spots or specks on the sides. These seem to be permanent parts of the colour pattern.

THE CRICKET FROG

Acris gryllus Le Conte.[1]

IDENTIFICATION CHARACTERISTICS

Colour: Variable and changeable. Usually some shade of brown, with a triangular dark mark between the eyes, a lighter band of colour in the midline of the back, and three obliquely-

---

[1] Cope says that there are two subspecies: *A. g. gryllus*, found from North Carolina to Florida, and *A. g. crepitans*, found north of this as far as New York. The two subspecies differ but slightly and the division is of doubtful validity.

" Hinder foot less tarsus less than half the length of the head and body; dermal tubercles larger; posterior femoral stripes less distinct." (*A. g. crepitans.*)

" Hinder foot less tarsus longer than half head and body; dermal tubercles smaller; femoral stripes very distinct." (*A. g. gryllus.*)

placed elongated spots on each side of the body. The spots and dorsal band may be green or red-brown, and are often outlined with light. There is a light line from the eye to the arm. Eye bright orange. Throat of male, in spring, yellow. Legs with three transverse bands, or irregularly spotted. Posterior face of femur conspicuously striped lengthwise. Underparts light-coloured. (See Fig. 184.)

Measurements: Size extremely small, i. e. length $\frac{5}{8}$ inch to $1\frac{1}{4}$ inches. Legs long; the length of the leg to the heel is greater than the length of head and body together. The tibia is longer than the femur. Foot scarcely longer than tibia. (See Fig. 184.)

Structure; Skin rough and warty. Head pointed, long from eyes to end of muzzle. The ear is indistinct; one-third the diameter of the eye. There is a fold across the breast and a curving fold over the ear from eye to shoulder. The foot is fully webbed. The inner and outer sole tubercles are both present, though small. The tubercles under the joints of the toes are fairly prominent. The disks on fingers and toes are so small that they are scarcely noticeable. Underparts granulated posteriorly only. (See Fig. 184.)

Range: The Cricket Frog is found in Eastern North America and through an extent of country including Florida, Texas, Kansas, and the Northwest. On the Atlantic coast it has not been reported north of southern New York and Connecticut.

———

The most conspicuously active of our small tree frogs is the Cricket Frog, a tree frog with wholly terrestrial habits. When it is frightened, it jumps high and far, repeating these leaps in remarkably rapid succession. It catches its insect food[1] by giving these prodigious leaps, after the moving insect has been sighted at a distance. This power of activity, combined with its small size and protective colouration, allows it to withstand its enemies, the small snakes and lizards of the ground. The Cricket Frog stands in special need of protection. Unlike the greater number of tree frogs, it cannot climb shrubs and trees to get out of danger, because the disks of the fingers and toes are

———

[1] " Among other insects, Chlorops, crane-flies, Thyreocoris, *Calocoris rapidus*, numerous pupæ and wingless Aphididæ and Orthoptera, have been determined from the contents of their stomachs." Bull. Ill. State Lab. Nat. Hist. H. Garman.

too minute. (Fig. 184.) The Cricket Frog remains on the ground throughout the year, preferably along the muddy margins of pools and rivers. It is diurnal in habit. If it is disturbed when near the water, it gives one or more of its remarkable leaps, swims vigorously a few strokes,— using to good purpose the large webs between its toes,— and is immediately buried at the bottom of the pond. Very soon, however, it is in activity again, leaping from one water-lily pad to another in search of insects.

Cricket Frogs may attain a size of an inch or more, but most of those we see are very small — three-fourths of an inch long, or even less. Specimens from Texas are usually considerably larger than specimens from Florida and the Eastern States. The small size and active habits of these frogs would seem to be the reasons why they have been named the Cricket Frog. However, the name is said not to refer to these characteristics, but to their song which bears a strong resemblance to the chirping of a black cricket. These tiny frogs sing in chorus in spring, and the isolated call may be heard during the summer. The sound resembles the rattling call of the Swamp Tree Frog but the notes are more rapidly given and are sharper in quality. The sound can be imitated by striking together two pebbles or two marbles, beginning slowly and continuing more rapidly for thirty or forty strokes. The series of notes is sometimes broken into groups of three notes each. The imitation may be so good that the frogs will answer as will the Pickering's *Hyla* when its call is whistled. The Cricket Frogs sing constantly in captivity; they become especially enthusiastic when they are sprinkled with water. The call has not great carrying power, either when given alone or when given in chorus.

The male Cricket Frog does the singing. The yellow throat is inflated enormously. Cricket Frogs are easily discovered while they are singing, because they do not, like Pickering's *Hyla* hide under moss and grasses, but swell their throats while they are in full view on some water-plant or floating twig.

This minute frog offers a marked difference from the ordinary frog form, in that the part of the head anterior to the eyes is unusually prolonged. Outside of this, the most striking peculiarity of the frog is its rough skin. The back usually has elongated wart-like elevations, which are large, relative to the small size of the frog.

The range of variation in colour is great, and the changes are

155

made rapidly. These frogs may have a colouring that is green, light red-brown, clay colour, or a brown so dark as to look black in general effect. The dark shades are taken on when the frogs aie in dark situations, and especially when the darkness is combined with a low temperature and moisture; the lighter colouration is assumed under the influences of bright light, high temperature, and dryness.

The colour pattern of the Cricket Frog is a very definite one, but at any given time it may be present in whole or in part, or may not show at all. The pattern is made up of a triangular dark patch between the eyes (the point of the triangle directed backward), and three obliquely-placed oval patches of colour, one just back of the eye and the other two on the sides of the body. The triangle between the eyes may be outlined with light colour, either green, reddish, or yellowish, and this light colour is continued in a band from the backward-projecting point of the triangle along the line of the back, to the posterior end of the body. This band of colour is likely to be broad at its anterior and posterior ends and narrow at the middle of the back, in the region just between the two posterior oval colour patches of the sides. These patches of colour on the sides are also usually bordered with light.

The Cricket Frogs breed late, although they are more or less active all winter. Their chorus is loudest in late April and early May, and it is then that the eggs are laid, attached to grass blades or leaves in the water. At this time the Swamp Tree Frog chorus has disbanded and the Pickering's *Hyla* is singing only at night.

The development of this frog is less rapid than that of the Common Tree Frog, the Eastern Wood Frog, or the American Toad. The tadpoles[1] may be found in the water as late as August. The final transformation takes place in September. The young tree frogs — as well as the older ones — seek shelter from the cold under stones and leaves at the margins of their brook or marsh. However, they have no long-continued hibernation, but renew their activity whenever the sun is warm or the south winds blow.

---

[1] The tadpoles of *Acris* may be identified, on close scrutiny, by the following characeristics: The upper lip bears two rows of horny teeth; the lower lip has the same number. The teeth are not notched at their tips. The border of the lower lip is not doubled in at the angles of the mouth.

THE SWAMP TREE FROG[1]
Chorophilus nigritus Le Conte.

IDENTIFICATION CHARACTERISTICS

Colour; Changeable from a colour so dark that it is nearly black, to flesh colour.   When light, the colouration may be bluish or ash grey, fawn colour, or even salmon or red in tone.   Iris golden or copper-coloured.   There is a dark stripe, which begins at the muzzle and extends through the eye and ear, and less conspicuously to the middle of the side of the body or beyond.   This dark colour is bordered below by a light band which extends to a point back of the arm.   The immediate edge of the jaw is dark.   There may be a pattern of dark lines or spots on the back, head, and legs.   This pattern consists typically of the following: 1.   Three longitudinal stripes (or series of spots).   The middle one of the three occupies the midline of the back and may fork posteriorly.   The two others extend backward parallel to this, from the posterior angles of the eyes.   2.   A transverse band between the eyes connected with the median stripe.   3.   Crossbands, or more or less irregular lines of spots, on the hind legs. The underparts are yellowish white.   The throat of the male is greenish yellow.   (See Studies of Chorophilus, Fig. 185.)

Measurements: Size small, i. e. length 1 inch, slightly more or less.   Body relatively long and slender.   Length of head variable.   The greatest length is presented by the Western and

---

[1] *Chorophilus nigritus* Le Conte, *Chorophilus feriarum* Baird, *Chorophilus triseriatus* Wied, Cope, Batrachia of North America.

The *Chorophilus* material is confusing, and insufficient to settle any problems. *Chorophilus nigritus, feriarum,* and *triseriatus* were described originally as distinct species. O. P. Hay, in 1892, called all three one species, making the latter two subspecies of the *nigritus* form (see quotation following).   Dr. Stejneger of the National Museum has identified a subspecies *septentrionalis* well represented by forms from the extreme North.   I have allowed *feriarum, triseriatus,* and *septentrionalis* to stand as subspecies of *nigritus*.   However, the whole subject is in need of investigation and is open to revision.

" Snout acuminate, width of head in length of head and body 2.8 to 3 times; heel reaching in front of orbit; size larger; colour leaden to fawn, with three rows of dark spots above, these sometimes united in continuous bands.   South Carolina to Mississippi." (*Nigritus.*)

" Snout shorter; width of head in length 3–3.25 times; heel reaching to front of orbit; length of body in total length of hind leg from 1.4 to 1.7; colour ash or brownish, eyelids involved in median stripe, three parallel stripes above seldom interrupted.   Eastern United States to Illinois. (*Feriarum.*)

" Snout drawn out; width of head in length 3.5 to 3.6 times; heel reaching only to tympanic disk; length of body in total length of hind leg 1.24 to 1.5 times; colour ash to brown, with three parallel dark stripes, median often forked behind, spot on each eyelid.   New Jersey to New Mexico and Idaho." (*Triseriatus.*) O. P. Hay.   1892.

Northern forms (*triseriatus* and *septentrionalis*), frogs from the South (*nigritus*) have a muzzle considerably drawn out, and those from the East (*feriarum*) are distinguished by relative shortness of the muzzle. Length of legs variable. In the southern and eastern forms (*nigritus* and *feriarum* Baird) the length of the leg to the heel equals or slightly exceeds the total length of head and body. In forms at the extreme North (*septentrionalis*), the legs are unusually short, the length to the heel not equalling the length of body forward to the ear. Those forms intermediate in distribution (*triseriatus*) have a leg measurement between these two.

Structure: Skin of upper parts finely tubercular; underparts granular. The head is narrow and pointed. Nostrils much nearer to the tip of the muzzle than to the eye. Muzzle extends beyond the line of the jaw. Ear small, only one-fourth to one-half the diameter of the eye. Eyes widely separated. Long slender toes scarcely webbed. Disks on fingers and toes very small. Inner and outer sole tubercles small; subarticular tubercles present.

Range: This member of the Hylidæ has the widest distribution of any member of its group in North America. It has been reported from every state, with the exception of those of northern New England, and Arizona, northern New York, Michigan, California, Oregon, and Washington. In Canada it extends quite to the Hudson Bay region.

Pickering's *Hyla* is not the only tree frog that sings in ringing choruses in early spring. In the Southern States the Swamp Tree Frog (Fig. 185) is heard singing in late January and early February, usually before Pickering's *Hyla* has begun peeping. The chorus of the Swamp Tree Frog proceeds from ditches, marshes, and pools, especially in low lands. These tree frogs are partial to temporary pools which are wholly shut in from approach by tangled growths of shrubs and woody vines. From such sheltered, sunny places they sing throughout many of the days, and of course during the night, until late April, when the breeding season is over.

The chorus is not so penetrating as that of the Pickering's *Hyla*, nor has it the ringing sleigh-bell character of the latter. It is soft, relatively low-pitched, and is said to have a soothing sound that swells and recedes " like the waves of the seashore."

However, the chorus is loud enough, so that it is usually attributed to some large frog (*Rana*.) The single call is a somewhat musical rattle that lacks great carrying power. It is not shrill. (The pitch varies with the individual between E above middle C and C above.) There is a slight rise in pitch, an increase in emphasis, and the crepitations are not especially rapid.[1] The call conveys to the mind something of the idea of gentleness and comfort so distinctly given by the trill of the Common Tree Frog. The call is given by the male only; the inflated throat-pouch is large.

The Swamp Tree Frog stays about the marshes throughout the summer and fall. We may sometimes hear the isolated call from marshy land during the hottest part of the summer, but on the whole, the species is rather silent except during the breeding season. These frogs seek refuge in the water when they are disturbed, but are very poor swimmers, and soon come back to the shore or crawl out on some miniature log. They are seldom seen after the spring months, owing to their minute size, their protective colouration, and their silence. They feed upon flies, beetles, and various insects that frequent marshy places.

The Swamp Tree Frog is slender and delicate in appearance. It has great power to change its colour between light and dark shades. It has a colour pattern that not only is variable but has the evanescent character common among the Hylidæ. That is, each tree frog has its own distinctive pattern of dress — we can scarcely find two alike among several dozens caught in the same locality — and in addition to this great variation, the given patterns may be wholly absent at one time, faintly outlined at another and prominently marked a third, all within the space of an hour.

The eggs are laid in shallow water in March or April.[2] They are in small bunches of from five to twenty eggs, and are attached to twigs and grasses in the water. Eggs laid March 22d hatched April 5th. The tadpoles, both at their time of hatching and later, are nearly black in colour. They can be distinguished from those of the Leopard Frog, which hatch at about the same time, by

---

[1] The call is not so loud nor so sharp in quality as that of the Cricket Frog (*Acris*); the crepitations are not so rapid.

[2] March 22, 1888, *Chorophilus triseriatus*. March 20, 1892, *Chorophilus feriarum*. Irvington, Ind. O. P. Hay.

March 13 and 24, 1890; February. 23, 1891. *Chorophilus triseriatus*, Baltimore, Md. T. H. Morgan.

their more slender shape and by the more lateral position of the eyes. By April 20th the legs are budded. The tadpoles are now one-half inch long, are black in colour, finely dotted with gold, and with the underparts very brilliantly copper-tinted.[1]

The final transformations take place from May 26th to June 12th, when the tadpole is slightly over an inch long.[2] The front legs appear, the toes furnished with their small disks. The stripes on the back do not appear until the creatures are actually on the point of leaving the water. Since the feet are so slightly webbed, the young frogs are very poor swimmers and are drowned unless they have opportunity to leave the water.

The young frogs are extremely delicate and timid. They look like the full-grown tree frogs, except that they are only one-half inch in length. They hide at once under convenient leaves, sticks, and stones about their marsh.

The genus *Chorophilus* is not found outside of the American region. It represents a tree frog that has suffered much retrogression in the structures for arboreal and aquatic life. The adhesive disks are ineffective because of their small size, and the toes are scarcely webbed. The species *nigritus* presents great variation in the different parts of the country. So great is the variation that four forms are easily distinguished, namely: *nigritus* Le Conte of the Southeast, *feriarum* Baird of the East, *triseriatus* Wied of the West and Southwest, and *septentrionalis* Stejneger, found at the extreme North, in the middle part of the continent (Manitoba and the Hudson Bay region). *Nigritus* and *feriarum* differ mainly in the relative lengths of the head. The great difference between these two forms and the other two (namely, *triseriatus* and *septentrionalis*) lies in the measurement of the hind legs; those at the South and East have legs that measure the longest, those at the North show an unusually short leg measurement, and *triseriatus* is intermediate in this characteristic.

---

[1] These tadpoles may be identified by a careful examination of the mouth; the upper lip has two rows of teeth, the lower has three. The teeth are notched at their tips. The border of the lower lip is not doubled in at the angles of the mouth.

[2] The main facts of the development are from the account by O. P. Hay (Amer. Nat., vol. 23).

CHOROPHILUS ORNATUS, HOLBROOK[1]

IDENTIFICATION CHARACTERISTICS

Colour : Upper parts olive, or dove-gray, or reddish brown. A black band extends from the end of the muzzle on each side through the eye and the ear, backward to the shoulder, and continues (more or less broken into spots) to the thigh. A light blotch on the side of the head above the dark margin of the jaw. There may or may not be elongated spots of dark brown on the back, a triangular spot between the eyes and smaller spots on sides and posterior back. These dark spots, when present, may or may not be margined with light. Undersurfaces light, unspotted, except for a few flecks of dark on the throat. Small yellow spots on the posterior sides, concealed by the thighs. Posterior femur spotted with yellow.

Measurements: Size small, i. e. length 1¾ inches. Head medium in length; its measurements contained slightly more than three times in total measurement. Leg short; leg measurement to heel equals length of body forward to ear. Tibia not longer than femur.

Structure: Skin smooth above, granulated below, less on throat region. Muzzle rounded, extending slightly beyond the line of the jaw. Canthus rostralis rounded. Ear smaller than eye (half diameter). Arms short and stout. Fingers short, dilatations minute. Foot with short web and a small inner sole tubercle.

Range: Reported from Texas (Helotes and Dallas) and Florida (Green Cove Springs)

This frog is said to live on land, in relatively dry places, such as corn-fields. That it shuns bodies of water except during the breeding season might be judged from the smallness of the webs on its feet.

CHOROPHILUS OCCIDENTALIS, BAIRD AND GIRARD

The description given for *Chorophilus ornatus* Holbrook applies almost equally here, judging from the type specimens in the

---

[1] See *Chorophilus occidentalis.*, p. 161.

National Museum. Cope, in " Batrachia of North America," says, " From the *Chorophilus ornatus* the *Chorophilus occidentalis* differs in colour entirely (it is described as chestnut instead of grey); the head is more acute and the cleft of the mouth deeper; the legs are longer and the granulation finer."[1]

Chorophilus occidentalis is reported from Georgia (Riceborough, Liberty County, Allapaha), Florida (Jacksonville), Mississippi (Bay St. Louis), and Texas (Dallas).

CHOROPHILUS OCULARIS, HOLBROOK

IDENTIFICATION CHARACTERISTICS

Colour: Chestnut-brown, with an obscure dorsal stripe of darker colour. This stripe extends from the end of the muzzle to the posterior back, forking posteriorly. There is a stripe on each side of this, and a more pronounced one below along the side of the head, through the eyes and ears and along the sides. Upper jaw edged with white; the white line extends backward to a point beyond the shoulder. Outer edge of tibia occupied by a light line set off by darker colour above. Below, yellowish, with obscure spots on breast and throat.

Measurements: Size small, i.e. length 1 inch or less. Legs long, length to heel equalling or exceeding the total length of the frog. Tibia longer than femur.

Structure: Skin smooth. Head pointed; eyes large; ear small, less than half diameter of eye.

Range: Specimens are from Charleston, South Carolina.

This species is said to be the smallest among North American *Hylas*. Its unusual characteristics seem to be the pointed jaw, the long legs, and the light line along the outer edge of the tibia. The colour pattern evidently agrees with that of *Chorophilus nigritus*.

These tree frogs are reported to frequent aamp places, such as the vicinity of stagnant pools. They are very active, covering two feet or more at a single leap. The rich brown of the upper surfaces has great metallic lustre.

---

[1] Although these differences are not marked in the type specimens in their present condition, they will have to be relied upon until further investigation is made upon fresh material.

FAMILY V. CYSTIGNATHIDÆ.[1]

LITHODYTES LATRANS, COPE

Identification Characteristics

Colour : Brownish olive or grey, with closely set dark brown spots. Spots rounded, those on the head and anterior and middle back may be elongated transversely. Colour surrounding the elongated spots of the top of the head bright salmon-pink. The bright colour of the middle back extends at right and left on the sides, and is conspicuous also on the elbows, so that there is produced the effect of a pink band across the middle of the back. Many small irregular dark spots on the front and sides of the head; rounded dark spots on the posterior back. One especially conspicuous dark spot under the eye widens downward to the line of the jaw. Arms and legs irregularly barred and spotted with dark. Iris bronze. Underparts greyish white, somewhat spotted along the jaw and on the breast. (See Colour Plate II.)

Measurements: Size relatively large, i. e. length may reach 3½ inches. Head relatively long, its length contained in total length two and a half times. Head wider than long. Leg not long; its length to the heel equals the length of the body forward to the ear or the eye. (Fig. 188.) Tibia as long as femur. Forearm unusually long. (Fig. 187.) Length of fingers in order from the shortest, 2–1–4–3. Length of toes from the shortest, 1–2–5–3–4.

Structure: Smooth everywhere; skin of extremely fine texture. Jaw acuminate rounded; head broad, with large eyes widely separated. (Fig. 188.) Truncate muzzle extends somewhat beyond the line of the jaw. Canthus rostralis prominent; long converging lines extend forward to the end of the muzzle. (Fig. 186.) Nostrils terminal or nearly so. Vomerine teeth oblique, between the large internal nostrils. Pupil horizontal. Ear distinct; vertically oval; large (its horizontal diameter slightly more than half the diameter of the eye); and very near the line of the jaw. Slight fold of skin from eye over ear to shoulder.

---

[1] Refer to pp. 7, 9 and 45.

Legs and arms slender. Fingers and toes long and slender. Two sole tubercles, the outer nearly as large as the inner. Conspicuous smaller tubercles on sole and under joints. Ends of fingers and toes blunt, with T–shaped disks. (See Fig. 186 to 188.)

Range: Found at Helotes, Texas (near San Antonio).

This smooth frog-like batrachian attains a surprisingly large size for one so delicately built. The arms and legs are peculiarly slender, and look out of proportion when seen on a frog three and a half inches long.

In fact, *Lithodytes latrans* is a very curious-looking creature. It rests on hands and feet only, the tarsus and other parts of the legs as well as the body being kept elevated some distance above the ground. If its tracks could be seen, they would show impressions of the soles and long toes, of the palms and long fingers only. It moves about slowly and seriously in this stilted fashion, a grotesque little creature indeed. Its grotesqueness is enhanced by the transversely elongated spots of the back, set in their light pink back- ground like two staring eyes.

This species lives in fissures of the limestone cliffs along the borders of the first plateau region of Texas. The method of proceeding with body elevated, instead of dragged on the ground, is perhaps correlated with its habit of living among the limestone rocks.

It is said to be very noisy after rains. The cry reminds one of a dog's bark, and when several are calling, the noise produced is loud enough to make the rocks resound.

LITHODYTES RICORDII, DUM. AND BIBR.

IDENTIFICATION CHARACTERISTICS

Colour: "Reddish brown. The loreal region, a band between the eyes, one above the tympanum, and some dorsal spots, darker. Beneath, light brownish."

Measurements: Size small, i. e. length little over one inch. Head longer than broad. Leg measurement to heel equals body measurement forward to the eye.

Structure: Skin smooth above and below. Sides roughened.

PLATE LIX

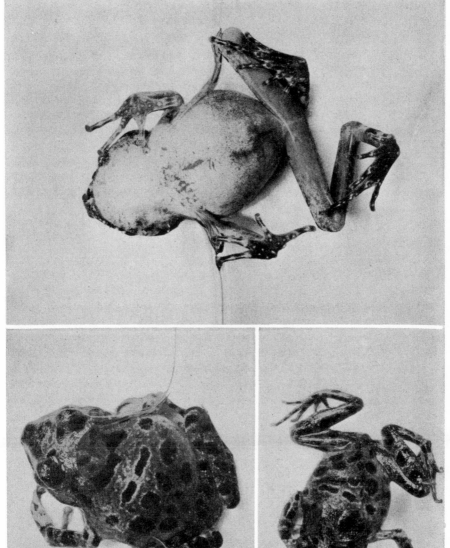

FIGS. 186 and 187.—*Lithodytes latrans* Cope. (Young specimen.) Helotes, Texas. Length 1¼ in. (For coloration see Plate II.)

FIG. 188.—*Lithodytes latrans*. Photographed (in water) to show characteristics of undersurface.

FIGS. 189 to 192 (1 to 4)—The NARROW-MOUTHED TOAD. (*Engystoma carolinense* Holbrook.) Raleigh, N. C. Length 1¼ in. The head is small and pointed. There is a fold of skin across the head back of the eyes. The feet are not webbed. (For coloration see Colour Plate II.)

FIG. 193 (5).—*Engystoma texense* Girard. Brownsville, Texas. Length 1 in. (See page 168.)

Lateral outlines of head curved. Muzzle truncate at end. There is a throat vocal pouch. Ear one-half the diameter of the eye. Sole and palm tubercles, two in number in each case. T-shaped disks at ends of fingers and toes small.

Range: Key West, Florida. A wanderer from Cuba.

SYRROPHUS MARNOCKII, COPE

IDENTIFICATION CHARACTERISTICS.

Colour: "Light purplish-brown, spotted with rather small, closely placed, and broadly defined dark spots. Spots less distinct on the head." Legs light, cross-banded with dark. Posterior femur brown, with a few light spots. Underparts light, unspotted.

Measurements: Size small, i. e. length $1\frac{1}{2}$ inches. Head long. Legs unusually short, length to heel scarcely equalling length of body forward to ear.

Structure: Skin smooth. Head acuminate rounded. Muzzle flat, long in front of the eyes, and projecting slightly beyond the line of the jaw. Space between eyes much greater than width of eyelid. Ear round, about half the diameter of the eye. Arms and legs slender. Fingers and toes blunt at the ends, with moderate sized T-shaped disks. Tubercles under the joints large.

Range: The only specimens known are from Helotes, Texas.

FAMILY VI. ENGYSTOMATIDÆ.[1]

THE NARROW-MOUTHED TOAD

Engystoma carolinense Holbrook

IDENTIFICATION CHARACTERISTICS

Colour: General colour may be black, brown, or grey. Usually the head and two oblique bands extending from the eyes to the posterior part of the body are bright brown (red or orange in tone). These brown bands are bordered with black above. The space on the back between these bands (narrow in front, broad posteriorly) is grey or dull brown, speckled with black. Sides of head, neck and body grey, finely spotted with black. Arms and legs bright brown. Leg crossed by two closely-placed narrow black bands, or spotted irregularly with black. Underparts lighter than sides, although completely sprinkled with small black spots. Throat of male black. (For colouration, see Colour Plate II and Figs. 189 to 192.)

Measurements: Very small, i. e. length of male 1 to 1¼ inches; female somewhat larger. Legs short, tibia slightly longer than femur. (Fig. 190.) Length of leg to heel not exceeding length of body forward to arm insertion.

Structure: Body broad, head pointed, obtuse at the end of the muzzle and extremely small. The upper jaw projects over the lower. The angles of the jaw are under the posterior part of the eye. Skin relatively smooth, or with minute tubercles distributed evenly over head, back, and legs. (Fig. 192.) A fold of skin extends across the head back of the eyes. (Fig. 192.) Eyes small and bead-like. Ear not visible. Arms slender; legs stout. Toes slender, not webbed. Fourth toe conspicuously longer than the others. Inner sole tubercle small; outer lacking. (Fig. 189.) Tubercles under toe and finger-joints relatively conspicuous.

Range: South Carolina, Georgia, and Florida westward to western Texas, northward into Missouri and southern Illinois.[2]

---

[1] Refer to pp. 8, 10 and 48.

[2] Micanopy, Clarcona, Lake Jessup, Little Sarasota Bay, Fla.; Charleston, S. C.; Raleigh, N. C.; Columbus and Riceborough, Ga.; New Madrid, Mo.; Dallas, San Antonio, Houston, Helotes, Fort Concho, and Hitchcock, Tex.

Members of the Salientia, popularly called frogs and toads, look remarkably alike; so much alike, that it requires fine discrimination to distinguish them one from another. *Engystoma carolinense* looks very different from the typical frog or toad. Its tiny head with dark bead-like eyes seems wholly out of proportion to its relatively large, squat body. (Figs. 189 to 192.) At first sight the creature is grotesque. It seems especially so when we take it up in our hands and find that the loose skin of the shoulders and body back of the head-fold pushes forward far over the head, making the creature resemble a turtle for the moment.

Engystoma is very alert and active, and although its legs are short, it is very difficult to catch. It proceeds by short jumps, given in surprisingly rapid succession.

It has been heard in September calling from ditches bordering the streets of Houston and San Antonio, Texas.[1] It has been found under old logs and under leaves in moist places in Florida.[2] At Raleigh, North Carolina, it begins the breeding season in May and continues it until August.[3] During this time it is found in pools of stagnant water, temporary or otherwise. It floats at the surface, with only the tip of its pointed head out of the water, so that on the approach of danger it can disappear beneath without leaving a ripple on the surface.

Engystoma is wholly nocturnal in habit. The *Engystoma* chorus is loudest at the time when the choruses of the American Toad and Spring Peeper (Pickering's *Hyla*) are diminishing somewhat in intensity — when these latter are singing at night only, instead of both day and night. Outside of the breeding season, *Engystoma* is seldom found, although one is occasionally discovered by chance under a dead log or a stone.

The isolated call sounds remarkably like the sound made by an electric buzzer. It is short, unmusical, and is vibrated very rapidly. It has been compared to the song of the American Toad, but when heard near at hand, seems as different as possible. Instead of being a sweet, tremulous note, it is a decided buzz, harsh and metallic in quality. *Engystoma carolinense*, when kept in

---

[1] Bulletin 20, U. S. Nat. Museum. " On the Zoölogical Position of Texas." E. D. Cope, 1880.

[2] Notes on Reptiles and Batrachians Collected in Florida in 1892 and 1893. E. Loennberg. Proc. Nat. Museum, Vol. XVII.
Also N. A. Herpetology, Holbrook.

[3] C. S. Brimley, Raleigh, N. C., 1905.

captivity, sings almost continually. A throat-pouch—which extends backward to a line between the points of the arm insertions—is inflated during the call. The chorus in full swing is said to be much louder than that of the Cricket Frog (*Acris gryllus*) or of the Swamp Tree Frog (*Chorophilus n. feriarum*).

That this batrachian is found in southern Illinois is an interesting fact, as it marks Illinois as part of a southern zoölogical region, very different from other places of the same latitude.

ENGYSTOMA TEXENSE, GIRARD

Engystoma texense Girard

IDENTIFICATION CHARACTERISTICS

Colour: Grey, greenish or brownish, speckled and spotted irregularly with black. Spots show a tendency to arrangement in lines running lengthwise of the back. Tibia crossed by two narrow black bands placed close together. (See Fig. 193.) Underparts covered with light-coloured transparent skin, which shows the dark organs through. Throat and breast obscurely spotted with brown.

Measurements: Size small, i. e. length 1 inch or slightly over. Distance from tip of muzzle to shoulder one-third total length, and greater than corresponding measurement in *Engystoma carolinense*. Legs relatively short. Tibia longer than femur.

Structure: Skin smooth. Fold of skin back of eyes relatively inconspicuous. Canthus rostralis prominent. Three carpal tubercles. Inner sole tubercle small; outer lacking.

Range: Rio Seco, Texas, is the type locality. Also reported from San Diego and Brownsville, Texas.

———

This active little batrachian was found in 1859.[1] It was described by Girard and given the specific name *texense*. Later it was grouped with *Engystoma carolinense* by Cope.[2] It differs from the Carolina *Engystoma* in many respects. It is smooth-skinned, instead of tubercular. It has a narrower and more pointed head, a more slender body, and shorter legs. (See Fig.

[1] Capt. John Pope.

[2] Probably owing to the poor condition of the type specimen in the National Museum.

193.) The distance from the tip of the muzzle to the shoulder is proportionately greater than in *Engystoma carolinense.* The canthus rostralis is more prominent. The colouration is dull greenish or gray, instead of warm shades of brown.

Engystoma texense was found during late June, 1905, in relatively large numbers at Brownsville, Texas. It was breeding in the same pools with *Scaphiopus couchii* and *Hypopachus cuneus.*

HYPOPACHUS CUNEUS, COPE

IDENTIFICATION CHARACTERISTICS

Colour: Brown, of greenish, yellowish, or greyish tone. There may be a broad band of brighter brown extending from the eye backward. This oblique band is bordered above and below by wavy lines of black. There is a black line below the angle of the canthus rostralis. A white band bordered with black passes obliquely downward from under the eye to a point in front of and below the arm insertion. There is much bright dark red on the femur, and some touches of it on the tibia, and on the body where it lies against the femur. Many black spots at the posterior end of the body and along the concealed part of the femur. Legs banded with black. (There are usually two bands placed close together.) An orange-yellow or white thread line along the middle of the back from the muzzle to the posterior end of the body. The lower sides are grey. The underparts are light, obscurely mottled with dark. Throat closely speckled with black. (For colouration, see Colour Plate II and Figs. 194 to 196.)

Measurements: Size small, i. e. length of female $1\frac{1}{2}$ inches, male smaller. Head small and short, its length (to fold) contained about eight times in total length. Legs short; length to heel equals length of body forward to the shoulder.

Structure: Body large and squat. Fold across head behind the eyes conspicuous, as is also the one from the eye to the shoulder. There is a fold across the breast from arm to arm. Ear not visible. Skin smooth, loose, and leathery on the back. The toes and fingers are slender. Feet with very short webs. (Fig. 195.) Tubercles under joints of toes prominent. Inner and outer sole tubercles large, each with a cutting edge.

169

Range: As far as known, reported only from San Diego and Brownsville, Texas. Abundant where found.

———————

Hypopachus cuneus is a bright-coloured, alert little batrachian that must be much more widely distributed than is known at present. At Brownsville, it has been found in shallow water in late June after heavy rains, at the same time that *Scaphiopus couchii* came from its underground burrow to deposit its eggs. Whenever this batrachian has been found, it has been in abundance, so that there was no difficulty in catching dozens of the diminutive creatures.

The skin of the back is loose and leathery, so that it can be thrust in a fold far forward, making the head look like a turtle's pointed head protruding from its shell. This frog shows a pattern of yellowish or whitish thread lines, corresponding exactly to the lines along which the skin naturally splits during the moulting. Not only is there the line along the middle of the head and back but there is a similar one along the midline of the ventral surface from the lower jaw to a point of meeting posteriorly with the line of the back. Branches from this main line extend along the middle of the posterior face of the femur to the tibia, along the back edge of the tibia to the heel, over this and out on the foot to a point just above the sole tubercles, where it is lost to the naked eye. There are also two branches opposite each other on the breast; they extend outward and forward to the humerus, thence out along the humerus and lower arm on to the hand. These lines may be obscure or very conspicuous. (Fig. 196.)

The habits and life history of *Hypopachus cuneus* are not on record.

PLATE LXI

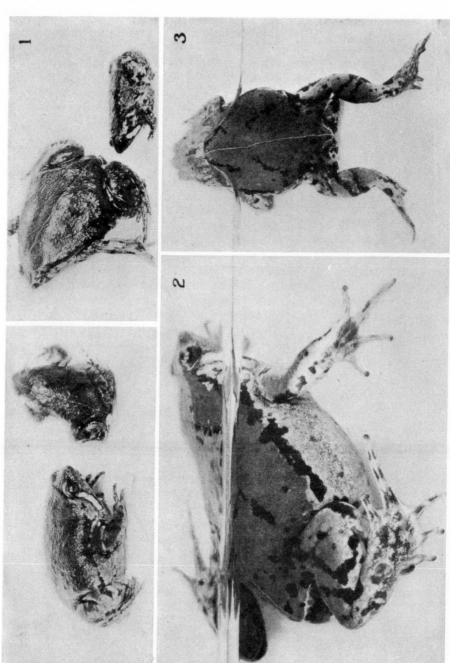

FIG. 194 (1 and 4).—*Hypopachus cuneus* Cope. Brownsville, Texas. Length 1½ in. (For coloration see Colour Plate II.) This diminutive creature has a fat squat body, a pointed head and a fold of skin on the top of the head back of the eyes. The males are much smaller than the females.

FIG. 195 (2).—Enlarged (in water) to show structure of foot and hand.

FIG. 196 (3).—To show the white vertebral streak and the arrangement of spots and bands of black on the upper surface.

The LEOPARD FROG lives in meadows and fields adjacent to brooks and marshes

FAMILY VII. RANIDÆ.[1]

THE COMMON LEOPARD FROG[2]

Rana pipiens Shreber[3]

IDENTIFICATION CHARACTERISTICS

Colour: Green, grey or brown, with somewhat rapid change from one colour to the other. Two irregular rows of rounded dark spots between the yellowish or bronze lateral folds. Two still more irregular rows of spots below the lateral folds on each side. Spots usually bordered conspicuously with lighter colour. Brown bands or disconnected spots on the legs. The underparts are white, possibly yellowish. (See Colour Plates XI and XII.)

Measurements: Size medium to large, i. e. male $3\frac{1}{2}$ inches; female larger. Body relatively slender. Head more or less pointed, its length contained in whole length of frog from three to three and a half times. Legs long, length to heel equal to length of head and body. Ear round, about two-thirds as large as eye.

Structure: Skin relatively smooth or somewhat tubercular. Line from nostril to eye prominent. Broad, flattened lateral folds are conspicuous. Two (or four) more or less broken folds of skin extend lengthwise along the back between the lateral folds. (Fig. 217.) Webs deeply indented. Tubercles under joints of toes rather prominent. Inner sole tubercle small; no outer tubercle. (Fig. 198.)

---

[1] Refer to pp. ° 11 and 48.

[2] The Leopard Frog is called "Spring Frog" in Florida and "Grass Frog" in New York.

[3] *Rana pipiens* Shreber is *Rana virescens* Kalm (Cope) and *Rana virescens brachycephala* Cope ("Batrachia of North America "). It has not been possible, in living material obtained from New England, New York, Michigan, Minnesota, Wisconsin, Colorado, Texas, and Arizona, to make a distinction into these subspecies. The variation of the frogs is remarkable, but no fundamental characteristic (such as proportionate length of head and body, leg measurement, etc.) remains stable when a large series of frogs from adjoining districts are examined. Eastern specimens are likely to be green or brown, Southern and Western specimens are more often grey. Eastern frogs, especially those that frequent the salt marshes of the coast, are more smooth-skinned and slender, and on the whole, more delicately moulded, while Southern and Western specimens are much more robust in build, have a rougher skin, and attain a larger size. The material is very confusing. With a smaller series, the subspecies might have been granted. With a still more complete series, it is possible that two or three intergrading varieties of the species *Pipiens* could be recognized. Much systematic study of such a series of frogs, combined with knowledge of their habits and life histories, could alone produce any definite conclusion in the matter.

Range: The Leopard Frog is the most common frog in North America, east of the Sierra Nevada Mountains. It is well-known in Florida; it is the edible frog in Texas; it is the only frog found between the eastern part of the Great Plains and the Sierra Nevada Mountains.

———————

The Leopard Frog is one of the most beautiful in colouring of all our common frogs. It is better known than others, not only because of its wider distribution and greater numbers, but because it has the habit of going considerable distances from its pond, or marsh. It is the frog met with when we walk across country, through fields and orchards. As we wander slowly through the meadow these frogs leap out from underfoot. They make long, low leaps, seldom appearing above the clovers and grasses. They are not satisfied with one jump for safety, but give three or four in succession, each probably in a somewhat different direction.

If we walk still more slowly and watch very carefully, we are likely to catch a glimpse of a spotted back and of squirted water as an especially large one makes a flying leap. If we try to catch a large one and meet with any success, we discover that this habit of squirting water — as though into the face of an enemy — may sometimes result in protection to the frog, since the water is disagreeable in odour.

Our greatest effort, however, comes in keeping a Leopard Frog, after the chase is over and when we have him in our very grasp. The slippery skin, the slender body, and strong hind legs serve him in just such emergencies. He gives most unexpected and vigorous jerks of the body to free himself. However, if he finds his efforts unavailing, and feels a firm hand about the posterior part of his body and the strong thighs, he stops struggling and begins to expostulate in a very decided but musical voice. We watch and listen in astonishment and admiration. Who knew that a frog could talk in so charming a fashion? Indeed, the sound is so musical, that we might almost say he sings. The vocal pouches swell into rounded projections behind and under the ears; they distend and collapse alternately as the musical notes are uttered.

The vocal pouches are elongated in shape, extending obliquely

172

above the arm.   They start from a point somewhat below the jaw in front, and extend upward on the sides of the frog, nearly or quite to the lateral fold.   (See Fig. 9, p. 20).   When the pouch collapses, the skin is left wrinkled and baggy in the given region. (Colour Plate XI, male   frog.)   The glandular band extending backward over the shoulder, marks the margin of a loose, drooping fold of skin.   The sound produced is a soft guttural in quality, low-pitched (about E, an octave below E of the first line), and vibrant,

The female has a voice, also, but it is less loud and vigorous. There is no distention of skin over the arm region.

The Leopard Frog makes a most interesting pet to keep for a few days in a small moss-garden enclosed with wire.   He is very handsome and alert-looking.   He eats worms and insects of all kinds.   He will not take fish or other food from under water.   It is reported that the Leopard Frog sometimes eats snails.   He sings vigorously whenever handled, but, more curious still, he sings in low purring tones when water is poured gently on his back.   He evidently likes it, and gives the same response that the cat gives when its fur is stroked.

The Leopard Frog (Fig. 197) is generally between three and four inches in length.   The white throat is in constant rhythmic motion.   The frog breathes just as the toad[1] does, though less rapidly.   The usual colour of the Leopard Frog of the eastern United States is metallic green above and pearly white below, sometimes becoming yellowish on the posterior portion.   There are two prominent bronze or yellow folds of skin extending almost parallel to each other from the eyes to the posterior end of the body. (Figs. 197, 212, and 217.)   Between the lateral folds are two rows of rounded olive-green or brown spots, each circled by a narrow line of yellow or white.   Below the folds along each side of the body there are two irregular rows of similar spots.   There is a dark spot above each eye, and there may be a dark spot in front of the eyes.   (Figs. 200 and 217.)   The eye itself is medium in size, with a wide orange-gold iris and a black pupil.   A prominent black band passes lengthwise through the iris.   There is a yellow or bronze stripe, which passes from the end of the muzzle to the shoulder, and another shorter one from the nostril to the eye. The upper jaw, which protrudes over the lower, is white, bordered

---

[1] For breathing of the toad, see p. 76.

above by black (which may be broken into spots). The black, in turn, has above it a yellowish glandular fold, which extends backward to the shoulder. There are two well-marked folds of skin between the bright-coloured lateral folds. There may be three or four dark cross-bands on the thigh, that are continuous (when the leg is folded) with similar bands on the lower leg and foot.

This description of colour is generally true, although there is often great divergence from it. As we walk across the meadows or skirt the marshes in August, hearing the summer song of the meadow-grasshoppers in the tall sedges and grasses, we can scarcely find two Leopard Frogs that look alike in details. The variation in the colour and pattern of their dress is pronounced.

The ground colour may be brown, or light grey, or green, either light and metallic or very dark. The space between the lateral folds may be green and the space below brown. The folds may be light golden-yellow or dark bronze. The spots may be ringed with green when the background is brown. The greatest variety appears in the spots and their arrangement. They may be small and round, or larger and irregular. They may be in two distinct rows, or sometimes in three, or even grown together so as to form irregular cross-bands between the lateral folds. We may find a frog that has the spots of one row distinct and those of the others so blended as to form a band running lengthwise along the back. There may or may not be a spot on the end of the muzzle in front of the eyes. The spots on the sides may encroach on the lateral folds. Finally, the cross-bands on the thigh may be incomplete or broken into irregular spots. There is likely to be an irregular black band extending upward on the lower arm from the base of the fifth finger. There may be a similar black band on the sole of the foot from the fourth and fifth toes to the heel. The female usually has some grey or brown on the under surface. The colour of the iris changes under different light conditions. In hibernation, the orange-gold becomes darker and darker until the iris can scarcely be distinguished from the black pupil, but under the influence of strong light the bright metallic colour returns.

The frog shown at the left in Fig. 197 is a typical specimen. This frog is one that was found at the bottom of the fifteen-foot entrance of a drive-well. It was impossible to tell how long he had been a prisoner, but something had tamed the poor creature remarkably. He was grateful for any attention in the way of worms or grasshoppers, and sang and talked most confidingly when taken in the hand or when showered with water. Soon after being taken from his prison, and before he had been released to the good hunting-fields near at hand, he moulted the skin. The process is exactly like that described for the toad (pp. 73-75). The frog sits up very high, with his back greatly humped. After the skin is split along the back of the head, he uses the front feet to get it from over the eyes, with movements like those of a cat when washing over its ears. He looks especially ludicrous when removing the hind legs from their sheathing coats, because of the length of the legs. They are drawn forward and then stretched back again and again during the process.

The Leopard Frogs are among the first of our frogs to come from their hibernation in the spring.[1] The eggs are usually laid in March.[2] The shallow water of marshes and of pond and lake margins resounds with their voices during the latter half of March and in early April, just when the bluebirds are deciding which cozy hole in the old apple-tree will make the best home for a family. Even when at the height of its power, the individual voice is not loud, although it is musical. The voice defies description in terms of familiar sounds. It has lately been described as a " characteristic snoring croak or rattle."

Let us go to the marsh or pond in late March or early April. It is a warm, sunny forenoon. The maroon hoods and grey, pointed leaf-buds of the skunk-cabbage are picturesque among

The maroon hoods of the skunk-cabbage are picturesque among moss and dead leaves at the time when the eggs of the Leopard Frog are laid.

[1] The wood frogs are likely to precede them.
[2] March 25, April 5, 1890. *R. virescens*. T. H. Morgan, Baltimore, Md.
March 22, April 1, 1897. *R. virescens*. R. G. Harrison.
" The Leopard Frog breeds in March." C. S. Brimley, Raleigh, N. C.

the moss and dead leaves. The water presents a rather desolate expanse, for it is too early for the appearance of much green. All seems silent as we approach. We walk on the firm foundation made by tangled sweet flag roots until we are at the very edge of the water. As we listen and watch, low, moaning, or grunting sounds proceed from everywhere about us. The pond is filled with Leopard Frogs. We can see their heads, with the bright eyes and distended ear-like vocal pouches protruding above the water. It is impossible to make one hear these talking voices unless he is already familiar with them. To say that the sound is low-pitched, throaty, and vibrant does not bring it to one's ears. The sounds are produced both by the male and by the female. Either will make the sounds when taken into the hand.

The eggs are laid in masses in the shallow water. They may be attached to sticks and grasses or left free in the water. Those drawn and described were laid on the morning of April 9th by a frog brought from the pond two days previous. They were attached to a fern leaf that bent over the water. The whole laying was in one mass about five inches in diameter and two and a half inches thick, which contained between five thousand and six thousand eggs. Each egg is very small ($1\frac{1}{2}$ mm. in diameter) and velvety black in colour. The eggs are so close together that the entire mass is dark-coloured, notwithstanding the fact that each is surrounded by a perfectly transparent sphere of gelatinous substance — (see Figs. 246 and 247)— three concentric spheres, in fact. This substance is so transparent that it does not prevent our watching the process of development. If we look closely at the eggs, we discover that they are black above only, and that the lower side — about one-third of the entire surface — is creamy white in colour. The egg contains not only the germ of the future frog, but yolk for its growth. The white lower part of the egg consists wholly of this food yolk.

Development begins within two or three hours after the eggs are laid. To the naked eye the change seems slight for the first two days. It begins by the egg becoming slightly larger. The black spreads until the visible white portion becomes no larger than a pin-point. However, if we increase the power of our eyes ever so little by the use of a magnifying-glass of any

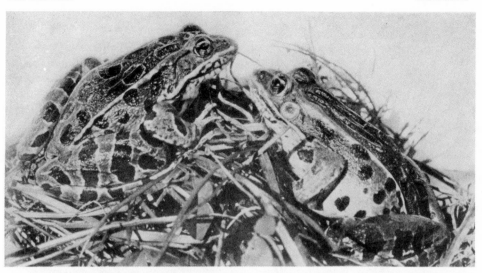

FIG. 197.—LEOPARD FROGS (*Rana pipiens* Shreber). The left is from Minnesota, the right from Michigan,

FIG. 198.—Structure study of foot and hand of *Rana pipiens* Shreber. Ithaca, N. Y.

FIG. 199.—YOUNG LEOPARD FROGS in July. The first has the typical spotted dress. The second is bronze with a few spots on the legs. The third is metallic green and unspotted. White Bear Lake, Minnesota.

FIG. 200.—The COMMON LEOPARD FROG is wild when young; alert, active and strong when fullgrown. In Texas it attains a larger size than does this species in other parts of North America. The lateral folds are conspicuous; the skin may be rough with elongated warts.

FIG. 201.—The COMMON LEOPARD FROG (*Rana pipiens* Shreber). Brownsville, Texas. Length 4¾ in. Light greyish brown with dark brown spots.

kind, we can see something more of the marvellous changes that have begun and will continue from the vital force of the life within until the egg has become a frog in miniature. If we examine the eggs with a lens very soon after they are laid, we can see that a groove appears in the midline at the top of each. It increases in length until it encircles the egg. The partition of which this is the external evidence divides the egg into two equal parts. (Fig. 202.) Many scientists believe that these correspond to what will be the right and the left side of the young frog. This groove is visible to the naked eye, though somewhat difficult to see. A second groove appears at right angles to the first and rapidly encircles the egg until the latter is divided into four nearly equal parts. (Fig. 203.) The next division is made by a horizontal partition instead of a vertical. This partition and its external groove are somewhat above the centre of the egg, so that the upper portion is smaller than the lower. From this time on the division is more rapid and more irregular. It is possible to follow it somewhat farther with just a hand-lens, but soon the parts (cells) become too small and too many to be distinguished. (Fig. 204.)

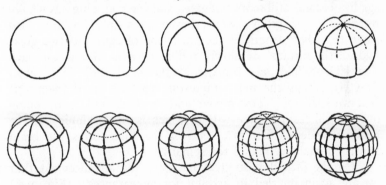

Fig. 204. Series of diagrams to show cleavage of the frog's egg. The second very nearly corresponds to Fig. 202. The third represents Fig. 203. The last is a stage just preceding that of Fig. 205, in which the cells are too small to be seen. (After Ecker.)

If we look carefully at the eggs on the afternoon of the second day after they are laid, we shall see a dark line of crescent shape on one side, just below the middle (equator). (Fig. 205.) Twelve hours later the crescent has become a circle. The black surface of the egg seems to have spread quite to the edges of this circle. The circle encloses a mass of white yolk, which protrudes like a small cushion.[1] (Fig. 206, A.) Throughout the development, our knowledge will be limited to what we can see on the outside. We can know very little, or nothing, about the rapid and wonderful happenings within. However, certain external changes will indicate internal conditions. This circle with its protruding plug of yolk is the external sign of a splitting or separation between cells, which is the beginning of the formation of the digestive tract. This digestive tract begins forming at its posterior instead of at its head end, therefore this yolk-plug marks a point very near the posterior end of the young frog.

Before the third day is over, the eggs have become elongated and on many of them a visible groove is being formed lengthwise along the top. (Fig. 206, B.) This groove marks the back of the developing frog; so that now we know which is to be the head and which the tail end, and which is the right and which is the left side.

By the fourth day, the eggs are greatly changed. The egg has become still more elongated and the yolk-plug has wholly retreated. The groove which began so simply has extended along the whole length of the back (top of egg) and two great folds of the surface are slowly rolling in over it, one on each side. These folds are broader at the head end. (Fig. 207.) This is perhaps the most interesting part of the development that we shall see. This groove and the folds which are rolling over it will form a tube within, which is the beginning of the nervous system. The head end of the tube forms the brain and the remainder makes the spinal cord.

On the fifth day, so great has been the advancement that we are again puzzled to account for appearances. (Fig. 208.) The elongation is still greater, and head and tail ends are curved somewhat to one side. The line of the back is nearly straight, the yolk side (front) is very convex. The nerve-tube seems to be wholly closed in, but the folds still persist to a certain extent over the head and along the back. The projection which is to form the tail is very apparent.

---

[1] For technicalities concerning the formation of the blastopore and its subsequent history, see Bibliography, pp. 241-250.

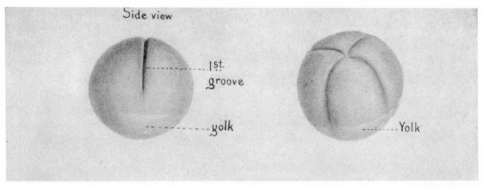

FIG. 202.—April 9, 1902. LEOPARD FROG'S EGG, greatly magnified. The upper portion is black; the lower in cream-white. The first vertical partition is forming. [Providence, R. I.]

FIG. 203.—Drawn to show first two vertical grooves corresponding to two partitions which divide the egg into four cells. (Egg tipped to show top.)

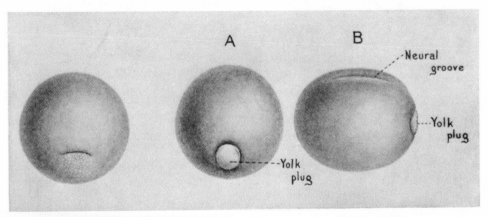

FIG. 205.—The cells are too small to be seen. A dark line of crescent shape appears on one side of the egg.

FIG. 206, A.—Morning of third day (April 11th). Egg drawn from posterior end. All of the yolk except a mere plug is covered by the dark living portion of the egg.

B.—Afternoon of the third day. Egg as seen from left side. Yolk-plug marks posterior end of embryo. Neural groove forming along the back.

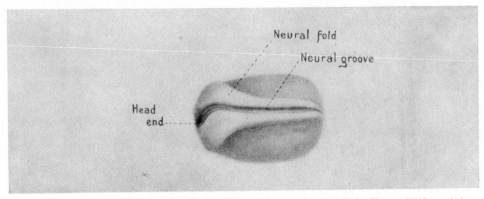

FIG. 207.—April 12th. Drawn from left side (as B, Fig. 206) but tipped to show back. The neural folds are closing in over the neural groove to form the nerve tube. The anterior of this will make the brain, the remainder will be the spinal cord.

PLATE LXVI

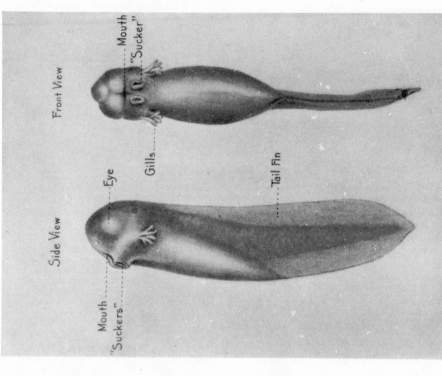

FIG. 210.—LEOPARD FROG TADPOLES, just hatched. April 17, 1902. Eggs laid April 9th. The tadpoles are black and measure 7¾ mm. in length.

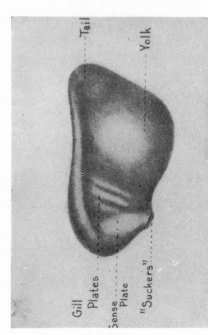

FIG. 208.—Afternoon of April 13th.—Fifth day of development. Embryo in same position as in figures 206, B, and 207.

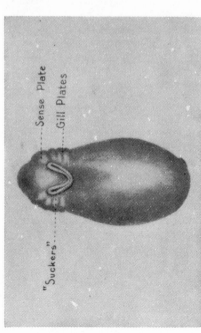

FIG. 209.—Frog embryo of figure 208 seen from the under or ventral surface.

If we now look at the embryo from above or below, the region of head and neck shows slight projections. (Fig. 209.) Examining these very carefully from the side, we see the appearance shown in Fig. 208. That portion in the most anterior and largest projection or swelling (sense plate), will become the facial part of the head, with upper and lower jaws, mouth, and nostrils. The three smaller elevated portions back of this are destined to make the gills. There is a blunt projection on the lower portion of the head end, which, on account of its position (the front margin of the sense plate), might be mistaken for a mouth. Viewed from the front (Fig. 209), it becomes one side of a horseshoe-shaped structure which will make, not the mouth, but a pair of " suckers," to be used by the tadpole to attach itself to water-weeds.

On the sixth day (April 14th) the young tadpoles are still longer and are more curved in the egg. The body seems much thinner. The head and tail ends are unmistakable, even to the casual observer. The projections on the sides of the neck are more distinct.

On the seventh day the tail is longer and distinctly finned at its edges. The head is more distinct from the body. The projections at the sides of the neck are longer. The tadpoles occasionally move in the egg, putting the head and the tail together and then jerking them apart. They seem little changed on the following day but move more often.

On the next morning (April 17th), nine days after the eggs were laid, we find most of the tadpoles out of the jelly, clinging by two conspicuous " suckers " to the deserted jelly-mass or to water-weeds. (Fig. 210.) These " suckers " are not what their name would seem to imply. They do their work of clinging, not by suction, but by means of a sticky substance or cement which they secrete. The jelly is much less stiff. Other tadpoles hatch as we watch: a vigorous wriggle, and the jelly sphere is ruptured and the tadpole becomes free. The tiny bit of life may lie flat on the jelly or at the bottom. But after a short time it is rested from the exertion and wiggles through the water aimlessly until it touches something that will act as a support. The tadpole is now about $7\frac{3}{4}$ mm. long, very slender and black. The transparent tail fin is conspicuous. The projections at the sides of the neck are easily seen as branched finger-like gills

179

that have grown out from the gill plates formed five days ago. If we examine the tadpole carefully with a lens, not only can gills and suckers be seen, but prominences that are to become the eyes (Fig. 210, side view), and an opening just forward of the suckers that is to be the mouth (Fig. 210, front view).

The low power of the compound microscope used now to examine the outside of the tadpole shows us many wonderful things. The blood is flowing in the gills. The current is easily traced out to the end of each finger-like extension and back again. The movement is in jerks or pulses, which are ryhthmic, corresponding to the pumping action of the heart. If we look still more closely, the current is seen to consist of minute circular bodies (blood corpuscles) that chase each other in most irregular fashion in a colourless liquid (blood plasma).

However, as we look at the blood movement, another motion catches our attention. There is a general wave-like motion of the water over the body of the tadpole in the direction of the tail. Careful examination reveals the presence of a coat of minute hairs (cilia) that are in continual motion, and so create this movement of the water. Cilia appear along the back of the embryo at the time of the formation of the nerve tube. They increase in number as development goes on, until the whole body is covered with them and strong currents of water constantly wash the surface of the tadpole from the head backwards. The most rapid streams flow over the back and in the region of the gills. This movement of the cilia, with the resulting circulation of water, aids the young tadpole in the process of respiration before the gills are formed. After the gills are well developed, the cilia are reduced in number so that they do not cover the whole body; they now serve mainly to bring fresh currents of water to the gills.

On the tenth day all the tadpoles are out of the eggs. They hang quietly from water-weed or other support, or circle about with vigorous wigglings of the tail whenever they are disturbed. The head becomes larger. This is due to backward growing folds on the side of the head. It is easy to see that the folds have progressed quite to the roots of the gills. (Fig. 211, April 18th.) On the eleventh day they have grown still farther back and have united underneath the throat. The tadpole is now 9 mm. long, the increase in length being mainly confined to the tail. On the

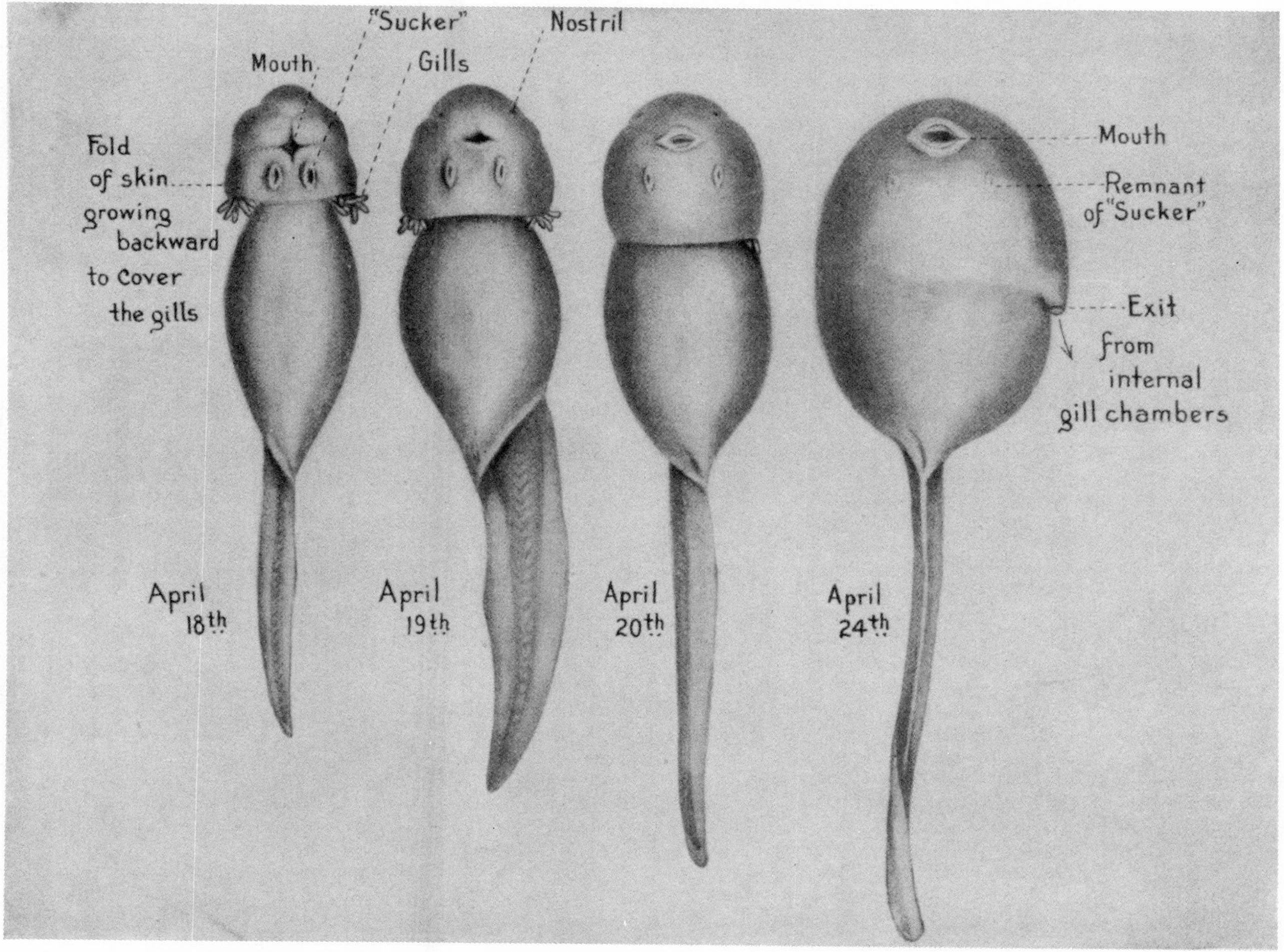

FIG. 211.—TADPOLES of the LEOPARD FROG. Providence, R. I. The ventral surfaces are drawn to show the growth of the membrane that eventually covers the external gills. The drawings also show changes in the mouth, and the reduction of the "suckers". (Greatly enlarged.)

PLATE LXVIII

Fig. 212.—The LEOPARD FROG protected by resemblance to grass and clover. (*Rana pipiens* Shreber. Male. Grand Rapids, Mich.)

Early July. The border of the pond where the young Leopard Frogs develop among the pickerel weeds and water lilies.

twelfth day the gills are entirely covered, except the very tip ends of two or three branches on the left side. (Fig. 211, April 20th.)

For two or three days from this time there is little visible change. The tadpoles (as black as toad tadpoles at the same age) remain clinging to convenient supports by the suckers, now greatly reduced in size. They sometimes start out on aimless circling trips, but, on the whole, are not very active. The body is now increasing greatly in diameter. This increase in diameter is due partly to the development of special organs within. Through the skin of the under side of the body can be seen the intestine, spirally coiled like a watch-spring. This increase is due also to the fold which covered the gills growing much farther back on the body. Here it has united with the body wall on sides and front, except for a small space on the left, where the tips of the gills were last visible. It remains unattached at this point all during the tadpole life. Thus is formed a spout for the exit of water (Fig. 211, April 24th) from the internal gills, which replace the external gills that we saw covered.[1]

When we look at the tadpoles on the morning of April 24th (sixteen days after the eggs were laid), we realize that the mouths are open. Hungry tadpoles are swimming rapidly, instead of aimlessly as before, and are nibbling the delicate ends of water-weeds or vigorously scraping the green slime from the stones and sticks at the bottom.[2] They are no longer jet-black, but are made to look dark brown because of a fine mottling of gold spots on the black.

Their life for the next few weeks seems to have only four needs: to swim rapidly, to eat almost constantly, to rest a little sometimes, and to grow. Their enemies are many, and their ranks are greatly thinned by them. It will be fortunate if they escape the monstrous sucking jaws of the water-tiger.[3] They glide up to nibble the end of a green stem, and the stem comes to life and sends out a powerful arm equipped with jaws that hold as in a vice, while smaller jaws[4] rapidly eat every part of the tadpole, except, perhaps, the long coiled intestine. An unsuspecting tadpole

---

[1] See Bullfrog, p. 236.

[2] The mouth structure of the Leopard Frog tadpole corresponds with that of the Bullfrog tadpole. (See footnote, p. 235.)

[3] The water-tigers are larvæ of the diving-beetles (Dytiscidæ).

[4] The larva of a dragon-fly (Libellulidæ).

approaches an inoffensive-looking brown stem, only to find it a house from which the owner[1] rushes with legs that grasp tightly and jaws that bite. The curious back-swimmer[2] pounces upon them and sucks their blood. There is small chance of escape from the jaws of the diving-beetle,[3] or from the sucking beak of the giant water-bug.[4] The undulating leech gets a deadly

A narrow escape from the jaws of the water-tiger

hold upon them while they rest. They are eaten by fish and turtles, by water-birds, and by their own kin.

What are apparently green stems come to life and send out powerful arms to capture the tadpoles.

[1] Caddis-worm, larva of a caddis-fly (Phryganeidæ). [2] Notonecta. [3] Dytiscus. Belostoma.

In early May, those that have lived through all these dangers are more than an inch long. The tail with its broad transparent fin is nearly twice as long as the rest of the creature. Soon the hind legs bud out and develop; the front legs appear; the mouth and eyes are transformed into those of a frog; the tail is absorbed.

In July and August the marshy borders of the lakes and ponds in which the Leopard Frogs breed are swarming with small

The back-swimmer is a powerful enemy of young tadpoles.

frogs. (Fig. 199.) Their home is in the shallow water among water-lilies and pickerel-weeds, or farther in, where sedges, grasses, and willows grow. They wander over the sand of miniature beaches or over the adjacent grassy places, in search of the small insect life they feed upon. Let any disturbance come and they rush for the water — three or four enormous low leaps, one after the other, and they disappear under the water with a splash so slight as scarcely to ruffle the surface enough to show where they are. We may look with great care, but we cannot find them. They hide at the roots of grasses or in the water-weeds, keeping under cover until we are tired and give up the search.

We can find many of them in wet meadows and in the long grass about wells, much farther from the water. They are active hunters, greedily eating spiders, beetles, crickets, grasshoppers, and other small creatures of the ground. Feed one of them with the young grasshoppers[1] that are so thick in the clover and grasses. He swallows them one after another — in fact, just as rapidly as he can dispose of the long spiny legs, which still stick out of his mouth after the body of the grasshopper is well swallowed. He will succeed in eating eight or more in a very few minutes, the look of satisfaction in his eyes increasing as his sides grow plumper.

Young Leopard Frogs are "aristocratic-looking." They seem especially long-nosed and slender. They show the greatest variety in dress. The lateral folds are rich yellow or bronze, as is also the line from the end of the muzzle to the shoulder. The spots are darkest at the edges,

Late March. The Leopard Frogs are croaking in the pond when the blue-birds are deciding on a home.

and are sometimes not yellow-rimmed as they are in the adults. Some are brown or tan in colour; others are green. And, strangest of all, a few of them have no spots at all. (Fig. 199.) Of these, some are metallic green on head, back, and legs, with sides strongly marked by golden longitudinal folds, but with no spot anywhere. Others are plain brown in colour, almost metallic enough to be called bronze, and have the same yellow lateral folds. These are more beautiful than the spotted ones. Some that have plain colour on head and body show irregular spots on the legs and arms.[2]

---

[1] Acrididæ, or short-horned grasshoppers.
[2] Much search has not revealed adults in this dress.

The boys who catch the young frogs to sell as bait to fishermen call the plain ones "policemen," the plain but brilliant colour and the metallic stripes giving, perhaps, the appearance of a uniform.

The young Leopard Frogs are sacrificed in hundreds and thousands as bait, wherever bass and pickerel fishing is carried on. Each boatman about the small lakes of the Middle West keeps a great wooden box containing hundreds of the little frogs, who desperately jump or climb, only to fall back captives. Boys search the lake margins, the marshes, and the meadows, and put their captives into bags or pails. They are paid perhaps five cents per dozen for them. When the frogs become more scarce, the price may be as high as twenty-five cents per dozen.

In the meantime the country about is overrun with grasshoppers to such an extent that it is difficult to grow even morning-glory vines about the houses. Nature's supply should not be so overwhelmingly drawn upon, but, as in all similar cases, the creature for which the demand is so great should be bred for the purpose. (See foot note p. 234.)

July. The Leopard Frogs eat the young grasshoppers that are so thick in the grass.

185

THE SOUTHERN LEOPARD FROG

Rana sphenocephala Cope [1]

IDENTIFICATION CHARACTERISTICS

Colour: Green or brown, but more often a combination of the two, with one colour abruptly invading the other in irregular fashion. (See Colour Plate XII.) Sometimes grey or fawn colour. Green or brown spots (small, irregular, or rounded), arranged in two irregular rows between the lateral folds, and still more irregularly on the sides. Spots usually not surrounded by light rings. Lateral folds light green, golden, or bronze. This colour of the lateral folds continues forward over the eye and along the canthus rostralis to the end of the muzzle. Also light metallic lines along the jaw from the shoulder to the end of the muzzle. These four converging colour lines meet in acute angles at the end of the muzzle. Eye golden or bronze, with a dark line through it. Ear bronze, with a white circular spot at its centre (not an irregular blotch, such as may be present in *Rana pipiens*. (Fig. 215.) Upper and lower lips dark, conspicuously spotted with white. Legs barred or spotted. (These bands or spots may be edged with light.) (Fig. 214.) Arms conspicuously spotted. Usually a dark band on the front of the humerus; also on the front of the femur (Figs. 215 and 220.) Concealed part of femur dark in colour, with yellow or white spots or reticulations. Underparts glistening white, yellow posteriorly. The throat and breast may be distinctly or obscurely mottled with brown. Whole frog iridescent.

Measurements: Size medium, i.e. $2\frac{1}{2}$ to $3\frac{1}{2}$ inches. Head long, its length contained two and a half times in the total length of head and body. (Figs. 219 and 220.) Leg long, its length to the heel exceeding the length of the body forward to the end of the muzzle. (Fig. 213.) Tibia much longer than femur.

Structure: Skin relatively smooth, very finely tubercular on back, sides, and tibiæ. Tibia may be ridged lengthwise. More or less unbroken lengthwise folds of skin — four in number— between the prominent lateral folds. (Figs. 214 and 220.) Glandular fold along jaw to shoulder. Head narrow, pointed.

---

[1] *Rana virescens sphenocephala* Cope.

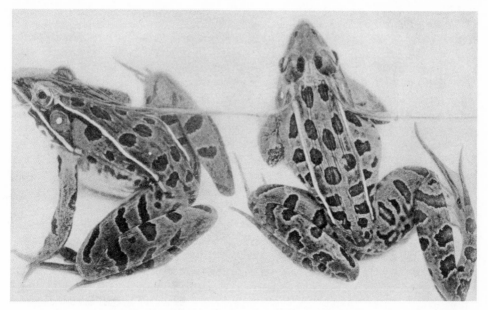

FIGS 213 and 214.—The SOUTHERN LEOPARD FROG (*Rana sphenocephala* Cope). The frog at the left is from Hitchcock. Texas ; the right from Ozona, Florida. Metallic green, brown or fawn color. A most beautiful frog in life, and extremely active.

FIGS 215 and 216.—*Rana sphenocephala* from Seven Oaks, Florida, at the left *Rana pipiens* from Providence, Rhode Island, at the right Note the relative lengths of head and body. *Rana sphenocephala* always shows a white circular spot at the centre of the ear.

FIGS. 217 and 218.—The COMMON LEOPARD FROG (*Rana pipiens* Shreber) Denver, Colo. The head is more or less pointed. Its length is one-third the total length. There may be a light blotch at the centre of the ear, and a dark spot on the head in front of the eyes.

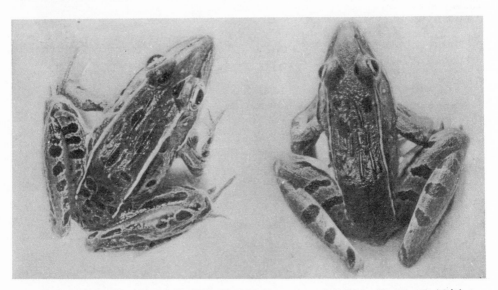

FIGS. 219 and 220.—The SOUTHERN LEOPARD FROG (*Rana sphenocephala* Cope). The frog at the left is from Ozona, Florida ; the right from Hitchcock, Texas. The head is long, narrow and pointed. The length is contained in the total length 2½ times. The ear has a circular white spot at its centre. The eyes are large. There is no spot on the head in front of the eyes.

Eyes large; space between them narrow. (Fig. 219.) Nostrils round, below the line of the prominent canthus rostralis, much nearer to the end of the muzzle than to the eye. Ear smaller than eye. Feet long, webs deeply indented. Fingers and toes long and slender. A tarsal ridge, and outer and inner sole tubercles are present. Thumb of male thickened at base.

Range: Rana sphenocephala is common in the Austroriparian subregion. It is reported from Georgia (Nashville, Saint Simon's Island, Liberty County), Florida (Georgiana, Ozona, Fort Myers, Seven Oaks), Louisiana (Prairie mer Rouge, New Orleans), and Texas (Hitchcock). One specimen is reported also from Wheatland, in southern Indiana.

———

The Southern Leopard Frog is perhaps the most beautiful frog in North America. It has not the delicate modest beauty of the Wood Frog, but it has distinction of form, richness of colouring, and intricacy of colour pattern. It has not, like the Wood Frog, an expression indicating gentleness and tameness. Instead, a creature extremely alert and wild, possessing great powers of activity, is seen in the unusually large eyes and in the attentive pose of the slender body. (Fig 215.)

The head is long and pointed, with the eyes set far back. This characteristic and the unusual length of the hind legs distinguish the frog at once from *Rana pipiens*, the Common Leopard Frog. It is peculiar, also, in possessing a circular white spot at the centre of the ear. This spot is never lacking, no matter what the colouration of the frog may be at the time. (Figs. 213, 215, 219, and 220.) *Rana pipiens* has sometimes a light blotch at or near the centre of the ear, but never this clean-cut circle of white.

The background of colouration varies greatly, but is seldom plain green or brown. Instead, it is a mixture of the two. The colours are equally intense, and meet each other in irregular lines, without any blending. The brown is usually a warm shade, not grey or ashy, and the green is most often pure green, without an unusual amount of either yellow or blue in it. An occasional frog is found which is light yellow-green. The spots may be dark green or brown, and are not margined with light colour,

187

except on the legs. The spots are irregular in shape and arrangement. Not only do the two sides of the frogs differ in the number, size and arrangement of the spots, but, what is more unusual, the two legs are sometimes totally different in these respects. (Fig. 219.) The colouring is everywhere highly metallic in character. The changes are not especially rapid. This species of frog in Texas is often beautiful in a dress of light dove-grey or fawn-colour. (See Colour Plate XII.)

The male *Rana sphenocephala* has large vocal pouches, one at each side, above the arm. These frogs are wild and active. They leap long distances, and are difficult to catch. The species is evidently a very distinct one, not intergrading with *Rana pipiens*, but holding its own with the latter frog in the same localities in the southern part of the United States.

THE PICKEREL FROG

Rana palustris Le Conte

IDENTIFICATION CHARACTERISTICS

Colour: Brown, with two more or less regular rows of conspicuous squarish spots between the lateral folds, and two irregular rows of smaller spots on each side below the folds. Legs barred or irregularly spotted. A conspicuous light line from muzzle to shoulder. The upper jaw is yellowish, marked with brown; the lower is white, marked with brown. The underparts are white in front, bright orange-yellow posteriorly. The yellow may extend forward along the sides and outward under the arms. (For colouration, see Colour Plate XIII.)

Measurements: Size medium; male, 2 to 2½ inches; female, 3 to 3½ inches. The legs are long, the distance from thigh to heel equalling the combined lengths of head and body. The ear is smaller than the eye.

Structure: Two relatively broad, non-elevated folds of skin extending from the eyes backward — the lateral folds. There are four folds of skin on the back between the lateral folds. These are not coloured differently from the surrounding parts, as are the lateral folds. The foot is distinctly webbed, but the webs are deeply indented and two joints of the fourth toe are free.

The brook and the meadows nearby make the home of the Pickerel Frogs.

Plate LXXII

Fig. 221.—PICKEREL FROGS live out of the water more than in it.

Fig. 222.—The PICKEREL FROG (*Rana palustris* Le Conte), Massachusetts. Just from the brook.

The inner sole tubercle of the foot is small; the outer still smaller. The palm of the hand has well-developed tubercles.

Range: The Pickerel Frog is found throughout the eastern part of North America, west to the Great Plains, and north to Hudson's Bay.

If we go to the meadow for blue flags in May, we are likely to hear the Pickerel Frogs (Figs. 221 and 222) croaking with low voices in the quiet shallows of the meadow brook or of the pond-margin near by. The prolonged note is very distinctive. It is well described by saying that it resembles the sound produced

The Pickerel Frogs are croaking when the blue flags are in bloom.

in tearing resisting cloth of some sort. The pitch varies with the individual, but is always low. The range is from G to A below middle C.

As we approach the brook, picking our way over the boggy ground with its sedges, sweet white violets and blue flags, many small spotted frogs leap astounding distances on both the near and the far side of the brook, striking the water in a series of successive splashes. The surface of the water is scarcely ruffled, and the frogs are immediately buried in the mud or hidden under shelving bits of moss at the brook's edge. The Pickerel Frogs are even more agile than the Common Leopard Frogs.

The brook and the fields and meadows near make the home of the Pickerel Frogs, and we shall find them here in all sizes, from those one year old and only an inch and a quarter long to large ones that are three inches in length.

There is perhaps no other of our frogs that presents a coat

189

of so brilliant a metallic lustre as the young Pickerel Frog after he has been in bright light for some hours. Shining gold and bronze make up his colour from the tip of his little pointed " nose " to the ends of his long back legs. On the other hand, the young Pickerel Frog just from a cold day's sleep in the mud is so dark that his spots are scarcely discernible.

The appearance of this frog will deceive us into believing that he is our familiar Leopard Frog, unless we are observing enough to see that the spots are square instead of round, and that as he makes one of his flying leaps there is a flash of orange under the back legs and posterior part of the body. These things mark him as a Pickerel Frog. He is in fact very closely related to the Leopard. However, he is always brown of some shade, instead of green. The head is usually less long and pointed than that of the Leopard. The spots do not have yellow rims. The Pickerel Frog has no large external vocal pouches, like those of the Leopard, but the throat, the region back of the eye and under the ear, as well as the sides, all expand considerably during the croaking. The male is much smaller than the female. It is he alone that does the croaking. This species has a distinctly unpleasant odour, due to the secretion of the skin. Because of this, it is not considered edible. The frog is used to a large extent as bait in pickerel-fishing, hence its name.

These frogs live out of the water (Fig. 221) more than in it, even at the breeding season. They go to the water to avoid their bird and snake enemies, to lay the eggs, to absorb the cool water through their shining coats. They spend the greater part of their time hunting, probably for caterpillars that feed on the violets and grasses, meadow caddis flies, butterflies and millers, flies, gnats, and beetles. It is likely that Pickerel Frogs find acceptable any insect that makes its home about the brook or that comes there to deposit its eggs in the water or to get honey from the flowers that grow there. They are known to feed on snails, small crayfishes, and aquatic amphipods and isopods. Pickerel Frogs are extremely common throughout the Eastern part of the United States. They are not to he found at all on the Great Plains of the West, where the Leopard holds supreme sway among frogs. They make their home not only in brooks and meadow marshes, but do good work in keeping pure the water of cold springs. We see their large eyes and palpitating white throats also in crannies at the mouths of surface drains.

The eggs of this species are laid in shallow water during the month of May. Frogs brought from the pond laid eggs on the nights of May 18, 23, and 26, 1902. The irregular egg masses are about two inches in diameter, and contain between two and three thousand eggs each. The upper half of the egg is rich brown in colour; the lower half cream-white. The eggs are small (1¼ mm.) and enveloped in triple spheres of transparent jelly. The earlier stages of the development take place very rapidly. The jelly holds its compact shape but a very short time; it softens, and the whole mass spreads and flattens. The tadpoles, which are light yellowish-brown in colour, leave the eggs very early. Eggs laid May 23rd were hatched May 27th. The tadpoles cling to the jelly side by side in rows and circles, with their heads up and their tails extending downward. The next day they are festooning the waterweeds as well as the jelly. Now they begin those circling tours, from which they settle to some new support, only to start off again in large circles, which give place to smaller ones until they find another support or drop lightly to the bottom. By the first week in June, the gills have become wholly covered, and the bits of life have grown to ordinary round-bodied " pollywogs," with the usual pollywog hunger.[1] From now on they vary greatly in size, some far outstripping the others, although all live under the same conditions. The larger ones change to the frog form in July and August; the smaller ones may be kept back in the process until September; and still others may delay the change until the following spring.

Large tadpoles of the Pickerel Frog have at first sight much the appearance of the Green Frog tadpoles. Looking more closely, we see that the head is much more pointed, the eyes are not widely separated, and the nostrils are close to the end of the muzzle, characteristics which distinguish this species. The younger tadpoles have small roundish spots irregularly placed on a greenish-brown background of body and tail. The dark pigment follows the lines between the muscle-plates of the tail so that for nearly one half its length the tail looks like a black feather. The tail fin is less than one-fourth of an inch wide

---

[1] The mouth structure of the pickerel frog tadpole is similar to that of the bullfrog tadpole. (See footnote, p 235.)

everywhere. The lateral line organs, especially in the region of the head, are very conspicuous. As soon as the hind legs are well grown, and before the front ones appear, the lines of the lateral folds begin to show, the square spots are blocked out on the back, and the legs become barred with dark. After the appearance of the front legs the swellings in the region of the gills are very noticeable, as are also the lines from the nostrils to the eyes.[1]

Just before the completion of the metamorphosis, while the stump of the tail is still present, and just as the swellings in the gill region disappear, the young frog moults its skin. It now leaves the water and wanders over the grassy places at the margin of the water. It is slender and delicate, and very shy. At our approach it escapes with enormous leaps into the protection of the pickerel weeds and cat-tails that grow in the shallow water.

RANA AREOLATA, B D. AND GIRD.[2]

IDENTIFICATION CHARACTERISTICS

Colour: Brown or olive, obscurely mottled and speckled with light. Many large or small rounded spots on head, back, and sides. There may be four irregular rows of these spots between the lateral folds. The spots usually do not encroach on the lateral folds. There may be yellowish-white outlines around the spots. Ear brown, with a white blotch at its centre. Upper and lower lips coarsely marbled with brown. Legs spotted, or crossed by four dark bars. Much yellow on femur and body where they fold against each other. Underparts white. (Figs. 223 to 225.)

Measurements: Size medium, i. e., length $2\frac{1}{2}$ to $3\frac{1}{2}$ inches. Length of head contained in total length three times. (Fig. 223.) Length of leg to heel equals length forward to eye or nostril. Tibia longer than femur. (Fig. 225.)

Structure: Skin rough, with elongated warts on back and sides. Lateral folds conspicuous. Tibia ridged lengthwise.

---

[1] See Bull Frog, pp. 236, 237.

[2] Judging from measurements made on the type specimens in the National Museum, *Rana areolata* Bd. and Gird. is the same as *Rana areolata circulosa* Rice and Davis and as *Rana areolata capito* Le Conte.

PLATE LXXIII

FIGS. 223 to 225.—*Rana areolata* Bd. and Gird. Immature frogs, Hitchcock, Texas. Brown or olive with many rounded dark spots. The spots may be either large or small, obscure or conspicuous. They may be outlined with light. Compare with FIGS. 226, 222, 218 and 213.

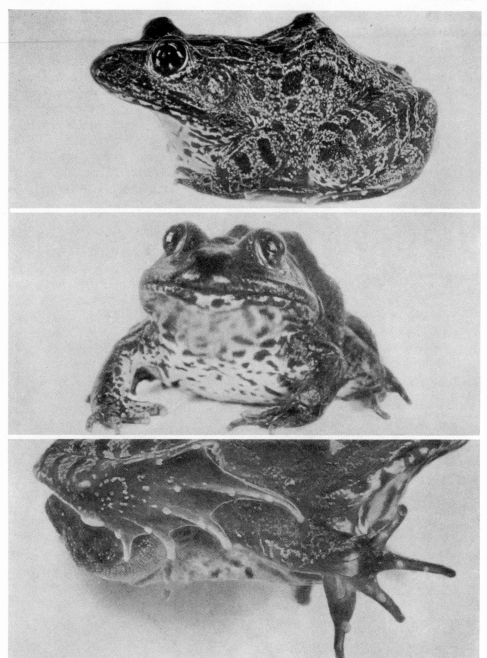

FIGS. 226 to 228.—*Rana æsopus* Cope. Ozona, Florida. (For coloration see Colour Plate XIV.) This frog lives solitary in the burrows of a highland turtle. Its greed is unequaled even by that of the American Bullfrog. (Note the development of the head and jaws.)

No glandular fold along the jaw. A distinct fold over the ear from eye to shoulder. Under and posterior surfaces of femur granulated. Head large; unusually thick through. Muzzle long; space between eyes greater than width of eyelid; nostrils nearer to the end of the muzzle than to the eye; eyes large; ear half to two-thirds size of eye. (Figs. 223 to 225.) Foot with a tarsal fold; webs short (three joints of fourth toe free); inner sole tubercle small, no outer tubercle, tubercles under toe-joints prominent.

Range: Rana areolata probably occupies the Austroriparian subregion. It is reported from Texas (Hitchcock, Indianola) and Georgia (Riceborough). There is also a record of single specimens having been collected in Indiana and Illinois.

This frog has the hiding instinct thoroughly developed, as has *Rana æsopus* of Florida. Like the Florida frog also, it has unusually large vocal pouches that can be extended from the shoulder regions. It is a silent, solitary frog, except at the breeding season.

The species can always be distinguished from *Rana æsopus*, by the lesser development of the jaws in width and massiveness, and because the ratio of head and body measurements are as one to three, instead of one to two and a half.

THE GOPHER FROG
Rana æsopus Cope
IDENTIFICATION CHARACTERISTICS

Colour: Brown, dark or light in shade. This colour may be purplish, greyish, or yellowish in tone. The broad lateral folds are bright orange-yellow. Warts on back and sides, often bright yellow. Many closely set black spots on the head and on the back between the lateral folds; many smaller black spots on the sides. The spots on the back and on the sides infringe upon the yellow lateral folds. Upper lip spotted, not light or dark bordered. Ear dark, with irregular spot of light in centre. Glandular fold along jaw to shoulder yellowish. Legs with four or five black or dark brown cross-bars. Foot and hand dark; tubercles of hands and feet light in colour. Underparts spotted, especially anteriorly. (See Colour Plate XIV.)

Measurements: Size medium to large, i. e. length 2½ to 4 inches; female larger than male. Head long, its length contained two and a half times in total length. (Fig. 226.) Head of a frog 3 inches long measures 1½ inches wide and 1¼ inches long. Length of leg to heel equal to length of body forward to ear or eye. Femur and tibia about equal. Foot long, fourth toe extremely long; web medium in size. (See Fig. 228.)

Structure: Body peculiarly short and squat. Skin leathery, and corrugated with elongated wart-like folds on back and sides. Tibia ridged lengthwise. Lateral folds broad and elevated. The glandular folds of the jaw end above the shoulder in peculiar large warts. Ridge from eye to shoulder (over ear) inconspicuous. Eye unusually large and prominent. Nostril equidistant between eye and jaw. Ear a vertical oval, half to two-thirds size of eye. Space between eyes less than width of eyelid. Fingers long and slender; the thumb of the male is thickened and horny at its base (Fig. 228); hand tubercles not notable for size. Legs stout and strong; inner sole tubercle relatively large and long, outer small or lacking; tubercles under joints of toes rather conspicuous (Fig. 228).

Range: Rana æsopus Cope is reported from Florida only (Micanopy, Orlando, Ozona, Lake Jessup, Clarcona).

The Gopher frog of Florida is very different from other frogs in its general appearance. It is squat and toad-like, having an unusually large head, with a prolonged muzzle, and eyes prominent and bulging even for a frog. Because of the unusual length and breadth of head, this frog has a mouth relatively larger than those of other North American frogs. (Fig. 227.) These structural characteristics give the frog so peculiar an appearance that although it may agree with *Rana palustris* and with *Rana pipiens* in colour and in being prominently spotted, there would never be any difficulty in distinguishing it as a different species. (See Colour plates XI, XIII and XIV.)

The male frog has two large vocal pouches (one at each

shoulder). These can be extended between the arm and the glandular fold above. When the pouch is not inflated, the region back of the angle of the jaw and between the arm and glandular fold (which extends fully one-half inch behind the jaw angle) is occupied by broad folds of thin dark-coloured skin.

The general colour of these frogs varies considerably. It may be grey or brown, somewhat yellow or purple in tone. The spots may vary in size and in number. In any individual frog, the colour changes are striking and rapid. The frog may change from nearly black to white, through shades of brown or purplish grey. The spots keep their intensity when the frog is light in colour. (Colour Plate XIV.) In the light-coloured frog, yellow colour is very prominent. It is not only on the elongated warts and lateral folds, but extends from the lateral folds over the eyes along the canthus rostralis to the nostrils. The secretion of the skin given off when the frog is annoyed is offensive in odour.

This frog is so wary and has such strong habits of hiding, that but few specimens have come to light. The wariness of this species has resulted in a habit of spasmodic instead of continuous activity. Its method, like that of the cricket grasshopper, is ludicrous to observe. It remains absolutely quiet for minutes at a time, relying on its protective colouration until the danger is well-nigh upon it. When the movement comes, it is with startling suddenness and despatch, leaving the frog statuesque again and observant, but in a new place.

Rana æsopus is comfortable in water, though not conspicuously a water-frog. It sits with head and shoulders protruding from water-weeds, invisible because of the colour and spotting of its dress. When the air becomes cooler than the water, it withdraws under the surface, and rests for hours, even days, at a time, with motionless flattened body, closed eyes, and arms and legs in hibernating position.

Outside of the breeding season, it lives solitary in gopherholes, hence its name. These so-called gopher-holes are the burrows of a Florida highland turtle. The burrow — about eight inches high, and fourteen wide, and sometimes as long as thirty feet — extends obliquely and irregularly through the sandy soil, starting under a clump of palmetto, or under a log, stump, or fence. The frog sits at the mouth of the burrow, watching for an unsuspecting insect, bird, or batrachian. It disappears so quickly at the approach of danger, that not only is it seldom seen, but, to be captured, must in all cases be dug out of the burrow.

This frog seems especially fond of toads as an article of diet. It ejects the poison from the mouth as soon as it has swallowed the toad. A toad of surprisingly large size can be managed, owing to the unusual development of the jaws and throat of this species. If the toad is too large to be all swallowed at once, so that the poison can be sent out through the mouth almost immediately, the frog gives up the attempt and disgorges the toad after about fifteen minutes. This time, however, is sufficient to allow some action of the poison to take place, and the frog shows many signs of discomfort. It has convulsive movements of the muscles, it leaps blindly upward, and finally, lowering the head and opening the cavernous mouth, uses the hands in frantic efforts to remove the irritation from there. During several weeks of captivity, *Rana æsopus* fed almost wholly upon toads, of species *lentiginosus*, *woodhousei*, and *fowleri*. This habit of eating toads may be duplicated in the case of *Rana catesbiana*. At least this frog has been found dead witn full-grown specimens of *Bufo fowleri* partially swallowed.

RANA ONCA, COPE [1]

IDENTIFICATION CHARACTERISTICS

Colour: Brown posteriorly; lighter anteriorly, often bright metallic green, especially on sides of head under the eyes and below the canthus rostralis. Iris golden. Ear bronze. Lateral folds light yellowish brown. Three or more irregular rows of spots between the lateral folds, and many spots placed irregularly below the folds. Spots light edged or not. Legs light brown, spotted with dark, even on the feet. Underparts white, yellow posteriorly. (See Colour Plate. II.)

Measurements: Size medium, i. e. length 2 to 3 inches. Leg short; length of leg to heel equalling length of body forward to eye. Tibia but slightly longer than femur.

---

[1] *Rana fisheri* Stejneger. Annotated List of Reptiles and Batrachians Collected by the Desert Valley Expedition in 1891. Leonhard Stejneger. North Amer. Fauna, No. 7. 1893.
Also *Rana draytoni onca* Cope. Cope's Batrachia of North America.

Structure: Skin smooth, except for lateral folds and a few inconspicuous elongated wart-like elevations on the back between the lateral folds and on the sides. Head rounded, thick through, with much the proportions and appearance of the head of *Rana clamitans*. (Fig. 257.) Ear larger than eye in male, slightly smaller than eye in female. No conspicuous ridge over ear. No glandular fold along jaw. Feet delicate; webs broad and long. Inner sole tubercle small; outer lacking.

Range: Rana onca Cope is reported from Utah and Nevada.

This species of frog (Fig. 257 and Colour Plate II) is not nearly related to the black-cheeked frogs of the Pacific Slope. It is apparently much nearer the eastern *Rana clamitans*, and the spotted frogs *Rana pipiens*. The general colouring, also the shape and proportions of head, body, and legs are remarkably like those of *Rana clamitans* (Fig. 230); the spotting reminds one of *Rana pipiens* (Fig. 197), but differs in that it represents a temporary colour pattern instead of a permanent one. *Rana onca* never attains the size of either of these other frogs.

Rana onca is a very bright, active little frog. It eats worms and insects greedily. It will try to take a worm away from a companion frog, biting at the frog's head again and again. In locomotion it proceeds by short hops, given in quick succession with short toad-like legs.

The power for rapid change of colour is considerable. The frog may be brown or green, of light or dark shade. The spots may or may not be rimmed with light colour. They may be darker or lighter than the background of colour. When lighter, they are shining gold or bronze. There is much iridescence in the colouration. In fact, the young frogs may wear a coat everywhere rich in metallic lustre.

The frogs examined have shown no external vocal pouches. The large webs and the unusually large tympanum make this frog easy of identification within its western range.

THE GREEN FROG

Rana clamitans Latreille.

IDENTIFICATION CHARACTERISTICS

Colour: Extremely variable and changeable. Typically, the colouring is brilliant metallic green on head and shoulders and dusky olive (perhaps spotted) posteriorly. There may be a yellowish band (widening anteriorly) along the lines of the jaw from the shoulder forward. Throat of the male bright orange-yellow; that of the female, white, spotted with dark. Sides of the body often marked with large blotches of dark. (This is especially true of the female.) Legs spotted or barred with dark. (See Plate XIII for colouration of the Green Frog.)

Measurements: Size somewhat above medium, i. e. male, 3 to 3½ inches, female 3 to 5 inches. Legs relatively short; the length of the leg to the heel being much less than the combined lengths of head and body. Tibia and femur about equal in length.

Structure: The skin may be rough. Head unusually thick through. Head somewhat pointed. Ear of male much larger than the eye; that of female no larger than eye, often smaller. (Figs. 229 and 230.) Body stout. Lateral folds conspicuous; a groove occupies the midline of the back. The web is broad; it leaves the last two joints of the fourth toe free. (Fig. 231.)

Range: Very common throughout eastern North America, including Canada and Florida.

As we walk along the path that skirts the meadow brook, we are surprised by a scream, followed by another and still another. Our curiosity demands that we investigate. The sound suggests a frightened bird, though there is almost no shrubbery for the concealment of a bird. We walk more slowly, and approach the brook. There is nothing to be heard now, except the occasional splashing of water as a startled tadpole rushes to safety from the shallow water; or the whirring of wings as a dragon-fly passes startlingly near to our faces. We walk on along the

---

[1] Called " Spring Frog " and " Pond Frog " in various parts of the country.

muddy bank of the little stream. Again we hear the sound ahead of us, and surely something is moving toward the water. Now we suspect that it may be a frog, and so we are on the lookout still more alertly as we proceed. This time we see the creature plainly — a small Green Frog. (Fig. 234.) It leaps high into the air and drops into the water, uttering the short, high-pitched cry. It is hard to believe that the sound which startled us was made by this small creature, but we remember that the " Screaming Frog " is one of the old names given to the Green Frog. Day after day confirms our experience. Year after year we become accustomed to the fact that young Green Frogs — especially in the spring months — give this short, frightened scream when they are alarmed.

The older frogs of this species (Figs. 229 and 230) make the same high jump, but they give a very different call when they take refuge in the water.[1] This sound is very familiar indeed to every person who has been in the country. It is a nasal " chu-n-ng," or " k-tun-n-ng," so low-pitched that it may be almost or quite an octave below middle C. It is a cheerful, vigorous call, somewhat musical in quality. The croaking of the Green Frog is a sound still different, and is given from shallow water. It is explosive, prolonged, and low-pitched and is likely to be repeated five or six times in succession. When we hear it given with less than its usual force, we may be deceived into thinking that we hear the drumming of a woodpecker. It may be imitated very well by cutting on a table, with heavy shears, some kind of coarse resisting cloth. Or it may be imitated less well by tearing heavy cloth in a jerky fashion. It resembles the croaking of the Pickerel Frog, but has more strongly accentuated notes in it.

The explosive character of the sound will be better understood if we watch the frog when he is croaking. He works hard; there is no appearance of external vocal pouches (as in the Leopard Frog, Fig. 9), but the yellow throat and the sides expand with such force as to jerk the whole body forward. Slowly the distended parts sink in as the vigorous sounds proceed. Then the throat and sides swell out again, and there follows another explosion of sound. And so on over and over. One yellow-

---

[1] They may give the screaming call also, but I have not heard it.

The Green Frog comes from his winter sleep soon after the red-wings appear in the marshes.

throated creature, hidden among the green slime and brown leaves of the pond margin, gulps out his ejaculatory remark; exclamatory responses come from other yellow throats hidden in other parts of the shallow water.

It is easy to confuse the Green Frog with the Bullfrog. This is not alone because the two look alike, but because both are more aquatic than most of the other frogs of eastern North America. From season to season they remain in the water or wander out on the bank only a few feet from the water. The Green Frog can always be identified by the conspicuous lateral folds of skin which extend from the eyes to the posterior part of the body. The Bullfrog has no such folds.

In the adult frog the head and the upper third of the body are brilliant metallic green. This colour merges into a dull brownish olive on the posterior portion of back and sides. This dull colour is likely to be irregularly spotted with dark brown. The young frogs (sometimes the older ones) lack the light metallic green on the head and shoulders. Instead,

FIGS. 229 and 230.—Adult GREEN FROGS (male and female). Rhode Island. The male [left] can be distinguished by the large size of the ear. (For coloration see colour Plate XIII.)

FIG. 231.—Structure study of the foot of the GREEN FROG (female).

FIG. 232.—The young GREEN FROG climbs out of the water on anything available.

FIG. 233.—The young GREEN FROG (the tail has just been absorbed) floats at the surface with eyes and nostrils above the water. [Enlarged.]

FIG. 234.—A young GREEN FROG can be distinguished from the young Bullfrog by the lifted fold of skin extending from each eye to the posterior end of the body

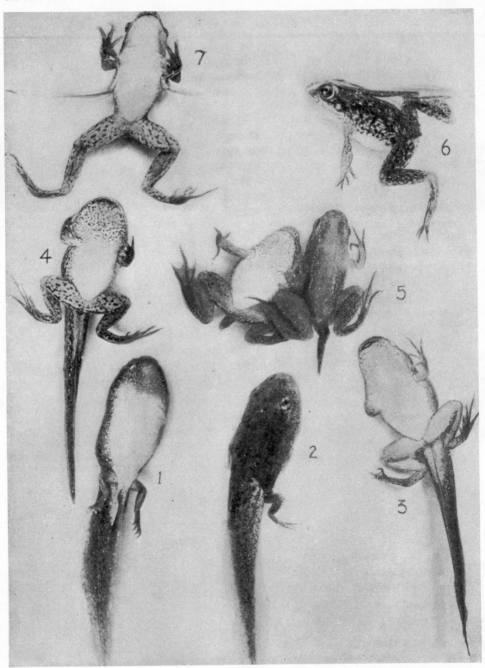

FIGS. 235 to 241 (1-7). Photograph to indicate the metamorphosis of the GREEN FROG (*Rana clamitans* Latr.). Compare the development of the legs in 1, 4 and 7. The left arm appears first, thrust through the breathing pore; the right arm breaks through the skin (3). Compare lengths of tail in 2, 5 and 7. Compare 3, 4 and 7 as to the size of the mouth.

there may be a well-defined band of the brilliant green on the sides of the upper jaw below the eyes and ears, but elsewhere the green is replaced by dull olive. (For colouration of the Green Frog, see Colour Plate XIII.)

The head is narrower than that of the Bullfrog, but it is unusually thick through. (The head of the female is narrower than that of the male.) The eye is very large and bright, with a golden iris and an oval black pupil. The ear of the male is much larger than the eye. (Fig. 229.) It is a conspicuous flat brown circle with a yellow spot at the centre. The ear of the female is smaller — about the size of the eye — and lacks the yellow centre. (Colour Plate XIII.)

The Green Frog moults the skin four or more times each year. If the frog is out of the water when the moulting takes place, the process is like that of the American Toad and of the Leopard Frog, and the skin is swallowed. If the moulting takes place in water, the skin may float off in large patches and is not eaten.

A small pond on a sunny day about the middle of April is a scene of much beauty and of great activity. There is a

Green Frogs may catch the dragon-flies that have left their larval skins

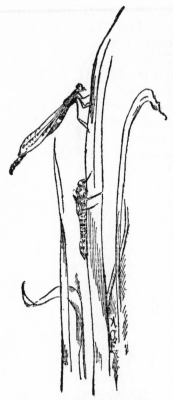

The Green Frog captures the damsel-flies before their wings are dried.

fringe of sombre alder enriching the brilliancy of a red maple and setting off the delicacy of a leaning grey birch. On one side the meadow slopes gently to the edge of the water. The bottom of the pond is a mat of delicate green, with lifted layers forming black openings leading to hidden caverns. The water is very clear. Suddenly the sun goes under a cloud, and the water becomes dark and impenetrable to the sight. A gust of wind sends the smooth surface into thousands of ripples that race toward the edge, but before they reach it a reverse wind hurries them off to one side, and all is still again. A song-sparrow sings from the shelter of the alders. Again the sun comes out, and the bottom of the pond is again illuminated. The smallest object can be seen distinctly. Brown tadpoles appear, and with vigorous tail-wigglings begin nibbling the green of the pond bottom. A few of them rise to the surface to rest in the sunshine. There creeps a caddis-fly larva, clumsily carrying its log house. Long-legged water-striders walk on the surface where there were none a moment before. Black, flat-bottomed whirligig beetles skate over the surface in interlacing courses that never end. From one of the dark cavern doors a black, yellow-spotted salamander [1] appears, moves slowly and gracefully over the green, to disappear within another arched doorway in the green. A painted turtle in the shallow margin water lumbers over the green with head bent downward, and disappears underneath. Suddenly frogs' heads are lifted above the green, and then above the water. They are Green Frogs; the water is so clear and so illuminated, that we

[1] *Amblystoma tigrinum*

can see the lateral folds on their sides. All is silent. Their eyes are watchful. Occasionally one moves a short distance in such a way — half-floating, half-swimming — that the water is undisturbed. One eats a water-strider, making a slight splash and ripple of the water as he uses his hands to help get the insect's long legs into his mouth. Having finished the first, he devours another. A second frog snaps up a back-swimmer (see p. 183) that has rushed to the surface for a breath of air. A large dragon-fly larva (see p. 182) creeps right under one frog's nose. He dives for it with a great splash of the water, and if we can judge by his look of satisfaction and the number of times the great eyes are lowered and lifted, success met his effort. A company of whirligig beetles circles near one of the frogs. He sees them at a distance of three or more feet, and swims slowly about half the distance towards them. They approach still nearer. There! He snaps up one, then another, then a third. The company takes alarm; some dive under the water (each with its silver bubble of air), others dash over the surface to join a second company farther away.

And so on. A small pond has infinite numbers of large and small forms of life, in a world practically concealed from us. In this world each creature is wholly intent on his one interest of the moment, whether it be escape from a devouring enemy, or the finding of a mate, or a snug retreat, or a breakfast. This little world reminds us of our own, in the fact that very often the interests of various individuals clash.

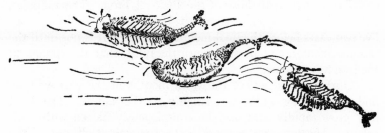

Green Frogs feed upon the fairy shrimps[1] of icy March pools.

The Green Frogs come early from their hibernation in the mud and moss about the ponds. They appear early enough to feed upon the delicate fairy shrimps[1] of icy March pools. The

[1] Branchipus.

truth is, they are more or less active throughout the winter, if the temperature is not too low. It is interesting to keep American Toads and Green Frogs together under the same conditions, to compare their hibernating habits. Even with the temperature at 60° F., the toads disappear early, and for weeks and months at a time will not so much as come to the surface. The frogs scarcely hibernate at all. They sit patiently in the water or on the moss, or possibly in shallow burrows in the moss. They take worms and small fish greedily all through the winter, whereas it is usually difficult to get toads to eat before the arrival of spring.

The eggs of the Green Frog are usually laid some time between the last of March and the last of April. The eggs are larger than those of the American Toad, and the jelly of the large mass (usually fastened to a twig or other support) is very firm, and remains so during the early development. The egg clusters are often laid during times of high water. Placed just below the surface of the pond and attached to the twigs of buttonbush, alder or other shrubs that are growing in the water, they are left some distance above the surface when the water recedes. If this receding comes before they are several days old and the jelly-mass considerably softened, here they continue to cling to their supports and soon dry under the influence of sun and wind.

The early development of the Green Frog eggs is rapid. The young embryos are light in colour and so may be distinguished from those of the Wood Frog and of the Leopard Frog, although easily confused with those of the Pickerel Frog. The tadpoles, (Figs. 235 to 241), like those of the Common Bullfrog, may live two years before the final metamorphosis.[2] It is not until the second summer, and possibly until the third, that the change to the frog form occurs.

During almost any of the warm months of the year we may find Green Frog tadpoles changing to the adults. The hind legs grow rapidly, and may be conspicuously barred with dark colour. The left arm appears first, thrusting itself out of the breathing-pore. (Fig. 237.) Then the right one breaks through the skin. The changes in mouth and eyes begin. The tail is slowly

---

[2] The mouth structure of the Green Frog tadpole is similar to that of the Bullfrog tadpole. (See footnote, p. 235.)

absorbed. (Fig. 239.) The ears are the last external sign to tell that the change is quite completed. The variation in the size, colour, and markings of the changing tadpoles is very great. Most curious is the fact that some tadpoles show the lateral folds and the colouring of the adult male or female long before the change is completed, while others take on the frog form entire before the lateral folds are well developed or before the sexual colouring is evident.

The activity and the spirit of adventure which characterize the Green Frog are evident very early, in fact before the tail is wholly absorbed. The young frog may sit contentedly in shallow water (Fig. 234) or float at the surface with only eyes and nose above (Fig. 233), but more likely he climbs out of the water on anything available. (Fig. 232.) Unlike the young Bullfrog, which constantly hides under water or moss, the young Green Frog is curious and alert, and always in evidence.

THE EASTERN WOOD FROG

Rana sylvatica Le Conte

IDENTIFICATION CHARACTERISTICS

Colour: Variable, changing from chocolate-brown to fawn-colour, through varying shades of reddish, yellowish, or greyish brown. Lower back and sides may or may not be irregularly spotted, legs may or may not be barred, with dark colour. There is a black or dark-brown patch of colour in the region of the ear. The dark colour may extend in a band (widening behind) from the snout to the shoulder. A light line extends along the jaw from snout to shoulder. The lateral folds may be light yellowish brown. Underparts yellowish or greenish white, sometimes mottled with dusky anteriorly. (See Colour Plate XIV.)

Measurements: Size relatively small, i. e. male 2 inches, female 3 inches. Ear smaller than the eye. (Fig. 245.) Distance between nostrils equal to the width of the head between the eyes. The legs are extremely long, measuring twice the length of head and body together. (Fig. 242.) The length of the leg to the heel considerably exceeds the total length of head and body. The lower leg (tibia) is more than half the combined lengths of head and body. (See Fig. 242.)

In June the Wood Frog is found where the fragrant pyrola stands on its carpet of oak leaves and pine-needles.

Structure: The body is flat. (Fig. 243.) The head is broad and pointed. The skin is relatively smooth and moist. There are a few tubercles on the lower sides and posterior back. (Fig. 250.) The lateral folds are conspicuous. (Colour Plate XIV.) The foot is light-coloured and delicate. The toes are long and slender. The web is extensive, but it leaves free the last two joints of the fourth toe and the last joint of each of the other four toes.

Range: Rana sylvatica is found in damp woods throughout the northeastern United States; it is not found west of the Great Plains, south of South Carolina, or north of Quebec, Canada.

Most of our frogs invite us to ponds or brooks, or river margins, if we would find them, but the Wood Frog (Figs. 242 to 245, and Colour Plate XIV) takes us to the shade of the pines and oaks of the forest.

It is June. The chestnut trees are waving fragrant plumed tops. The red-eyed vireo, now in one tree, and then in another, is talking incessantly of the beauty of things. A slight wind sways the curving branches of low-growing hickories and chestnuts, their leaf shadows falling cool on the moss and brown leaves below. As we walk up the wooded hillside, getting our garments covered with bedstraw burrs, tiny frogs jump out from our feet, in front, at the right, and at the left. But stand still, and you will see only the brown pine-needles and oak leaves, the erect, fragrant pyrola, and the nodding waxy pipsissewa. The frogs are small, and their colours are so thoroughly matched with those of their surroundings as to make them almost invisible.

The home of the WOOD FROG (*Rana sylvatica* Le Conte).

FIG. 242 (1).—The WOOD FROG covers more ground in a single leap than do most of our other frogs. Photographed to show length of hind legs, also the lateral folds and other distinctive characteristics.

FIG. 243 (2).—The WOOD FROG in resting position.

FIG. 244 (3).—Very alert. The WOOD FROG can always be known by its dark cheek patches.

FIG. 245 (4).—The WOOD FROG (*Rana sylvatica* Le Conte) is a typical land frog. Rhode Island.

Step forward ever so little, and bend down to pick a spray of red-tipped pyrola flowers, and a frog will leap almost from under your very hand. It is hard work to catch a half-dozen of them, and good fun to make them swim in the near brook. The work comes first, for the ground is uneven and these atoms of frogs leap enormous distances, never twice in the same direction. Besides, they are not easy to keep after they are caught. They are strong and slippery, and they are so delicate that they must be handled with great carefulness. The fun comes when we release them in the water. They are powerful swimmers, and kick out their hind legs vigorously. However, they make for the nearest miniature island, or for the shore, where they are hidden, and we have at once lost all but one or two. It makes us very active indeed to keep trace of these; before we are aware of it, they, also, are gone.

However, we saw them long enough to realise that they were slender and delicate in shape, grey or brown in colour, and that they had black or dark-brown cheek-patches. They are one-year-old Wood Frogs. Wood Frogs are more truly land frogs than are any of the others among our North American frogs.

In addition to these very small frogs, we are certain to come upon larger Wood Frogs, two years old or more. We are most likely to find them along wood paths or at the edge of the brook.

Land-life, and the broader experience resulting therefrom, seems to have produced a somewhat higher development in this frog. It not only looks much more intelligent, but it is certainly less unintelligent in some of the ways of its living, than other frogs. It jumps farther than most of the

The waxy flowers of the pipsissewa. June.

207

others, and has the habit of turning during the movement, so that when it strikes the ground it is facing the enemy. It is much more alert in getting food, resembling the toad in this respect. It sees the moving insect at a distance of several feet, stealthily walks or creeps toward it, and perhaps follows it some distance, before making the capture. Besides, the Wood Frog is our most silent frog, in this, again, resembling the toad. It is only at the early breeding-season that its hoarse croaking can be heard. When a creature lives on the ground, and has no manner of defense, and none of escape, except jumping (and that always on the ground), silence must be a great protection.

The Wood Frog may measure $2\frac{1}{2}$ or 3 inches in length. Its head is pointed. The body is broad and flat. (Fig. 243.) The legs are extremely long, measuring twice the length of the head and body together. The hind feet are strongly webbed. The upper parts are light or dark reddish, yellowish, or greyish brown in colour. This frog is distinguished within its own range by the dark-brown or black cheek-patches. A distinct dark line reaches from the front of the eye to the end of the muzzle. A golden yellow line extends along the sides of the upper jaw and is continued to the shoulder. The eyes, which are larger than the ears, are very prominent, and possess an alert but gentle expression. The golden iris shows a lower half much darker than the upper. The light-brown lateral folds, extending from the eyes to the posterior end of the body, are very conspicuous. (Colour Plate XIV.) The male Wood Frog, when held in the hand, talks in a vigorous purring voice, something like that of the Common Leopard Frog.

Very early in the spring, the Wood Frogs come from their winter sleep under the leaves and mossy logs. In fact, they are the first to be enticed by the spring sunshine. In February or March, after only a few days of moderate temperature (40° to 60° F.), the frogs are out and the eggs are laid[1] in the pools of the woods or of the open country adjacent. The eggs are laid in masses which measure about four or five inches in diameter, and which contain from one thousand to three thousand eggs each.

---

[1] March 23, April 2, 1882. W. H Hinckley, Milton, Mass.

February 23, March 8, 1890. T. H. Morgan, Baltimore, Md.

April 4, April 10, 1904. After an unusually severe and prolonged winter. (The eggs were hatched by April 23.) M. C. Dickerson, Providence, R. I.

(Figs. 246 and 247.)   The masses may be attached to twigs and grasses in shallow water, or they may be free.

After the eggs have been in the water a week or more, the mass flattens and spreads greatly, and rests on the surface of the water.   There are likely to be several masses close together in the water.   The jelly about the eggs becomes green in colour, and thus the egg-masses bear a close resemblance in position and appearance to the floating masses of green pond-scum.   The green colour of the jelly about the eggs is due to the presence of innumerable microscopically small green plants.   The relation between these plants and the developing egg is one of mutual advantage.   The plants feed upon the large amount of carbon dioxide breathed out by the young tadpoles, and the tadpoles get, as their share in the partnership, the free oxygen that the plants give out as a waste product from their starch-forming process.   This oxygen must be of infinite value, produced everywhere in the midst of the egg-mass, because it supplies sufficient pure air for breathing, in spite of the crowded condition of the two thousand or more growing tadpoles.

These egg-masses are not easily found, partly because they are so inconspicuous, and partly because our attention is rivetted on the very conspicuous jelly masses (Fig. 249) of the spotted salamanders,[1] or of the marbled salamanders[1] (which choose the same time and often the same place for depositing eggs).   Eggs that are laid in water that afterwards freezes are not killed, and will develop as soon as a higher temperature returns.

As has been said, the hoarse croaking of the Wood Frog is heard only at the breeding-season.   At that time, however, dozens of the frogs croak together in a most clamorous fashion. The repeated notes are low-pitched (about an octave below middle C).   The notes have been compared to the quacking of ducks, but near at hand, at least, they are much  less unmusical.   The males alone do the croaking.   They have no external vocal pouches, but, as in the Pickerel and Green frogs the throat and sides of the body over the lungs distend considerably as the sounds are produced.   The breeding-season is likely to

[1] *Amblystoma punctatum* or *Amblystoma opacum.*

be over before the first of May. (Fig. 250.) After that time their voices are never heard.

In colour, the eggs are chocolate-brown above and white below. If laid early, they develop very slowly, requiring at least a month to reach the hatching stage. (Fig. 248.) If laid later, when the temperature of the water is much higher, the development is so much more rapid that the tadpoles may hatch in nine or ten days. The development is especially rapid in shallow temporary pools. The young tadpoles are nearly black in colour. The external gills become considerably longer and more branched before their absorption than do those of the Leopard Frog. (See Fig. 210.)

The tadpoles of the Wood Frog eat[1] not only the green jelly-mass from which they themselves hatch, but also the soft green spheres within the jelly-masses vacated by young salamanders. Like other tadpoles, they act as scavengers by greedily devouring all dead animal matter of the pond.

In late May, the margins of the ponds will be found swarming with young Wood Frogs with tails of varying lengths. The frogs (minus the tails) are ¾ inch long, about the size of a male adult Pickering's *Hyla*. Their hind legs are extremely long, and the webs are fully developed. The lateral folds show red-brown on a dark wood-brown background. The young frogs are active and shy.

In permanent ponds or in deep or well-shaded temporary pools, the development is more slow, because the pool endures longer, and the frog is somewhat larger when it leaves the water.

In late June, the brown leaves of the bottom of such a pond are covered with Wood Frog tadpoles that just match the leaves in colour. Many of them have the legs well developed, perhaps the arms also. With their plump " pollywog " bodies and their long waving tails, they are much larger than the young frogs that have left the water.

The variation in colour among the Wood Frogs is great indeed, and the colour changes are fairly rapid. The young frogs are likely to be dark in colour, more often than light; and when light, they are more nearly grey than brown. The older ones vary from a colour so light that it might be called flesh-

---

[1] The mouth structure of *R. sylvatica* is like that of *R. catesbiana* (see footnote, p. 235), except that the lower lip is broader and bears four rows of teeth, instead of three.

colour, to a brown that is almost black. The female is usually much lighter than the male. The Wood Frogs may be either conspicuously spotted and the legs conspicuously barred, or they may show perfectly even colour without trace of spots or bars. Indeed, conspicuously spotted and barred frogs may lose all trace of the markings within the space of half an hour. The change from light brown to dark, or the reverse, may take place in fifteen minutes only. (See Colour Plate XIV.)

Like the chickadee, the Wood Frog is a gentle spirit of the woods.

The Wood Frog is beautiful at all times It has a high-bred and delicate air. It is to the ground what the chickadee is to the trees — a gentle spirit of the woods. Its appearance and ways are always in harmony with the subdued light, the quiet, and the delicate mosses and frail ferns that live in the shade of great trees.

THE NORTHERN WOOD FROG

Rana cantabrigiensis Baird

IDENTIFICATION CHARACTERISTICS

Colour: Dark brown to yellowish grey. A dark line from the end of the muzzle extends backward on each side along the canthus rostralis through the eye, to form a large patch of colour in the region of the ear. A light line along the jaw from the end of the muzzle to the shoulder. There may be a light dorsal streak from near the end of the muzzle to the posterior part of the body. Lateral folds light-coloured, and bordered below by irregular line of black. Legs barred or spotted with dark.

211

Underparts light, more or less mottled with dark, yellowish posteriorly.

Measurements: Size below medium, i. e. length 2 to 2½ inches. Distance between nostrils greater than width of the head between the eyes. Legs long, length to heel just equalling total length of head and body. (Legs shorter than are those of *Rana sylvatica*.) Tibia equal to the femur and equal to one-half the total length of head and body.

Structure: Skin smooth. Head pointed. Ear smaller than the eye. Lateral folds not greatly elevated. Web large.

Range: The distribution of *Rana cantabrigiensis* is wholly northern. It is reported from Illinois, Michigan, Wisconsin, and Minnesota northward to Great Slave Lake on the west and St. James Bay on the east.

Rana cantabrigiensis would be recognised at once as a species closely related to *Rana sylvatica*, the Eastern Wood Frog. It differs only slightly in colouration and general form. It can be distinguished at once by the leg measurement; the leg to the heel just equals in length the total measurement of head and body.

This frog has the same delicacy of beauty, the same gentleness and alertness of expression, possessed by the Eastern Wood Frog. It would be surprising to find any great difference in its habits. It is probably silent, except at the breeding-season, and is more thoroughly a land frog than are most of the species of *Rana*.

Its relationship to *Rana sylvatica* is also shown by its northern distribution, which provess ability to endure a lower temperature than most frogs. (*Rana sylvatica* is the earliest frog to appear in the spring in the northeastern United States.)

West of the range of *Rana cantabrigiensis*, that is, from the Great Slave Lake to Alaska, inclusive, the representative of this frog is a subspecies, *Rana cantabrigiensis latiremis* Cope. The leg measurement will always distinguish this frog from the Northern Wood Frog. The western form has short, stout legs, the measurement to the heel never being more than three-fourths the combined lengths of head and body (length to heel equals distance forward to eye.) There are a few other differences plainly visible; for instance, distance between the nostrils

PLATE LXXIX

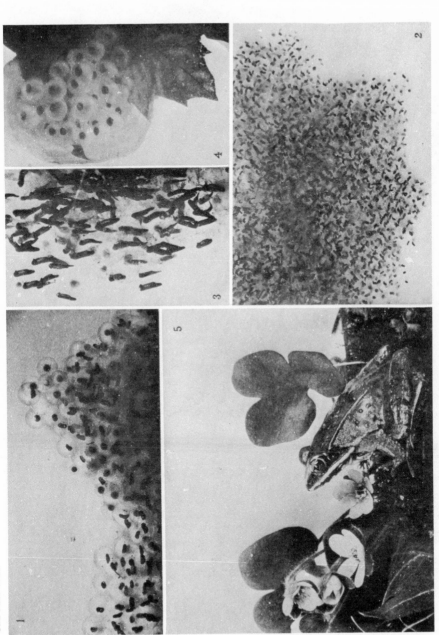

FIGS. 246 and 247 (1 and 2).—The eggs of the WOOD FROG are in masses that float at the surface of the water.   Each egg is enclosed in a sphere of jelly.   (FIG. 247 represents ⅔ mass, reduced.)

FIG. 248 (3).—Hatching WOOD FROG TADPOLES.   They wriggle out of the jelly and cling to its outer surface.   (Enlarged.)

FIG. 249 (4).—SALAMANDER (*Amblystoma punctatum*) eggs fastened to oak leaf.   Frog eggs never have an outer mass of jelly surrounding the jelly spheres. [Compare with FIG. 246 (1).]

FIG. 250 (5).—The WOOD FROG leaves the pond while the hepatica is still in bloom.

FIG. 251 (1).—Structure study of *Rana draytonii* Bd. and Gird. (Female. Half-grown.) South San Francisco, Cal.

FIG. 252 (2).—Photograph of foot of *Rana draytonii* (female) to show size and number of the tubercles on the sole and under the joints of the toes. (In water.)

FIG. 253 (3).—Frog of Figs. 251 and 254. Note the length of the fingers.

FIG. 254 (4).—Photograph (in water) to show one possibility in size and arrangement of spots.

is considerably greater than the width of head between the eyes, and the webs are much larger than in either *Rana cantabrigiensis* or *Rana sylvatica*.

RANA DRAYTONII, BAIRD AND GIRARD

IDENTIFICATION CHARACTERISTICS

Colour: Female — Reddish brown on the upper parts, with or without darker spots.   The region below and behind the eye (including the ear) may be dark brown in colour.   A yellowish band along the jaw from the shoulder to the eye.   Arms, legs, and upper sides irregularly spotted with dark;   the legs may be transversely barred.   Underparts light, spotted, and marbled with dark.   Lower sides of body and underparts of legs and feet bright red.   Rich mosaic arrangement of black and yellow on upper leg and side of body where they rest against each other.   The male is less rich in colouring.   It is greyish brown or yellowish, is more likely to be distinctly spotted, and has much less red. In both sexes, the palm of the hand and the sole of the foot are purplish grey in colour.   (See Colour Plate XV.)

Measurements: Size large, i. e. adult males 2½ to 4½ inches (Figs. 255 and 256), females still larger.   The length of the head is contained three times in the total length of head and body. The lower leg is somewhat longer than the upper leg.   The length of the leg to the heel is not as great as the combined lengths of head and body.

Structure: The skin is tuberculated, especially in old specimens. (Fig. 255.) Buttocks granulated. Head broader than long, rounded in front. Body broad and heavy. Canthus rostralis fairly prominent. The ear is smaller than the eye. (Fig. 251.) A glandular ridge extends backward from under the eye, narrowing to the arm. This ridge is interrupted at the angle of the jaw, and also back of this, where the curving ridge descends from the eye to the shoulder. (See Fig. 255.) The lateral folds are distinct, and are perforated with minute pits. There is a conspicuous fold of skin over the ear from eye to shoulder. The legs are massive in full-grown specimens. The tubercles under the toe-joints are especially conspicuous. The inner tubercle of the sole is medium in size; the outer, small or lacking. (Fig. 252.) A distinct tarsal ridge. The fingers are

213

unusually long. (Fig. 253.) The first is thickened at the base (male).

Range: Rana Draytonii is reported from various parts of California, also from the mountains of Lower California. (From Petaluma, El Dorado, Presidio, Fort Tejon, Carmel, San Francisco, and South San Francisco, California.)

This Western species, when half-grown, is a frog of much beauty of form as well as of colouring and texture of skin. It is very alert and intelligent-looking, and becomes tame in captivity. (Fig. 251.) When it has attained its full size, it is much less attractive in appearance. The eye, although very lustrous, seems too small for the size of the frog; the skin has toughened and coarsened until it is leathery in appearance, and is tubercular in structure (see Fig. 255), and the colouring is much less delicate and beautiful.

This frog is hardy. It is partially aquatic in its habits, remaining in shallow water much of the time and taking food from under the water. It eats fish greedily, as does the Eastern Bullfrog, and therefore must prove a menace in fish-ponds.

It is a very awkward frog, because of the massive build and great length of its hind legs. (Figs. 255 and 256.) When walking, it is ludicrous in appearance, and it is still more ridiculous when it captures a fish from under the surface of the water and swallows it. The frog tries to brace himself on the long hind legs so as to use the hands, both at the same time to keep the fish away from the angles of the jaws and to push it into the mouth. To brace himself against slippery mud is not easy, and besides, the frog loses his balance because both hands are lifted at once, so he makes a great kicking and splashing before he finally swallows the fish. This frog eats not only fish, but also various water-insects, tadpoles, and smaller frogs. This species is said to be one of the most cannibalistic of our North American frogs. He eats worms and air insects, also; among the latter, sow-bugs are said to be favourites.

Both male and female " talk " vigorously in a low-pitched musical voice, when they are taken in the hand so that the feet are unsupported. There is no appearance of distended vocal sacs when the frog croaks.

This frog can be recognised at once because of the presence and distribution of red colour on the underparts. This colour is vividly displayed on the sides when the frog is in sitting position; considerable red is sometimes found on the upper surfaces of the body and legs, blending with the rich chocolate-brown of the upper parts. (Colour Plate XV.) The dark brown or black patch of colour in the region of the ear will help to identify the frog sometimes, but very often this spot is no darker than the background of colour elsewhere. The iris is rich orange-bronze, instead of yellow, as in its near neighbour, *Rana pretiosa.* But from this species the smooth, firm texture of the skin on the soles of its feet will at once distinguish it. (See Fig. 252. Compare with Fig. 263.) The tubercles under the joints of fingers and toes are unusual in size. There is great variety in the size and appearance of the spots on different individuals. Some are almost plain in colour and some are conspicuously spotted. The spots may be of large size (see Fig. 256) or very small. They may be spots of solid colour or may have lighter centres. (Fig. 254.) The spots may infringe on the lateral folds, in fact, sometimes small spots are aggregated along the lateral folds.

For the exact webbing of the toes, see Fig. 252. The web of the male is broader than that of the female. The first finger on the hand of the male is thickened and hardened at its base, and is dark-coloured and horny, especially on its upper surface. All of the fingers are unusually long. (Fig. 253.)

Rana draytonii hibernates in the mud at the bottom of ponds and creeks in winter, when the air is colder than the mud and water. Here the frogs would be at the mercy of their enemies — the large water-beetles, water-snakes, and especially the leeches, except that the cold affects these enemies in the same fashion, and they are sleeping also.

In the region of middle California, this frog comes from its hibernation in late January or in February. The large egg-clusters are laid at once in the shallow water of ponds. It is said that the eggs hatch in about six weeks, and that the tadpoles become young frogs in four or five months.[1]

The young frog is very small in the first year and still during the second and third years,— in fact, it takes four or five years

---

[1] Facts given by S. C. Coombes, Frog Ranch, South San Francisco, Cal.

for it to attain a length of two and a half to three inches, and eight years or more to become full-grown. It is said by people of the Western Coast that *Rana Draytonii* is the best edible frog in North America, and that the flesh of the Eastern Bullfrog is tough and coarse compared with it.

RANA AURORA, BAIRD AND GIRARD

IDENTIFICATION CHARACTERISTICS

Colour: Brown, yellowish, or olive, often matching the colour of dead leaves. There may be small spots or specks of dark brown or black on head, back, and sides. Space behind the eye and including the ear may be black. A black line below canthus rostralis from eye to jaw. Iris golden yellow. Glandular fold from under eye to shoulder, yellowish. Upper and lower lips spotted with dark. Arm may be crossed by 3 to 5 narrow dark bands. Much red in the colouration, showing on the parts of legs and feet which are concealed when folded, on the sides of the body, and under the arms at their insertions. Reticulations of yellow and black on body and femur where they lie against each other. Throat and underparts light, obscurely mottled with dark. Hand and foot may be purplish grey in colour. (For colouration, see Plate XIV.)

Measurements: Size medium, i. e. length $2\frac{1}{2}$ to $3\frac{1}{2}$ inches. Length of head enters total length three and a quarter to three and a half times. Leg very long, its length to the heel exceeding the total length of the head and body. Tibia much longer than femur. (See Colour Plate XIV.)

Structure: Skin very smooth, finely pitted. Buttocks granulated. Broad lateral folds perforated with pits. Groove along the middle of the back. Body flat, long, and slender. (Fig. 258.) Muzzle rounded. Canthus rostralis prominent. A glandular fold of skin along jaw from under the eye to the shoulder. Eyes large, prominent, facing outwards. Space between eyes equal to or greater than the width of the eyelid. Ear round, one-third to one-half the diameter of the eye; it is likely to be inconspicuous when the cheek-patch is dark. Ridge from posterior angle of eye to shoulder not prominent. Tibia ridged lengthwise. Arms and legs slender. Fingers long and slender;

FIGS. 255 and 256.—Male frog of *Rana draytonii* Bd. and Gird., eight or more years old. Slightly under natural size. South San Francisco, Cal. The massive legs are conspicuously banded and the back has many large dark spots. The skin is leathery and tubercular.

FIG. 257.—*Rana onca*, Cope. Las Vegas, Nevada. Immature frogs, 1½ in. long. (For description see page 196 ; for coloration see Colour Plate II.)

FIG. 258.—*Rana aurora* Bd. and Gird. Seattle, Washington. (For coloration see Colour Plate XIV.)

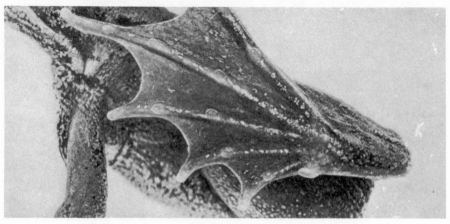

FIG. 259 —*Rana aurora* Bd. and Gird. (For description see page 216.)

base of first finger greatly thickened in male (Fig. 258); tubercles under finger-joints fairly conspicuous. Foot not thick, web delicate, with two joints of fourth toe free; inner sole tubercle small, outer small or lacking. (Fig. 259.)

Range: Rana aurora occupies the Pacific Slope. It is reported from Washington, Oregon, and California. In California, where *Rana Draytonii* is the common frog, *Rana aurora* is said to be found in the high Sierras only; in Oregon and Washington, it is abundant, but is less so in many parts of these states than is *Rana pretiosa.*

Rana aurora is a delicately formed, smooth frog, less hardy than most frogs of North America. (See Figs. 258 and 259, also Colour Plate XIV.) It is shy and wild, and difficult to keep in captivity, except in a perfect imitation of its environment. In such a place, it seems to enjoy equally sitting under the shade of ferns or in the water, and eats earth-worms greedily. Both male and female give high-pitched, jerky cries, expressing fright, when taken in the hand. One unusually large specimen opened his mouth wide and gave a prolonged high-pitched scream, reminding one of the similar sound produced by the Common Bullfrog.

Judging from the radical difference in the sizes of the frogs to be found in the spring, this frog requires four or five years to become full-grown. It changes colour rapidly, from dark rich browns to delicate shades of rosy tan. *Rana aurora* is a delicate, timid-looking frog, but, notwithstanding the promise of its name, it does not always compare in beauty with many of the other frogs of North America. It seldom has the richness of colouring that may be possessed by *Rana draytonii*, its neighbour on the Pacific Slope.

Rana aurora is easily confused with *Rana draytonii* (Fig. 251 and Colour Plate XV), because of the likeness, both in colouring and proportions. The former frog can be distinguished by the following characteristics: It has a longer leg, the greater length especially noticeable in the tibia. Its skin is very smooth, while that of *Rana draytonii*, especially in the full-grown frogs, is always tubercular, and may be extremely so (even on the ear). *Rana aurora* has a longer foot with a broader web, but with a much smaller inner sole tubercle.

THE WESTERN FROG

Rana pretiosa Baird and Girard

IDENTIFICATION CHARACTERISTICS

Colour: Variable; dull or bright yellowish or reddish brown on head, back, and upper surfaces of arms and legs. Few or many irregular, roundish black spots — like splashes of ink — on the back between the lateral folds. Lower sides light yellowish grey, unspotted. Underparts light, obscurely or conspicuously marbled with greyish brown. Salmon-red on undersurfaces of legs, and in a more or less conspicuous U-shaped marking on the belly. A light glandular streak from under the eye to the arm, interrupted at the end of the jaw. Iris bright yellow, not orange-coloured or bronze. (See Colour Plate XVI.)

Measurements: Size medium, i. e. male 2 to 3 inches; female 3 to 4 inches in length. Leg to the heel as long as the body (i. e. forward to the ear). Foot conspicuously longer than lower leg. (Figs. 260 and 262, also Colour Plate XVI.)

Structure: The skin is everywhere rough, even in the region of the ear. Lateral folds distinct. Head rounded, broader than long. Ear smaller than the eye. Head not conspicuously angled along the lines between eyes and nostrils. Nostrils round. Eye not large, set obliquely, so as to be but slightly elevated, and so as to face more dorsalwards than is usual. The foot has broad webs extending to the tips of all the toes, except the fourth, which has the short terminal joint free. (Fig. 260.) The whole lower surface of the foot, as well as the buttocks and outer surfaces of legs (especially of lower leg), very rough with crowded tubercles. The inner tubercle of the foot is small, and there is a small tubercle opposite this on the sole. (Fig. 263.)

Range: Northwestern North America, as far east as the foot of the Rocky Mountains in Montana, north to Puget Sound, and south to southern California.

The Western Frog has been found during the winter, sleeping in the mud under a foot or more of water, along marshy lake margins. It appears in the Puget Sound region from the last of February to the middle of March. A few scattered individuals may, however, be seen on sunny days throughout the winter. These are usually among the lily-pads along the marshy borders of the lakes.

As soon as they appear in March, they set up a noisy croaking, and the eggs are laid between this time and the first of April. The egg-masses (Fig. 261) are unattached. They vary greatly in size, but average about a pint in bulk. In one case where the eggs were counted, a laying consisted of over fifteen hundred eggs. The eggs are relatively large, measuring nearly 2 mm. in diameter. Each egg is in a transparent sphere of jelly measuring one-half inch across. The eggs are placed in the shallow, marshy pools near a lake, but never in the deep lake-water itself. The length of time required for hatching is from one to two weeks, varying with the temperature; those in the warm, shallow water hatching earlier than those in deep water. The later development is slow, and it is not until after the summer is passed that the tadpole becomes a frog. This slow development is perhaps correlated to the conditions of the region of the frog's range. There is an abundance of water in this region, even in summer, so that the development is not hastened by the drying up of the pools.

From this time on the growth is slow; at least, there can be found, each spring, frogs of four or five different sizes, so that it would seem as though they require four or five years to reach the adult size.

The adults are easily captured during the breeding-season. As soon as we approach them, they dive into the mud of their shallow pool, burying the head and shoulders, but leaving the legs exposed in good position for capture. Their colouring is highly protective. It is difficult to see them when they are sitting among the alternating lights and shadows of the reeds. They depend so much on their protective colouration, that they lie low and allow themselves to be touched before taking alarm.[1]

This frog is distinguished from other Western frogs by its round nostrils, the tubercular character of the soles of the feet, the long foot and large web, and the lack of prominent lines

[1] Many facts concerning this species were kindly furnished by Prof. J. F. Illingworth, Seattle, Wash.

from the nostrils to the eyes. The frog shows no salmon-red colour when in sitting position, and so one's surprise is great on discovering so much brilliant colour on the under surface of the frog's body and legs. The undersurfaces of the arms may have the same colour. The lack of red on the side distinguishes it at once from *Rana Draytonii* (see Colour Plate XV), and from *Rana aurora*, as does also, the lack of dark cheek-patches. The position of the eyes also aids in the distinction.

As to colouration, this frog may be any shade of yellowish or reddish brown, from the lightest to the darkest. The sides are always lighter than the back. The legs are irregularly barred and spotted with brown. The knees are likely to possess the same light yellowish grey colour of the lower sides. The male is considerably smaller than the female, and is likely to be more spotted. The forearms are muscular, and the first finger is thickened and hardened at its base. The feet and webs are enormous for the size of the frog. (Fig. 260.) The web has a spread of one and one-half inches on a frog only two and one-half inches long.

When taken in the hand so that its feet are unsupported, this frog " talks " vigorously, as do many of the frogs and toads. This is true of both male and female, but the voice of the male is louder and more emphatic. External vocal pouches do not show when the frog croaks.

The Western Frog is thoroughly aquatic in its habits. It gets its food largely from the water, feeding greedily on small fish, as does its near neighbour on the Western coast, *Rana draytonii*, and as does the Eastern Bullfrog.

It is interesting to watch the male swim in very shallow water. With flattened body and lowered head, he searches for something under which he can hide. Finding nothing, he kicks out his powerful legs, alternately spreads and folds the extremely large webs, and continues the search. He sometimes turns so sharply, that the body is entirely turned around before the legs have had time to turn, and so for the moment one leg ludicrously measures itself straight forward along the body. Finally, some bit of moss is found under which the frog can push his head, and there consider himself safe. So safe does he feel, that almost immediately he lifts his head till nostrils and yellow eyes are above the weeds and water. The eyes are

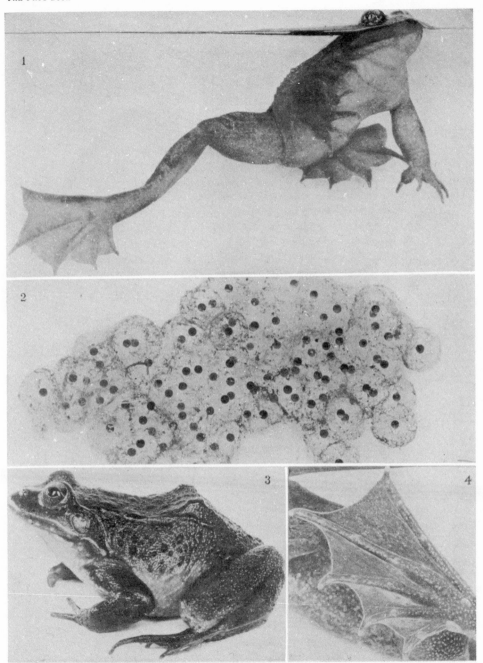

FIG. 260 (1).—*Rana pretiosa.* (Male). Seattle, Washington. The first finger is thickened, the webs are unusually large

FIG. 261 (2).—A portion of the egg-mass of *Rana pretiosa.*

FIG. 262 (3).—*Rana pretiosa.* (Female). Seattle, Washington. Distinguished by round nostrils, warty skin long foot and light lower sides.

FIG. 263 (4).—*Rana pretiosa.* (Female). Structure study of foot.

PLATE LXXXIV

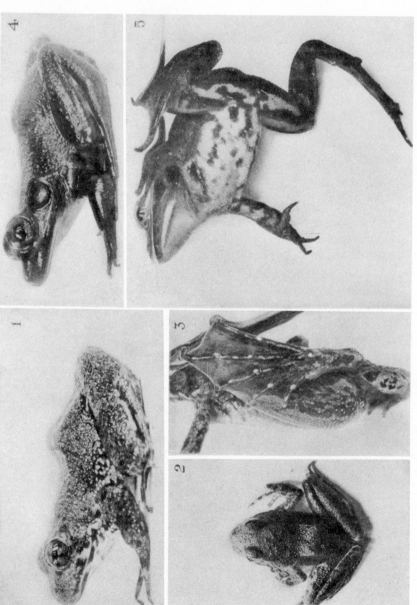

Fig. 264 (1).—*Rana boylii* Bd. and Gird. Mill Valley, Cal. Enlarged to show some structural characteristics, i. e., outline of head, size of eye, ear obscured by tubercles, etc. (For coloration see Colour Plate II.)

Fig. 265 (2).— To show tubercular surface, relative lengths of **femur and tibia**, etc.

Fig. 266 (3).—Foot to show extensive web and the sole and subarticular tubercles.

Fig. 267 (4).—*Rana virgatipes.* Male. Lakehurst, N. J. (Somewhat enlarged.) To show outline of head, size of eye and of ear, length of foot, etc. (For coloration see Colour Plate XIII.)

Fig. 268 (5).—To show relative proportions of body and leg, and the markings of the underparts.

peculiar, in that they are little elevated at their upper margins, and so face upward more nearly than sideways. This is one of the many characteristics that adapt this frog to a thoroughly aquatic existence.

RANA BOYLII, BAIRD AND GIRARD

IDENTIFICATION CHARACTERISTICS

Colour: Dull olive or greyish brown; sometimes brick-red. Upper surface may be obscurely spotted with dark. Upper jaw spotted irregularly. Iris metallic yellow. Legs and arms barred with dark. Underparts white, mottled anteriorly, and bright yellow posteriorly. Much yellow around the arm insertion. Webs yellow (See Colour Plate II.)

Measurements: Size small, i. e. length 1½ to 2½ inches. Head short and broad. (Fig. 265.) Legs very long; length to heel equals the total length of the frog, and sometimes exceeds it. (Fig. 265.) Tibia longer than femur.

Structure: Skin thick and coarse; unusually warty over all upper parts. (Fig. 264.) Underparts smooth; buttocks granular. Lateral folds broad, not elevated, very inconspicuous. Muzzle projects beyond lower lip. Nostrils small. Ear round, smaller than eye, indistinct because covered with fine warts, as is the surrounding skin. (Fig. 264.) The fold extending over the ear from eye to shoulder is indistinct. Canthus rostralis prominent. Space between the eyes greater than the width of the eyelid. Arms well developed; fingers long, with small tubercles under the joints. Foot with broad webs extending quite to the expanded tips of the toes. Inner sole tubercle medium in size; outer tubercle small. (Fig. 266.)

Range: Rana boylii Baird and Girard, is reported from California and Oregon.[1]

Rana boylii, which, in California, is called the Yellow-legged Frog, has perhaps the most toad-like appearance of any frog of North America, although it does not sit erect in toad fashion. (Fig. 265.) The likeness lies in the texture of the skin. The

---

[1] Eldorado County, Ashland, Ore Shasta County; Mill Valley, Marin County, Cal.

short, flat body is completely covered with small warts, from the tip of the nose to the ends of the feet, producing a surface that at first glance has somewhat the appearance of coarse sandpaper. The frog is usually olive, grey, or yellow-brown, obscurely spotted on the back (Colour Plate II), but often the whole tubercular upper surface is bright brick-red. This red is sometimes to be seen on the lateral folds and on the tibia, when the frog is brown or olive elsewhere.

Rana boylii is excessively shy and wild. Its first instinct is to hide. It scuttles head-first under cover at any approach. If there is no place of concealment, or if its hiding place is disturbed, it leaps great distances, and the enemy who can capture it must be alert of sight and grasp. This frog emits a curious, oily odour, greatly like that given out by the California Toad, *Bufo halophilus*.

It has great power to change its colour from dark to light, appearing nearly black at one moment, and light reddish or yellowish grey half an hour later.

Rana boylii is one of the most distinct species of frogs in North America. Within its own range, the yellow colour of the underparts will suffice to distinguish it, since *Rana draytonii*, *Rana aurora*, and *Rana pretiosa*, the other frogs of the Pacific Slope, have red instead of yellow in the colouration. Compared with all the frogs of North America, it is peculiar in the tubercular character of the skin, though some specimens of *Rana draytonii* approach it in this characteristic. *Rana boylii* is like *Rana pretiosa*, *Rana catesbiana*, *Rana grylio*, and *Rana septentrionalis* in the extensive webbing of the feet.

RANA VIRGATIPES, COPE

Identification Characteristics

Colour: Chocolate-brown or brownish olive, with four narrow lengthwise stripes of bright golden brown. There are two of these stripes on each side. One occupies the position usually held by the lateral fold (i. e. from the posterior part of the eye backward); the other lies below this, and extends along the middle of the side. The lower stripe is continuous with a stripe of bright golden brown extending from the shoulder forward along the jaw. Throat yellow, speckled with bronze. The sides of the frog have large dark spots on a metallic, brownish yellow back-ground. There are small black spots on the back and sides between the stripes. The belly and undersurfaces of the arms are yellowish white, spotted and mottled with rich brown. Under-surfaces of legs vividly striped lengthwise with yellow and brown; stripes continued on tibia and foot. (See Colour Plate XIII.)

Measurements: Size somewhat below medium, i. e. length 2 to 2½ inches. Head long; length contained three times in total length. (Fig. 267.) Space on top of head between eyes unusually narrow (half width of eyelid). Leg short (Fig. 268); length of leg to heel equals length of body forward to the ear. Tibia and femur equal. Foot relatively long; fourth toe much the longest; third longer than fifth.

Structure: Skin relatively smooth and wet. Head pointed, upper jaw projecting over the lower. Canthus rostralis prominent. Eye peculiarly bulging (Fig. 267); extends beyond the jaw on the sides of the head, so that it can be seen from below. Ear larger than eye, and very distinct, surrounded by a circular ridge of skin. Inconspicuous fold of skin from eye over ear to shoulder. No lateral folds. A groove marks the middle of the back. Fingers slender; first thickened at base. Web broad and conspicuous; two joints of fourth toe free. Inner sole tubercle of medium size; outer lacking.

Range: Reported from Atlantic City and Lakehurst, New Jersey.

Rana virgatipes (Colour Plate XIII and Figs. 267 and 268) was first discovered by Cope, at Atlantic City, in 1891. It was found in company with Leopard Frogs and Green Frogs, in stagnant water, where sphagnum moss, bladderworts, and water-lilies grow. In the summer of 1905, it was reported as very abundant near this type locality.[1]

These frogs have been seen at Lakehurst, at intervals from May to September. They occur rather abundantly in the ditches about the cranberry-bogs, as well as in the lake itself. They are often found seated on a lily-pad or on the sphagnum moss.[2]

[1] Fowler, Acad. Nat. Sci., Philadelphia.

[2] I am indebted to William T. Davis, New Brighton, N. Y., for these facts, as well as for material.

Rana virgatipesis decidedly a water frog, and is one of the least hardy of the North American species. It has only average powers of leaping and swimming, but its instincts for hiding are strong. When disturbed, it disappears at once under floating water-weeds.

It differs from the other smaller frogs of North America in the great development of the eyes and ears. It is like the bullfrogs in lacking the lateral folds. It resembles the Leopard Frog, in that the male frog has large vocal sacs that can be extended at the sides behind and under the ears. It shows close relationship in structure and habit to *Rana grylio* (pp. 227 to 227).

THE NORTHERN FROG
Rana septentrionalis Baird

IDENTIFICATION CHARACTERISTICS

Colour: Light olive, with or without coarse vermiculations of darker colour. There may be large irregular blotches of brown on the sides and posterior back. No light stripe along the jaw. Legs blotched or transversely banded. Underparts light yellowish, unspotted. Buttocks yellow, with dark blotches. Posterior surface of femur may be strongly reticulated with dark colour.

Measurements: Size medium, i. e. length 2 to 3 inches. Leg measurement to heel equals body measurement forward to the eye. Tibia and femur about equal in length.

Structure: Skin relatively smooth; finely pitted when examined closely. Underparts smooth. Buttocks but slightly granulated. Body rather stout. Head narrow, rounded in front. Space between the eyes narrow. Nostrils large, halfway between eyes and tip of muzzle. Ear larger than the eye in the male, smaller than the eye in the female. No lateral folds, or only slight traces of them. Feet long, toes provided with long, broad webs. Inner sole tubercle medium in size.

Range: Rana septentrionalis is wholly northern in its distribution. It is reported from the Adirondack Mountains, from Lucknow, Ontario, and Fort Ripley, Minnesota, and from Moose River and the Hudson Bay region.

It is thought that this species is intermediate in its characteristics between some more primitive form and nearly all the

North American species of *Rana*. From some such form might have come all of our frogs, except, perhaps, the black-cheeked ones, such as *Rana sylvatica, Rana draytonii*, and the like. It shows close relationship to the Green Frog (*Rana clamitans*) and to the Bullfrog (*Rana catesbiana*).

The Northern Frog is described as decidedly a river frog; it is never captured in lakes and ponds. It is silent and unobtrusive, solitary in habit, and thoroughly aquatic. We do not see it in meadows or woods, but if we walk along the brook margin or river bank, it will dive into the water, much as does the Pickerel Frog (*Rana palustris*) in a similar situation. It hides under stones, among water-plants, or in the mud near the centre of the stream, and may not return to the surface for fully a half-hour. In this habit of remaining long under water when frightened, it resembles the Common Leopard Frog (*Rana pipiens*). When it does appear, just head and shoulders are thrust out among the water-weeds at the border of the stream. The Northern Frog eats water-insects, and sometimes small fish.

The breeding-season is in June and July.[1] The egg-masses adhere to water-plants, and wave back and forth with the current half-way between the surface of the water and the bottom. Two years are required for the development and metamorphosis of the tadpole. The full-grown tadpole with developing legs may measure four inches in length, two and one-half inches being the measurement of the tail. The tadpoles are the scavengers of the brooks and rivers. For instance, they will greedily eat a dead brook-trout, leaving only a perfectly cleaned skeleton.

Both the frogs and the tadpoles give off a strong, disagreeable odour when annoyed. This odour is said to be like the scent of the mink, and this species of frog is often called the Mink Frog.

---

[1] June 24 and July 30, 1883. Dr J. H. Garnier, Lucknow, Ontario.

THE SOUTHERN BULLFROG

Rana grylio Stejneger

IDENTIFICATION CHARACTERISTICS

Colour: Head and shoulders usually vividly green; olive posteriorly, with many irregular black spots. The whole frog may be olive or rich dark brown. Ear orange-brown, with green centre. Middle and posterior back may have four longitudinal bands of bright orange-brown, alternating with bands of olive. Small black spots on legs. Underparts light, unspotted, except posteriorly. Throat of male bright yellow. Undersurfaces of legs may be mottled and reticulated in coarse pattern with black and yellow.

Measurements: Size large, i. e. length 4 to 5 inches. Head long, its length contained little more than two and one-half times in the total length. (Fig. 269.) Legs medium in length; length to heel equals length of frog forward to a point anterior to the eye. Tibia same length as femur.

Structure: Skin smooth on the head, slightly rougher elsewhere on upper parts (Fig. 274); when examined closely, seen to be everywhere finely pitted. Head with pointed outlines, gradually diverging backward to the widest part of the head in the region of the middle point of the ear. (Fig. 271.) Eyes greatly elevated and unusually large. (Fig. 273.) Space between the eyes narrow. Ear of male greatly larger than the eye (twice the diameter) (Fig. 269); that of the female about equals the eye in diameter. (Fig. 270.) Nostrils prominent, near together; slightly nearer to the muzzle than to the eye. Elevated fold of skin over the ear to the shoulder. (Fig. 274.) A groove runs along the midline of the back. Arms and legs very muscular. Fingers long. (Fig. 271.) Foot broad; webs large, extending fully to ends of toes (all except fourth toe relatively longer than corresponding toes of *Rana catesbiana*). (Fig. 272.) No outer sole tubercle; inner sole tubercle small. Palm tubercles and all subarticular tubercles small.

Range: Reported from Florida (Pensacola, Kissimmee, Ozona) and Mississippi (Bay St. Louis).

This frog was first found in 1900 at Bay St. Louis, Mississippi, but was not recognised as a distinct species until more material

FIG. 269.—The SOUTHERN BULLFROG (*Rana grylio Stejneger*). Ozona, Florida. A beautiful frog, very retiring and thoroughly aquatic in habit. Usually vivid metallic green on head and shoulders, olive posteriorly. Head long and pointed. Ear of male greatly larger than the eye.

FIG. 270.—Female of the SOUTHERN BULL-FROG. The ear is no larger than the eye.

FIG. 271.—Photographed (in water) to show the long narrow head, and the smooth character of the undersurfaces of the fingers and toes. The breathing movements of the throat are suspended under water.

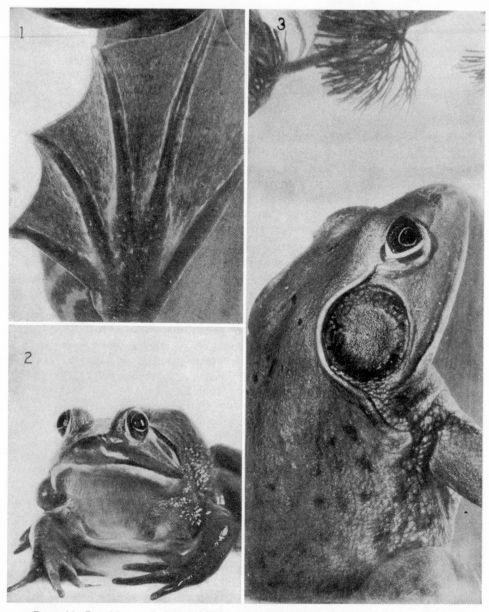

FIG. 272 (1).—Foot of *Rana grylio*. Toes long with inconspicuous tubercles and long broad webs.

FIG. 273 (2).—Head pointed ; eyes greatly elevated and close together.

FIG. 274 (3).—Structure study of *Rana grylio*. (Enlarged.) To show texture of skin, relative size of eye and ear, and fold of skin from eye to shoulder. The photograph shows the transparent nictitating membrane of the eye.

was obtained some time later from Kissimmee, Florida. The frog might be unknown now, if it had not been for the persistent reports of its voice. The sounds produced are said to resemble the grunting of a herd of pigs, thus differing entirely from the familiar bass notes of the Common Bullfrog.

The frog is really very different in appearance from the Common Bullfrog, not resembling it in shape, porportions of body, or colouring. The long, narrow, pointed head, with its large eyes set close together, tell the story at once. But other evidences lie in the ratio of the lengths of head and body (compare Figs. 269 and 278), in the greater length of toes (except the fourth) (compare Figs. 272 and 282), and in the finely pitted texture of the skin. In addition to all these points, there is that of colouration. *Rana grylio,* in its brilliant phases of colouring, furnishes one of the most charming studies in blended shades of yellow, green, and brown, all of these colours showing metallic lustre. Especially beautiful is the colouring of the undersurfaces. This species shows great power of changing colour. It may be brilliant or dull, light or dark, green or brown. There may be green as vivid as that of the anterior head region on the breast, at each side, about the arm insertion.

The frog is shy and wary, and is seldom seen, except by those who are looking for it. It lives in deep water, among pond-lilies and other vegetation of the lake. It seldom leaps; its strong instinct, when frightened, is to dive and hide.

Rana grylio shows close relationship to *Rana virgatipes* of New Jersey in shape and proportion, metallic colouring, texture of skin, large size of eyes and ears, in lacking the lateral folds, and in aquatic habits.

THE COMMON BULLFROG

Rana catesbiana Shaw

IDENTIFICATION CHARACTERISTICS

Colour: Green or greenish brown, of light or dark shade. The back and sides may be plain in colour or may be spotted with dark. (Figs. 276 and 277.) The spots, when present, may be distinct or connected. Arms and legs spotted or barred with dark. Underparts white, distinctly or obscurely spotted and mottled with dark. The throat of the male may be yellow. The iris is either golden or reddish bronze.

Measurements: Size large, both male and female often reaching a length of 7 to 8 inches. The leg to the heel is not as long as the combined lengths of head and body. The femur is about equal to the tibia.

Structure: The head is broad and flat. The body is stout and flat. Ear of male much larger than the eye (Fig. 277); the ear of the female is about the size of the eye. (Fig. 276.) The lateral folds are lacking. (Figs. 276 and 278.) A strong fold of skin extends from behind the eye to the arm, curving around the ear. (Figs. 277 and 278.) Toes broadly webbed; no joints free, except the last of the fourth toe. (Fig. 282.)

Range: Rana catesbiana Shaw is found in North America, east of the Rocky Mountains (including Florida and Texas).

Bullfrogs are late in coming permanently from their hibernation.[1] It may not be until late May or early June that we hear their deep bass voices from the ponds, or that we see their gigantic green bodies perched on partially immersed logs or floating among water-weeds at the surface. They prefer large ponds or lakes, where they can find deep water as well as shallow, screened from the shore by low willows, alders or other water-loving plants. They like such places, also, because of the sheltering growths of pickerel-weed, arrowhead, and water-lilies. (Fig. 275.) These make good hiding-places, and about the roots and stems and under the leaves are to be found crayfishes, water-beetles and bugs, snails and shrimps, the larvæ of dragon-flies and May-flies, and, in fact, all sorts of delicacies for a water frog's *mênu.* For the Bullfrog differs from the Leopard and Pickerel frogs, in that it does not hunt in any place except the body of water which makes its home. We shall not find Bullfrogs when we go for country walks across meadows and through orchards, even though the meadows and orchards may be near ponds or lakes. We are more likely to see them if we go rowing on river or pond. The Bullfrog is more thoroughly

[1] Solitary individuals may remain active throughout the winter, in spring houses or large springs, in the vicinity of Philadelphia.

FIG. 275.—Under the pickerel weed. The BULLFROG is the most aquatic frog of Northeastern North America. [*Rana catesbiana* Shaw. Rhode Island.]

June—We are likely to hear and see BULLFROGS if we go rowing on river or pond.

BULLFROGS prefer large ponds where the water is screened from the shore by willow, alder and other water-loving plants.

aquatic than any of the other frogs of northeastern North America. However, if we happen to be walking across country, or even along a country road during a long-continued heavy rain, we may overtake a large Bullfrog who seems to be making the same journey. Whether the continued wet weather has tempted him to go hunting beyond his usual bounds, or whether he is migrating from pond to pond, it would be difficult to say. He proceeds by successive leaps, about three feet each in length. He can cover a distance of five or six feet without difficulty, notwithstanding his large, heavy body. A wet Bullfrog leaping

across a dry surface leaves curious tracks, interesting in that they show how large a part of the under portion of the body and thighs strikes the ground forcibly after each leap, and how the frog " toes in " with its front feet.

The Bullfrog is our largest frog. (Fig. 277.) He may measure six or seven inches from the tip of the muzzle to the posterior end of the body. A young frog of this species, which had been raised in the laboratory, measured four inches in length on his first birthday. However, size is not a good criterion by which to judge the age of a Bullfrog, or even its identity. The variation in this particular is marvellous. A frog one year old may be no more than two inches long. Much depends on the size attained by the tadpole before the transformation, and of course much also depends on the food and other conditions of the environment, and the ability of the individual frog to cope with these conditions.

The Bullfrog (Figs. 276 to 278) is very easily distinguished from other frogs, however, whatever may be its size. The head is broad and flat. (The head of the young Bullfrog is relatively less broad than that of the adult.) The ear is much larger than the eye. There are no lateral folds. There is a short fold of skin extending backward from the eye, over the ear, and down to the shoulder. The hind feet are fully webbed. (Figs. 281 and 282.)

The colour varies greatly, not only according to the sex, but also among individuals of the same sex. The Bullfrog has power to change colour considerably. The general colour of the upper parts is dull olive-green, marked with irregular, dusky spots of brown. However, when the frog is in warm air, and exposed to bright light, the skin may become a beautiful spotless yellow-green, very light in tone. The Bullfrog just from the mud, or from some place of concealment in deep water, is so dark-coloured that he is nearly black. Experiments prove that light has much to do with these changes of colour; at least, that these changes in colour take place with changes of light, when temperature and moisture conditions remain the same.[1]

The female is usually more brown and spotted, and the male more nearly plain green. The under parts of both are white, with distinct or indistinct mottlings of brown. The male has a bright yellow throat; that of the female is dirty white, mottled with brown. The ear of the male is much larger than that of the female.

This description holds regarding the Bullfrog of northeastern North America. In southern New York, and still farther south, the Bullfrog is more likely to be spotted, and the male lacks the bright yellow on the throat. The Bullfrog of Texas has the underparts vividly marked everywhere with irregular, connected black spots. This frog of the Southwest has also a more tubercular and leathery skin. There are probably three or four distinct varieties of this species in different localities of North America. It is certain that the Bullfrog of Wisconsin and adjoining regions is different enough to be classified as a variety. (Fig. 278.) It is finely spotted with dark on all parts except the head. There is much more bright yellow in its colouration than in that of Bullfrogs from other parts of North America. The male has this colour not only on the throat, as in the case of the Eastern Bullfrog, but also along the sides of the body and on the legs and feet to the tips of the toes. The head is relatively more pointed than that of other Bullfrogs. The body is relatively longer; the head is contained

---

[1] See pp. 22 to 27 for discussion of change of colour in the Batrachia.

three and one-fourth to three and one-half times in the total length, whereas the usual proportion is one to three. The eyes are surprisingly small and little elevated, giving the flat head an expression greatly lacking in intelligence and alertness. The longitudinal diameter of the eye in a frog $6\frac{1}{2}$ inches long is a short $\frac{3}{8}$ inch, while it is fully $\frac{1}{2}$ inch in an Eastern Bullfrog measuring $5\frac{3}{4}$ inches. The smaller size of the eye results in a greater space between the eye and the nostril and a longer fold of skin above the ear. In this frog the vocal sacs of the throat extend backward over the arm so that when the frog croaks, not only does the throat swell, but pouches appear between the ear and the arm as in the case of the Leopard Frog. The increase in vocal powers in this frog is shown also in the fact that the female croaks in a manner similar to that of the male, but without quite the same force and without the appearance of pouches at the sides of the head.

The Common Bullfrog is a powerful swimmer, with great strength and length of hind legs (which may measure from seven to ten inches long) and with very large webs. It is interesting to see one dive under the water. The legs are straightened powerfully, and then slowly drawn forward into position for the second stroke. The huge web is alternately extended into a flat resisting membrane and folded again as the leg is drawn forward. The eyes are shut; that is, they are flattened until they are level with the head, by being lowered in their sockets, which project downward from the roof of the mouth. (Fig. 279.) This takes the eyes out of danger during the swift motion through the water, but also makes it necessary that the frog shall swim rapidly but a short distance at a time. He must stop, or slacken speed and open his eyes to see where he is, and then, perhaps, may make a new plunge with eyes lowered, if an enemy is near. The frog, like the toad, has no outer ear to hinder him in swimming. The ear-drum is at the surface of the head, covered and protected merely by the moist skin.

Something else is seen to take place, also, as the frog dives under water. Large bubbles of air are given off from the nostrils, which are then closed tightly. The frog does not use the lungs in breathing under water; the nostrils are kept closed, and the throat shows none of the swallowing movements so conspicuous when the frog is breathing air. The frog's moist skin is like a great gill stretched over the whole body. In consequence the frog not only can live under the water for months at a time, but will, by preference, spend a very large portion of his time lying, with flattened body and closed nostrils, at the bottom of the pond.

If we go rowing on river, lake, or park lagoon some moonlight night in late June, we are certain to hear the deep-toned call of the Bullfrog many times. Coming as it does at unexpected intervals and from unexpected directions, it seems startlingly weird in the quiet of the night. For June nights are quiet. The insect orchestras are not yet in full swing and the frog choruses have disbanded. The toads are still calling, though much more feebly than earlier in the season, and the voices of only a few can be heard, whereas there were hundreds in May. The Bullfrog does not sing in chorus; the call is an isolated one. The notes are so low in pitch that we think of him as the bass viol among the batrachia. The call resembles, to a considerable degree, the roar of a distant bull, but it has a more musical ring, and the notes are less blended and slurred. The pitch varies with the individual. The following are four interesting annotations of the bullfrog's call:[1]

The call can be imitated well by saying with a hoarse, deep-toned voice the syllables of various interpretations of it, such as, " Be drowned," " Better go round," " Jug o' rum," or " More rum." The imitation is especially good if the slurred words are repeated in front of some reverberating hollow body. That the call has a musical quality was once illustrated most ludicrously. During the rehearsal of a chorus of female voices, a big yellow-throated Bullfrog, in an adjoining room, began vigorously ejaculating, " Jug o' rum, jug o' rum, jug o' rum." Several persons were deceived for the moment into thinking that the bass voice of the director had joined the chorus, for it happened that the first few notes of the frog were in time and harmony with the chords of the selection. A tame Bullfrog

---

[1] Familiar Life in Field and Forest. F. Schuyler Mathews. D. Appleton & Co.

PLATE LXXXIX

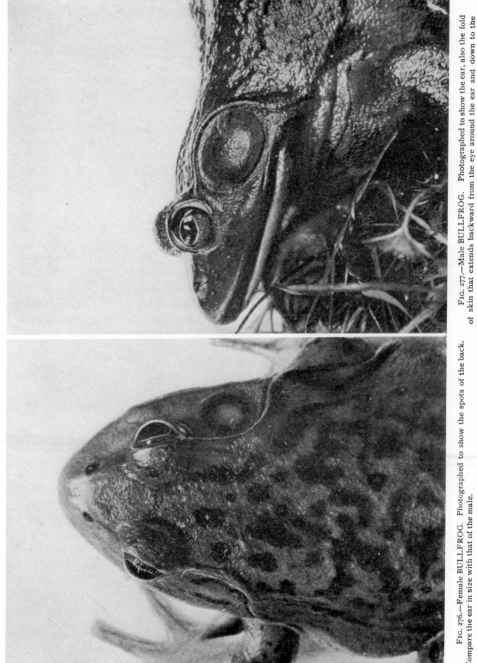

FIG. 276.—Female BULLFROG. Photographed to show the spots of the back. Compare the ear in size with that of the male.

FIG. 277.—Male BULLFROG. Photographed to show the ear, also the fold of skin that extends backward from the eye around the ear and down to the shoulder.

FIG. 278.—The BULLFROG (*Rana catesbiana* Shaw) is heard in the ponds by the first of May. Oshkosh, Wisconsin. (See page 230.)

will always sing when other sounds are being produced, whether these are musical or not. He always becomes enthusiastic at the sound of running water.

The Bullfrog has two internal vocal sacs, which act as resonators. These are in the pouch of the throat, and the openings into them are on the floor of the mouth. (See Fig. 279.) When the frog croaks, the yellow throat over the vocal sacs, and the sides of the body in the region of the lungs, are forcibly distended with air drawn in through the nostrils. Throat and sides immediately relax as the air passes out over the vocal cords of the throat and the sound is produced.

The frog's vocal powers do not stop with the croaking described. If we live in the country, or if we are given to camping and fishing, it is possible that at least once in a lifetime we shall hear this species of frog give voice to quite another sound. This comes when he is forcibly seized by a huge enemy, such as a hawk or an otter. The unexpected sound given at such a time is most distressing to hear. It is a loud, prolonged, high-pitched scream, containing anguish and antagonism, to such an extent that we cannot but think that the cry is made by the human voice. Sometimes, when we take into our hands a masterful, untamed Bullfrog, just brought from the pond, he gives this same cry with wide-opened mouth. The scream of distress is so penetrating, and so prolonged, that we hasten to release the frog, for fear our neighbours will accuse us of cruelty to children.

However, as the mouth is held wide open while the cry is given, we find a most excellent opportunity to see various things about which we may have been curious. (Fig. 279.) The tongue has a forked posterior end, and has its front end fastened just back of the lower lip.[1] There is a circle of small, sharp teeth on the upper jaw. Two large openings at the sides back of the tongue lead into the vocal sacs. Two smaller openings on the roof of the mouth are the openings of the tubes leading from the nostrils. Their situation so far in front of the throat makes it clear why it is that the frog must swallow the air that passes in at the nostrils in order to get it down to the lungs. The great rounded elevations on the roof of the mouth are made by the eyes. These extensions from the roof of the mouth

---

[1] See description of toad's tongue, p. 81.

appear when the eyes are flattened to a level with the top of the head.

The Bullfrog feeds upon the insects and other small life of the pond, as has been stated. But this does not make up the greater part of his food. He is the green dragon of the pond to the fish, the small turtles, the young water-birds, and, alas, to the frogs also. The Bullfrog will eat any moving object that he can swallow or partially swallow. It does not take long to find out the cannibalistic traits of this frog, and to learn that we must not keep a large specimen in the same place with smaller frogs. When we open the collecting-pail on arriving home from a trip to the pond, we learn our lesson, for several of the smallest frogs have disappeared, and the feet and legs of one of the largest are protruding from the capacious mouth of the big fellow.

The Bullfrogs are found throughout the United States, east of the Rocky Mountains. They are less common than many other frogs. This is not entirely owing to the many enemies of the adults, i. e. snakes, otters, hawks and owls, herons, turtles, and (at the South) alligators. Nor is it wholly due to the fact that the tadpoles and the young frogs are preyed upon by fish and by all sorts of small enemies of the pond — to say nothing of their own greedy kin. It is probably due in some measure to the fact that their large size has made them especially valuable as food for man, and that their large size, together with their greed, has made them easy of capture. They bring a price of from one to four dollars per dozen at the markets.[1]

The Bullfrog is solitary in habit, except at the breeding-season. This breeding-season is late, extending from the last of May into July. The tadpoles do not develop into frogs during the first season, as do those of the Leopard and Pickerel frogs. It is not until the second season, and sometimes the third, that a Bullfrog tadpole makes its final transformation.[2] Giant Bullfrog tadpoles can be found any month in the year. It is

---

[1] Frog hunting is carried on in all parts of the United States. The states supplying the largest amounts for the market are New York, Maryland, Virginia, Indiana, Ohio, Missouri and California This work yields $50.000 annually to the hunters, but threatens the practical extinction of our native frogs. It has been demonstrated on Frog Reserves or "Frog Farms" in Wisconsin, California and elsewhere that frog raising is a practicable and profitable industry. (See Notes on the Edible Frogs of the U. S. Extract from Report of 1897 of the Commissioner of U. S. Fisheries)

[2] This fact is interesting to persons actually concerned in frog culture.

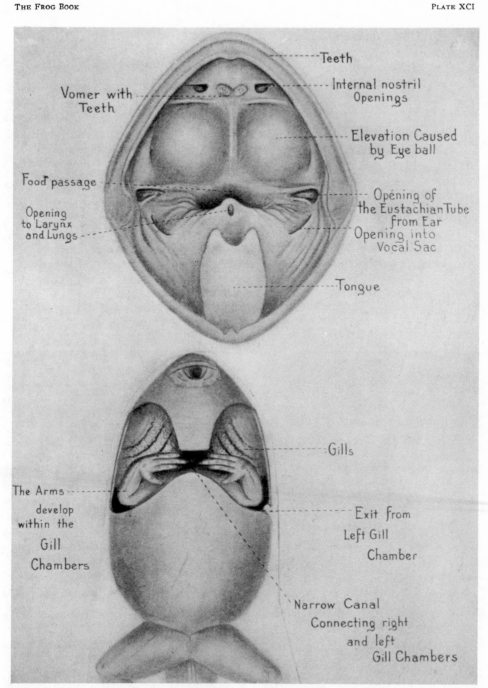

Teeth

Internal nostril Openings

Vomer with Teeth

Elevation Caused by Eye ball

Food passage

Opening of the EustachianTube from Ear

Opening to Larynx and Lungs

Opening into Vocal Sac

Tongue

Gills

The Arms develop within the Gill Chambers

Exit from Left Gill Chamber

Narrow Canal Connecting right and left Gill Chambers

FIG. 279.—Drawing to show the floor and the roof of the Bullfrog's mouth.

FIG. 280.—BULLFROG TADPOLE, one day previous to the time of activity of the arms. Drawn to show the connection of the gill chambers. (This canal lies directly in front of the heart.) [Enlarged.]

PLATE XCII

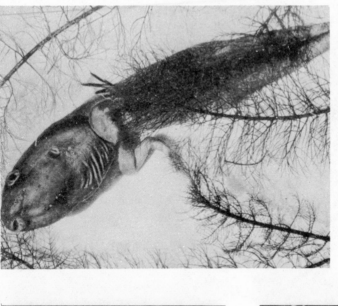

FIG. 283.—July 3, 1901. BULLFROG TADPOLE. The hind legs are well developed. The breathing pore shows plainly on the left side.

FIG. 284.—The elbow of the left arm shows in the breathing pore. July 4th. [Enlarged.]

FIG. 281.—The hand of a BULLFROG has only four fingers. It is not webbed.

FIG. 282.—The foot of the BULLFROG is fully webbed.

perhaps during June and July, however, that most of the final transformations are made.

If we bring tadpoles from the pond in early July, we shall find that many of them have hind legs. The size of the tadpole is surprisingly large. It may measure six or seven inches from the mouth to the end of the tail, the tail alone being three or four inches long. Let us examine one of these tadpoles (Fig. 283) closely to see how he is fitted to live his life in the water, surrounded by innumerable enemies. If we take one into our hands, we find it slippery and soft. The skeleton is cartilaginous. The creature has no means of defence, but must depend wholly on hiding and on flight. Fortunately, he is well provided for both. The marbled speckled brown of his moist skin makes him almost invisible on the muddy bottom, or among brown stems and leaves in the pond. The long tail has a broad fin, and is provided with strong muscles. With this equipment the tadpole can swim rapidly and vigorously, and can splash the mud of the bottom so as to obscure his course, and make it possible for him to glide off unseen in some new direction. The hind legs are fairly well developed, and the broad feet are webbed to the ends of the toes, so they give effective help in swimming. The eyes are large and conspicuous; in fact, they seem already to show a slight elevation, as though they were beginning to take on the characteristics of the frog's eyes. The mouth is small. It consists of fleshy lips covered with rows of tiny teeth.[1] The lower lip is especially broad and ruffled, and bears along its lower edge rows of fleshy papillæ, which, probably, serve for determining the nature of substances when the tadpole is seeking food. Between the lips, and somewhat within them, is a horny beak, which, though very small, is much like a bird's beak in shape. It consists of an upper and a lower jaw, strong, and very thin and sharp at their edges. The mouth is well fitted to bite off the delicate ends of leaves and stems, or to scrape off the tender green or brown plants from sticks and stones. It is equally adapted for eating animal food. The Bullfrog tadpole (like that of the Green Frog and of the Wood Frog) is especially fond of any animal food

---

[1] The mouth structure of the bullfrog tadpole is as follows: The upper lip is relatively narrow, and bears only one complete row of teeth; the lower lip is very broad, has three rows of teeth and a border of papillæ; rder of the lower lip extends upward to the upper lip, and is doubled in at the corners of the mouth. This structure corresponds almost exactly with that of the tadpoles of three other water-frogs, *R. pipiens, R. palustris, and R. clamitans.*

available. Thus these tadpoles act as scavengers and dispose of dead fish, or dead tadpoles even, that otherwise would become a menace to the living creatures of the pond.

On the left side of the tadpole is a conspicuous opening: the breathing-pore. (See Fig. 283.) The breathing is done by means of internal gills on each side of the throat, in a position like that of a fish's gills. They are concealed, however, by the outer skin. (Fig. 280.) This is the fold of skin which grows back from the sides of the head in the young tadpole and covers the external gills.[1] There are three sets of these internal gills on each side. They are feathery tufts extending into cavities between the walls of the throat and the outer skin of the sides of the head. These cavities, or gill-chambers, are connected with each other by a passage underneath the skin of the throat. (See Fig. 280.) Alternating with the tufts of gills, there are three openings in the throat-wall. These openings (gill-slits) connect the throat and mouth with the gill-chambers at the sides of the head. Water is constantly passing in at the mouth and nostrils, through the gill-slits into the gill-chambers, over the gills, and out at the breathing-pore. The water of the gill-chamber on the right passes into the gill-chamber on the left, and thence out of the breathing-pore on the left side.

One important way in which the tadpole is fitted to cope with the difficulties of his life is his power of reproducing the tail, should a hungry fish or other enemy bite it off. When you collect tadpoles for the aquarium, do not collect and put in with them the giant diving-beetles or any other of the tadpole's enemies. If you do so, on the first morning after the aquarium is arranged the beetles will be looking very hearty and the tadpoles will be scared, wobbling, tailless creatures, which demand quick rescue before the beetles complete their destructive work. However, if the beetles are removed, the tadpoles soon recover their assurance, and in a very few weeks their waving filmy tails are nearly as long as they were before the disaster.

The lateral-line organs are easily made out because of the large size of the tadpole.[2]

On the second day of our observation (July 4th) the mouth is beginning its transformation. It is much wider, and as it is con-

---

[1] See Leopard Frog, Fig. 211.
[2] For figure, and discussion of lateral-line organs, see p. 6.

FIG. 285.—July 5th. Developing BULLFROG TADPOLE.   The right arm breaks through the skin after the left one comes out of the breathing pore.

FIG. 286.—July 9th.   The absorption of the tail has begun.   The legs do all the work of swimming.   Compare with FIG. 288.

PLATE XCIV

FIG. 287.—July 9th. He is very comfortable out of water.

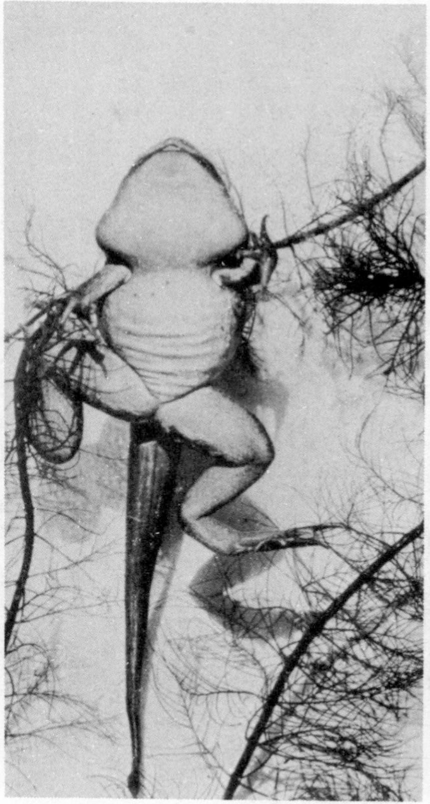

FIG. 288.—July 9th. BULLFROG TADPOLE constantly rushes to the surface for air.

FIG. 289.—July 13th. Tail merely a black stub. Ears not yet showing.

stantly opened and shut in breathing, the rudimentary tongue is visible on its floor. The fringe of the lower lip is still present, but the horny beak within seems to have disappeared. From this time to the end of the change the tadpole does not eat.

The elbow of the left arm is now visible within the breathing-pore. (Fig. 284.) The skin of the right side has become thinner, so that the movement of the right arm is plainly visible, and before night the movement has worn a hole through the skin, and the right elbow is plainly visible also. We are not surprised in the morning to see the left arm projecting through the breathing-pore. Two hours later the right arm is pushed out so that both arms are now free. (Fig. 285.) These arms begin their growth at the time when the back legs appear, but are concealed within the gill-chambers. (See Fig. 280.)

On this day the tadpole breathes with much effort. The mouth, which is still increasing in width and shows the developing tongue within, is opened and shut constantly. The gills have begun to be absorbed, and the lungs, although developed, are not yet fully in use. The left arm blocks up the breathing-pore, so that little of the water sent to the gills can escape there. (Fig. 286.) The water is taken in at the mouth and nostrils to the gills of the throat, and is expelled through the mouth, instead of through the breathing-pore. The lungs are used somewhat; the tadpole very often comes to the surface of the water and gives out a bubble of air from the mouth. In a very few days (by July 9th) a decided change takes place: the gills are wholly absorbed; the lungs are fully in use; the mouth is kept closed, and the tadpole is an air-breather. Now the tadpole spends much time at the surface of the water, sometimes rushing madly from the bottom to exchange a bubble of impure air for fresh. (Fig. 288.) He is very comfortable out of water. (Fig. 287.)

The developing tadpole is white on the under side of the body and yellow on the under side of the legs. The mouth is open back to a point on a line with the front of the eye. The legs are greatly developed, and the tail is becoming shorter and narrower. It is dark in color and almost black at its end. The tail is no longer used in swimming, but the legs do all of the work. (Fig. 288.) The process of absorption has begun by which all the living part of the tail retreats into the body of the tadpole and helps in the formation of new organs. The wandering white-blood corpuscles (phagocytes) accomplish this retreat of the tail substance in such a manner that the external skin of the tail is not broken, and in fact, nothing of the process, except the result, is visible from the outside. These corpuscles move out into the tail and carry the particles one by one into the body to serve as food for the tadpole. It is therefore true that a tadpole "eats" its tail, though not at all according to the customary manner of eating. The decrease in the size of the tail proceeds rapidly until there is a mere black stub left (Fig. 289), and our tadpole looks no longer like a tadpole, but, instead, like a fully formed frog. The skin is more distinctly mottled. That about the eyes and nose is green and iridescent. The eyes are more elevated, showing rounded black centres surrounded by a broad iris, reddish gold in colour. The mouth is open to a point on a line with the back of the eye. The lines where the membrane of the gill-chambers joined with the body wall are still visible around the arms. The head is kept above the water; the nostrils are constantly moving and the throat pulsating.

It is not until four days later that the ear membrane is visible. Now the tail is wholly gone (July 16th). The frog begins to show hiding and burrowing habits. In fact, young frogs at this stage remain concealed under water, mud, or moss most of the time, except at night. During the first summer the young Bullfrog eats insects of all sorts, but by fall it is capable of disposing of small fish. The Bullfrog, whose transformation has been traced, was heard to croak for the first time in early July, one year after its change. At this time the ears had gradually increased in size until they were considerably larger than the eyes. Head and body together measured over four inches in length.

Each of us has actually before him, or in memory, a typical pond or small lake, for our country is everywhere made picturesque by them. We have waded there for lilies, or fished from its sheltered coves for pickerel, or perhaps for frogs. It is called, indiscriminately, "the lily-pond," or "the frog-pond." The lilies make a large part of its beauty, the Bullfrog a large part of its life. The Bullfrog is the spirit of the place. (Fig. 290.) Independent, self-composed, silent, he may sit for hours with no slightest movement to tell that he is alive. But he is fully alert to every disturbance of the water and to every shifting shadow.

PLATE XCV

We have waded there for lilies or fished from its sheltered coves for pickerel, or perhaps for frogs.

FIG. 290.—The BULLFROG—independent, self-composed, alert—is the spirit of the place.

Not only is he alert in sight and hearing, he is ready in muscle for a sudden movement at any second. If a dragon-fly skims over the water's surface in front of him, the insect is swallowed quickly. If a sparrow comes for its daily bath beside what seems to be a moss-covered stone, its brown tail feathers are seen a moment later protruding from the frog's mouth, while the frog is sitting sedately in just the same spot. Sometimes a bird drops from the overhanging bough above, because of the correct aim of some gunner and becomes a trophy for the frog instead of for the man.

However, it is not appetite alone that brings into play the alert senses and muscles of the Bullfrog. Let a bear approach from the wooded shore ever so stealthily, when his paw comes down suddenly over the frog, he finds he has nothing but water-weeds and mud to pay him for his trouble.[1] A heron hunting frogs has no chance of catching the Bullfrog, if the frog is on the bank. It is only when the Bullfrog is in the mud that he is speared by the powerful beak. Ages of generations of contest with this enemy have not taught the frog to bury the hinder portion of his body when he plunges into the mud. He may not see the snake, his greatest enemy, and so, at last, he is lost. But what eyes could see its sinuous body moving so cautiously, neither shape nor motion differentiated from the surrounding water and the waving plant stems?

And so, in pond and marsh, the contest goes on, as it always has in past ages. Each day the life of the individual is given to maintain the life of the species, and the balance of life among the races is kept, although the scales may tip somewhat now in one direction and now in another. Very definite and very emphatic is our admiration for the individual. Each represents high specialization along a given line of development, and seems perfected to the minutest detail in its fitness for its life. Each is so invisible in its environment that it seems wonderful that an enemy ever finds it at all. Each is supplied with the power of extremely rapid movement. However, certain characteristics may be of the greatest advantage to a given individual, but of the greatest danger to that individual when the same powers are possessed also by an enemy. Thus the rapid flight of a bird or insect is

---

[1] William J. Long.

counteracted to its disadvantage by the invisibility and rapid movement of the frog, and these characteristics of the frog are offset fatally for him by the same characteristics and the power of stealthy approach in the snake.

So life goes on, and gladsome but arduous days are passed by the denizens of the pond.

BIBLIOGRAPHY

ABBOTT, C. C.

1882. Notes on the Habits of the Savannah Cricket Frog (*Acris crepitans*). Amer. Nat., vol. xvi, pp. 707–711.

1884. Recent Studies of the Spadefoot Toad. Amer. Nat., vol. xviii, pp. 1075–1080.

ALLEN, G. M.

1899. Notes on the Reptiles and Batrachians of Intervale, N. H. Bost. Soc. Nat. Hist. Proc., vol. xxix, pp. 63–75.

ALLEN, J. A.

1868. Catalogue of Reptiles and Batrachians found in the vicinity of Springfield, Mass. Proc. Bost. Soc. Nat. Hist., vol. xii, Dec., 1868.

ASSHETON, R.

1894. On the Growth in Length of the Frog Embryo. Quar. Jour. of Micr. Sci., vol. xxxvii.

1895. Notes on the Ciliation of the Ectoderm of the Amphibian Embryo. Quar. Jour. Micr. Sci., vol. xxxviii, p. 465.

BAIRD, S. F., and GIRARD, C.

1853. Characteristics of Some New Reptiles in the Museum of the Smithsonian Institute. Jour. Acad. Nat. Sci., Phila., vol. vi, p. 173.

1853. List of Reptiles Collected in California by Dr. J. L. Le Conte with Description of New Species. Acad. Phila., vol. vi, p. 30.

1853. Communication from Baird. and Girard. Acad. Phila., vol. vi, p. 378.

BAIRD, S. F.

1854. Description of New Genera and Species of North American Frogs. Jour. Acad. Nat. Sci. Phila., vol. vii, p. 59.

BALLOU, W. H.

1887. Migration of Frogs. Amer. Nat., vol. xxi, p. 388.

BAUR, G.

————, Ueber die Homologien einiger Schädelknochen der Stegocephalen und Reptilien. Anat. Anz. 1. No. 13, pp. 348-350.

BEDDARD, F. E.

1892. Animal Coloration. London.

BORN, G.

1893. Ueber Druckversuche an Froscheiern. Anat. Anz., vol. viii.

BOULENGER, G. A.

1882. Catalogue Batrachia Salientia s. Ecaudata in the Collection of the British Museum, London, 1882.

1892. The Poisonous Secretion of Batrachians. Natural Science, i, pp. 185-190.

1896. The Tailless Batrachians of Europe, London: Printed for the Ray Society. Two volumes.

Bibliography

BREHM.

    1878. Thierleben Bd. I. Abth. 3.

BRIMLEY, C. S.

    1896. Batrachia found at Raleigh, North Carolina. Amer. Nat., vol. xxx, p. 500.

BRONN, H. G.

    ——, Klassen und Ordnungen des Thierreiches, Wirbel-thiere. Bd. VI, Abth. 2, pp. 533-565.

BUMPUS, H. C.

    1885, 1886. Reptiles and Batrachians of Rhode Island. Random Notes on Natural History, vols. ii and iii, 1885, 1886.

CASE, E. C.

    1899. The Development and Geologic Relations of the Vertebrates. Univ. of Chicago Press, 1899. Reprint from Jour. Geol., vol. vi, No. 4, to vol. vii, No. 2.

CHAMBERLAIN, F. M.

    1897. Notes on the Edible Frogs of the United States and their Artificial Propagation. Extract from Report of Commissioner for 1897, U. S. Commission of Fish and Fisheries.

COOMBES, S. C.

    1902. Frog-raising. As Good and Better than Gold Mines. How to Breed and Feed It, and How to Protect It from its Enemies. (South San Francisco, San Mateo County, Cal.)

    (This is a pamphlet sold in sealed packages at a price of five dollars. It is almost valueless.)

COPE, E. D.

    1863. On Trachycephalus, Scaphiopus, and other American Batrachia. Proc. Acad. Nat. Sci. Phila., p. 43.

    1866. On the Reptilia and Batrachia of the Sonoran Province of the Nearctic Region. Acad. Phila., 1866, p. 301.

    1867. On the Structure and Distribution of Genera of the Arciferous Anura. Jour. Acad. Nat. Sci. Phila., pp. 67-97, 1867.

    1867. On the Families of Raniform Anura. Jour. Acad. Nat. Sci. Phila., pp. 189-206, 1867.

    1870. Synopsis of Extinct Batrachia and Reptilia of North America. 3 parts.

    1874. Catalogue of the Air-breathing Vertebrates from the Coal Measures, of Linton, Ohio. Supplement to the preceding.

    1875. Check-list of North American Batrachia and Reptilia. Bulletin of the U. S. National Museum, No. 1, 1875.

    1875. Synopsis of Extinct Batrachia of the Coal Measures. Geol. Survey of Ohio, vol. ii, Paleontology.

    1880. On the Zoölogical Position of Texas. Bulletin U. S. Museum Nat. Hist., No. 17.

    1882. The Reptiles of the American Eocene. Amer Nat., vol. xvi, p. 979.

    1884. Batrachia of the Permian Period of North America. Amer. Nat., vol. xviii, pp. 26-29.

1885. Batrachia. Standard Nat. Hist. Vol. III, p. 322.

1888. On a New Species of Bufo from Texas. Proc. U. S. Nat. Museum. 1888.

1888. Catalogue of Batrachia and Reptilia. Brought by William Taylor from San Diego, Tex. Proc. U. S. Museum, 1888.

1889. Batrachia of North America. Bulletin of U. S. Nat. Museum, No. 34.

1890. Synopsis of the Families of Vertebrates. Amer. Nat., vol. xxiii, p. 849.

1892. The Batrachia and Reptiles of Northwestern Texas. Proc. Acad. Nat Sci. Phila., 1892, pp. 331–333.

1896. Primary Factors of Organic Evolution. Chicago, 1896.

1896. The Geographical Distribution of Batrachia and Reptilia in North America. Amer. Nat., vol. xxx, pp. 886–902, and pp. 1003–1026.

Origin of the Fittest. D. Appleton & Co.

COX, PHILIP.

1898. Batrachia of New Brunswick. Bulletin 16, Nat. Hist. Soc., New Brunswick vol. iv, part 1.

DAVIS, N. S., and RICE, F. L.

Batracha found East of the Mississippi. Illinois State Lab. of Nat. Hist. Bulletin 5.

DAVIS, WILLIAM T.

1904. Note on *Hyla Andersonii* Baird. Proc. Nat. Sci. Ass. Staten Island. Vol. ix, No. 8.

DAWSON, J. W.

1863. Air Breathers of the Coal Period.

DE KAY, JAMES E.

1842. Natural History of New York. Zoölogy of New York. Vol. iii, part 3, Reptiles and Amphibia.

DITMARS, R. L.

1905. Batrachians of the Vicinity of New York City. Guide Leaflet No. 20. Amer. Museum Nat. Hist. Reprinted from Amer. Museum. Jour. Vol. V, No. 4.

ECKEL, E. E. and PAULMIER, F. C.

1902. Catalogue of New York Reptiles and Batrachians. Bulletin 51, N. Y. State Museum.

ECKER, DR. ALEXANDER.

1889. The Anatomy of the Frog. Oxford: Clarendon Press.

EMERSON, H. and NORRIS, C.

1805. "Red-leg," An Infectious Disease of Frogs. Jour. Exper. Medicine, vol. vii, No. 1, 1905, pp. 33–58.

FLEMING, W.

1896. Ueber den Einfluss des Lichts auf die Pigmentirung der Salamanderlarve. Archiv für mikroskopishe Anatomie. Band 48, pp. 369–374.

FOGG, B. F.

1862. List of Reptiles and Amphibia found in State of Maine. Portland Soc. of Nat. Hist., Proc. vol. 1: 86.

GADOW, HANS F.

1901. Amphibia and Reptiles. Macmillan & Co., Cambridge Nat. Hist.

1901. Color in Amphibia. Paper before the Royal Institution of Great Britain, April 26, 1901.

GAGE, S. H. and S. P.
1886. Combined Aerial and Aquatic Respiration. Science, vol. vii, 394–395.

GAGE, S. H. and NORRIS, H. W.
1890. Notes on the Amphibia of Ithaca. Proc. Amer. Ass. Adv. of Sci., vol. xxxix, p. 339.

GAGE, S. H.
1898. The Life History of the Toad. Teachers' Leaflet, No. 9. The College of Agriculture, Cornell University, Ithaca, N. Y.

GARMAN, H.
1891. Synopsis of the Reptiles and Amphibia of Illinois. Bulletin Illinois State Lab. Nat. Hist.
1894. Preliminary List of the Vertebrate Animals of Kentucky. Bulletin Essex Institute, vol. xxvi, Nos. 1, 2, and 3.
1801. The Food of the Toad. Kentucky Agri. Exp. Station, Bulletin No. 91.

GARNIER, J. H.
1882. The Mink or Hoosier Frog. Amer. Nat., vol. xvi, pp. 945–954.

GAULLE, DR.
1882. The Cell Parasite of the Frog. Révue Scientifique, Jan. 28, 1882. Abstr. Amer. Nat., vol. xvi, pp. 323–326.

GAUPP, ERNST.
1901. Ecker's und Wiedersheim's Anatomie des Frosches.

GIACOSA, P.
1884. Chem. Comp. of the Egg and its Envelopes in the Common Frog. Jour. R. Microsc. Soc., London, series 2, vol. iv, p. 1, pp. 203–204.

GILL, THEODORE.
1897. E. D. Cope, Naturalist. A Chapter in the History of Science. Amer. Nat., vol. xxxi, pp. 831–863.

GUNTHER, A.
1858. Catalogue of Batrachia Salientia in the Collection of the British Museum.

HARGITT, C. W.
1888. Recent Notes on *Scaphiopus Holbrookii*. Amer. Nat., vol. xxii, pp. 535-537.

HARRISON, R. G
1898. On the Growth and Regeneration of the Tail of the Frog Larva. Papers from the Anat. Lab. of Johns Hopkins University, vol. iii, pp. 430–483.

HAY, O. P.
1889. Notes on the Life History of *Chorophilus triseriatus*. Amer. Nat. vol. xxiii, pp. 770–774.
1890. On Certain Species of the Genus Chorophilus. Proc. Amer. Ass. for Adv. of Sci., vol. xxxix.
1892. Batrachians and Reptiles of the State of Indiana. Report of the Geol. Survey of Indiana, 1892.

HAY, W. P.
    1902. A List of Batrachians and Reptiles of the District of Columbia and Vicinity. Vol. xv, pp. 121–145.
    1903. On Batrachia and Reptiles. Forest and Stream May 16, 1903, p. 425.
HENSHAW, S.
    1904. Fauna of New England. List of the Batrachia. Occasional Papers. Bost. Soc. of Nat. Hist., vol. vii.
HERTWIG, RICHARD.
    1897. General Principles of Zoölogy. Henry Holt & Co.
HINCKLEY, M. H.
    1882. On Some Differences in the Mouth Structure of Tadpoles of Anurous Batrachians found in Milton, Massachusetts. Proc. Bost. Soc. Nat. Hist., vol. xxi, pp. 307–314.
    1882. The Development of the Tree-toad. Amer. Nat., vol. xvi, p. 636–640.
    1883. Abstract of Article on Mouth Structure of Tadpole. Amer. Nat., vol. xvii, p. 670.
    1883 The Development of the Tree-toad. Proc. Bost. Soc. Nat. Hist., vol. xxi, p. 104.
    1883. Notes on the Peeping Frog, *Hyla pickeringii* Le Conte. Memoirs Bost. Soc. Nat. Hist., vol. iii, pp. 311–318.
    1884. Notes on the Development of *Rana sylvatica* Le Conte. Proc. Bost. Soc. Nat. Hist., vol. xxii.
HOLBROOK, J. E.
    1842. North American Herpetology. Philadelphia.
HORNADAY.
    1904. American Natural History. Scribners.
HOWE, R. H.
    1899. North American Wood Frogs. Proc. Bost. Soc. Nat. Hist., vol. xxviii, No. 14, pp. 369–374.
HUXLEY, T. H.
    1875. Article on Amphibia, Encycl. Britann. 9th Edition. pp. 750–771.
JORDAN, D. S.
    1899. Manual of the Vertebrate Animals of the Northern United States. Chicago.
JORDAN, E. O., and EYCLESHYMER, A.
    1892. The Cleavage of the Amphibian Ovum. Anat. Anz., bd. vii.
    1894. Journal of Morphology, vol. ix.
KING, H. D.
    1902. The Gastrulation of the Egg of *Bufo lentiginosus*. Amer. Nat., vol. xxxvi, pp. 527–548.
    1902. Experimental Studies on the Formation of the Embryo of *Bufo lentiginosus*. Bryn Mawr College Monographs, vol. i, No. 2, pp. 545–563.
    1904. The Formation of the Notochord in the Amphibia. Bryn Mawr Monographs. Contributions from the Biological Laboratory. Reprint Series, vol. i, No. 3.

245

Bibliography

KIRKLAND, A. H.
  1897. Habits, Food, and Economic Value of the American Toad. Hatch Experiment Station, Bulletin 46.
LE CONTE, J. L.
  1855. Descriptive Catalogue of the Ranina of the United States. Jour. Acad. Nat. Sci., Phila., vol. vii, pp. 423–431.
LE CONTE, JOSEPH.
  1900. Comparative Physiology and Morphology of Animals. D. Appleton & Co.
LEE, F. S.
  1898. Functions of the Ear and the Lateral Line in Fishes. Amer. Jour. of Phys., vol. i, No. 1.
LEUNIS.
  1883. Synopsis der Thierkunde, bd. i.
LOCKWOOD, S.
  1883. *Bufa americanus* at Play. Amer. Nat., vol. xvii, p. 683.
LOCKINGTON, W. N.
  1884. Review of the Progress of Batrachology in the Years 1880–1883. Amer. Nat., vol. xviii, pp. 149–154.
LOEB, J.
  1900. On the Transformation and Regeneration of Organs. Amer. Jour. Phys., vol. iv, No. 2, pp. 60–68.
LOENNBERG, E.
  1894. Notes on Reptiles and Batrachians Collected in Florida in 1892 and 1893. Proc. U. S. Nat. Museum, vol. xvii, pp. 317–339.
MACKAY, A. H.
  1896. Reptiles and Batrachians of Nova Scotia. Nova Scotia Inst. of Science, Proc., vols. ix, xli, xliii.
MARSHALL, A. MILNES.
  1893. Vertebrate Embryology. G. P. Putnam's Sons.
MEARNS, E. A.
  1898. Study of the Vertebrate Fauna of the Hudson Highlands. Amer. Museum of Nat. Hist., Bulletin 10, pp. 303–352.
  1899. Notes on the Mammals of the Catskill Mountains, with General Remarks on the Fauna and Flora of the Region. Amer. Museum of Nat. Hist., Proc., xxi, pp. 341–360.
MEEK, S. E.
  1899. Notes on Collection of Fishes and Amphibians from Muskoka and Gull Lakes (Ontario). Field Columbian Museum. Zoölogical Series, vol. i, No. 17.
MILLER, G. S., JR.
  1899. New Tree Frog from the District of Columbia. Proc. Biological Soc., Washington, vol. xiii, pp. 75–78.
MORGAN, C. LLOYD.
  1900. Animal Behavior. London.
MORGAN, T. H.
  1891. Some Notes on the Breeding Habits and Embryology of Frogs. Amer. Nat., vol. xxv, p. 753.

246

1801. The Problem of Development. International Monthly, 1901, pp. 3-47.

The Development of the Frog. Macmillan & Co.

MORGAN, T. H. and TSUDA UMÉ.

1893. The Orientation of the Frog's Egg. Quar. Jour. Micr. Sci., vol. xxxv.

MORGAN, T. H., and DAVIS, S. E.

1902. The Internal Factors in the Regeneration of the Tail of the Tadpole. Bryn Mawr College Monographs, Reprint Series, vol. i, No. 2.

MORSE, MAX.

1904. Batrachians and Reptiles of Ohio. Contributions from the Department of Zoölogy and Entomology. Bulletin Ohio State Univ., series 8, No. 18, pp. 96-123. Reprinted from Boc. Ohio State Acad. Sci., vol. iv, part 3, paper 9, pp. 91-144.

NEEDHAM.

1905. Mayflies and Midges. Bulletin No 86. New York State Museum. (Food of Bullfrogs.)

NELSON, JULIUS.

1890. Descriptive Catalogue of the Vertebrates of New Jersey. State Geol., N. J. Final Report, vol. i, part 1, pp. 643-648.

ORR, H.

1888. Notes on the Development of Amphibia. Quar. Jour. Micr. Sci., vol. xxix, p. 316.

PARKER, G. H.

1802. Hearing and Allied Senses in Fishes. Bulletin U. S. Fish Commission, pp. 45-64.

1803. The Sense of Hearing in Fishes. Amer. Nat., vol. xxxvii, No. 435, pp. 185-204.

1803. The Skin and Eyes as Receptive Organs in the Reaction of the Frog to Light. Amer. Jour. Physiology, vol. x, pp. 28-36.

PIKE, COLONEL NICHOLAS.

1886. Notes on the Hermit Spadefoot (*Scaphiopus holbrookii* Harlan; *S. solitarius* Holbrook). Bulletin of Amer. Museum of Nat. Hist., vol. i, No. 7, pp. 213-221.

POULTON, E. B.

1890. Colours of Animals. London.

PUTNAM, F. W.

1871. Some Statements concerning the Frogs and Toads Found at Cambridge, Massachusetts. Proc. Bost. Soc. Nat. Hist., vol. ix, pp. 229-230.

ROBERTS, H. L.

1889. Frogs Eating Snakes. Amer. Nat., vol. xxiii, p. 74.

ROMANES, G. J.

1884. Mental Evolution in Animals. New York: D. Appleton & Co.

1884. Animal Intelligence.

RYDER, J. A.

1888. "Ventral Suckers" or "Sucking Disks" of the Tadpoles of Different Genera of Frogs and Toads. Amer. Nat., vol. xxii, p. 263.

Bibliography

SAMPSON, L. V.
    1900. Unusual Modes of Breeding and Development among Anura. Amer. Nat., vol. xxxiv, pp. 687–715.
SEDGWICK, W. T.
    Variations, etc., Induced by Changes of Temperature. Studies Biol. Lab. Johns Hopkins Univ., vol. ii, No. 3, p. 385.
SEMPER, KARL.
    1881. Animal Life. D. Appleton & Co.
SHERWOOD.
    1898. Frogs and Toads Found in the Vicinity of New York. Proc. Linn. Soc. of New York, No. 10. 1898,
SHIPLEY, A. E., and MCBRIDE, E. W.
    1901. Elementary Text-book of Zoölogy. Macmillan Co.
SMITH, F. S.
    1879. The Spadefoot in New Haven, Connecticut. Amer. Nat., vol. xiii, pp. 651–652.
SMITH, W. H.
    1879. Catalogue of the Reptiles and Amphibia of Michigan. Supplement to Science News. 8vo. New York, 1897.
    1882. Reptiles and Amphibia of Ohio. Geological Survey of Ohio, 1882, pp. 629–734.
    1901. *Hyla andersonii* Baird. Proc. Phila. Acad. Sci., vol. liii, p. 342.
SPENCER, W. B.
    1885. Some Notes on the Development of *Rana temporaria*. Quart. Jour. Micr. Sci., vol. xxv.
STEJNEGER, LEONHARD.
    1890. Annotated List of Reptiles and Batrachians Collected by Dr. C. Hart Merriam and Vernon Bailey on the San Francisco Mountain Plateau and Desert of the Little Colorado, Arizona. North Amer. Fauna, No. 3, pp. 103–118.
    1893. List of Reptiles and Batrachians Collected by the Death Valley Expedition in 1891, with Descriptions of New Species. North Amer. Fauna, No. 7, pp. 157–228.
    1899. Description of a New Genus and Species of Discoglossoid Toad from North America. Proc. U. S. Nat. Museum, vol. xxi, pp. 899–901.
    1902. A New Species of Bullfrog from Florida and the Gulf Coast. Proc. Nat. Museum U. S., vol. xxiv, pp. 211–215.
    1905. A Résumé of the Geographical Distribution of the Discoglossoid Toads. Amer. Geographical Soc. Bulletin, vol. xxxvii, No. 2, pp. 91–94.
    1905. The Geographical Distribution of the Bell-toads. Science, Oct. 20, 1905, p. 502.
STONE, WITMER.
    1801. *Hyla andersonii* Baird. Proc. Phila. Acad. Sci., vol. liii, p. 342.
STORER, H. W.
    1843. On the *Bufo lentiginosus* of Shaw (B. l. *fowleri* Putn.). Proc. Bost. Soc. Nat. Hist., vol. i, p. 136.

STREETS, THOS. H.
 1877. Contributions to the Nat. Hist. of the Hawaiian and Fanning Islands and Lower California. U. S. National Museum, Bulletin 7.

TATNALL, E.
 1889. Home Instinct in Toads. Amer. Nat., vol. xxiii, p. 1032.

TEST, F. C.
 1890. Contribution to the Knowledge of the Tree Frog *Hyla Regilla*. Proc. U. S. National Museum, vol. xxi, pp. 477–492.

THIELE, J.
 1887. Der Haftapparat der Batrachierlarven. Zeitschr. Wiss. Zool. XLVI, pp. 67-79.

TORELLE, E.
 1903. The Response of the Frog to Light. Amer Jour. of Phys., vol. ix, No. vi, pp. 466–488. Also, Bryn Mawr Monographs, Reprint Series, vol. i, No. 3, 1904.

TOWNSEND, C. H.
 1900. Statistics of Fisheries of the United States.

TRUE, F. W.
 1893. Useful Aquatic Reptiles and Batrachians of the United States. Fisheries and Fishery Industries of the United States, sec. 1, pp. 141–162.

UNITED STATES GOVERNMENT.
 1860. Reports of Explorations and Surveys to Ascertain Route for Railroad from Mississippi River to Pacific Ocean. 1853–55. Printed in Washington, D. C., 1860.

VAN DENBERGH, J.
 1896. Additional Notes on the Herpetology of Lower California. Proc. Cal. Acad. Sci., Second Series, vol. v, part 2.

VERRILL, A. E.
 1863. Catalogue of Reptiles and Batrachians Found in the Vicinity of Norway, Oxford County, Maine. Proc. Bost. Soc. Nat. Hist., vol. ix, pp. 195–199.

WASHBURN F. L.
 1899. A Peculiar Toad. Amer. Nat., vol. xxxiii, p. 139.

WERNER, F.
 1892. Untersuchungen über die Zeichnung der Wirbelthiere. Zoologische Jahrbücher, band vi, pp. 155–229; band, vii, pp. 365–410.

WHITE, GILBERT.
 1876. Natural History of Selborne.

WIEDERSHEIM, ROBERT.
 1886. Comparative Anatomy of Vertebrates. Macmillan Co.

WILDER, H. H.
 1896. Amphibian Larynx. Zoologische Jahrbücher, neunter Band. 1896.

WILSON, C. B.
 1896. The Wrinkling of the Frog's Eggs during Segmentation. Amer. Nat., vol. xxx, pp. 761–773.

WILSON, H. V.
 1900. Formation of the Blastopore in the Frog's Egg. Anat. Anz., bd. xviii.

Bibliography

YARROW, H. C.

1882. North American Reptiles and Batrachians. Bulletin 24, U. S. Nat. Museum.

YERKES, ROBERT M.

1903. The Instincts, Habits, and Reactions of the Frog. Reprint from Harvard Psychological Studies, vol. i, Jan., 1903, pp. 579–638.

1905. The Sense of Hearing in Frogs. Reprint from Journal Comparative Neurology and Psychology, vol. xv, No. 4, 1905, pp. 279–304.

INDEX

Index